Elections and Political Order in Russia

To Kylie

Elections and Political Order in Russia

THE IMPLICATIONS OF THE 1993
ELECTIONS TO THE FEDERAL ASSEMBLY

Edited by
PETER LENTINI

Central European University Press
Budapest   London   New York

First published in 1995 by
Central European University Press
1051 Budapest
Nádor utca 9

Distributed by
Oxford University Press, Walton Street, Oxford OX2 6DP
Oxford New York Athens Auckland Bangkok Bombay Toronto
Calcutta Cape Town Dar es Salaam Delhi Florence Hong Kong
Istanbul Karachi Kuala Lumpur Madras Madrid Melbourne
Mexico City Nairobi Paris Singapore Taipei Tokyo Toronto
and associated companies in Berlin Ibadan
Distributed in the United States
by Oxford University Press Inc., New York

This volume and Chapters 1, 3, 4, 11 and Appendix © Peter Lentini 1995

Chapter 2 © Ian D. Thatcher 1995; Chapter 5 © Daphne Skillen 1995; Chapter 6 © Matthew Wyman, Bill Miller, Stephen White and Paul Heywood 1995; Chapter 7 © Elena Omel'chenko and Hilary Pilkington 1995; Chapter 8 © Richard Sakwa 1995; Chapter 9 © Stephen White 1995; Chapter 10 © Troy McGrath 1995.

All rights reserved. No part of this publication may be reproduced, stored in a retrieval system or transmitted, in any form or by any means, without the prior permission of the copyright holder. Please direct all enquiries to the publishers.

British Library Cataloguing in Publication Data
A CIP catalogue record for this book is available from the British Library

ISBN 1-85866-017-3 Hardback
ISBN 1-85866-018-1 Paperback

Library of Congress Cataloging in Publication Data
A CIP catalog record for this book is available from the Library of Congress

Typeset by Mayhew Typesetting, Rhayader, Powys
Designed and produced by John Saunders
Printed and bound in Great Britain by Biddles of Guildford

Contents

List of Contributors	vii
Acknowledgments	xi
1 Introduction *Peter Lentini*	1

Part I: Elections in Russia and the USSR: A Historical Overview

2 Elections in Russian and Early Soviet History *Ian D. Thatcher*	15
3 Reforming the Soviet Electoral System *Peter Lentini*	36

Part II: The 1993 Election Campaign

4 Overview of the Campaign *Peter Lentini*	63

Part III: Influences and Trends of the 1993 Campaign

5 Media Coverage in the Elections *Daphne Skillen*	97
6 Parties and Voters in the Elections *Matthew Wyman, Bill Miller, Stephen White and Paul Heywood*	124
7 Stabilization or Stagnation? A Regional Perspective *Elena Omel'chenko and Hilary Pilkington*	143

Part IV: The Framework of a New Political Order

8	The Development of the Russian Party System: Did the Elections Change Anything? *Richard Sakwa*	169
9	The Presidency and Political Leadership in Post-Communist Russia *Stephen White*	202
10	The Legacy of Leninist Enforced De-participation *Troy McGrath*	226
11	Conclusion *Peter Lentini*	246

Appendix: Electoral Associations and their Programmes 260
Peter Lentini

Index 282

Contributors

Paul Heywood is Professor of Politics at Nottingham University. He previously taught at Glasgow University and Queen Mary College, London University. He is the author of *Marxism and the Failure of Organised Socialism in Spain, 1879–1936* (1990), *Spain's Next Five Years: A Political Risk Analysis* (1991) and *The Government and Politics of Spain* (1995), and co-editor of *West European Communist Parties After the Revolutions of 1989* (1994).

Peter Lentini lectures in the Department of Politics and Centre for European Studies, Monash University, Victoria, Australia, and has published articles on Soviet and contemporary Russian politics. An honorary research associate of the Institute of Russian and East European Studies, Glasgow University, his earlier lecturing appointments were at the Centre for Russian and East European Studies, Birmingham University, and the Central European University, Prague. He is a consulting editor of the journal *Political Expressions*.

Troy McGrath lectures in the Department of International Relations and European Studies, Central European University, Prague. He previously lectured at New York State University, Palacky University, Czech Republic, and Tirana University, Albania, and was Chair of the Department of Politics and Law, Shkoder University, Albania. At present, he is also a contributing consultant to the Open Media Research Institute's weekly publication *Transition* and is conducting research on minority nationalism in the Russian Federation.

Bill Miller is Professor of Politics at Glasgow University. He is the author of books and articles on British politics, public opinion and electoral politics. With Stephen White and Paul Heywood he supervised a five-nation study on Public Opinion and Democratic Consolidation in Russia and Eastern Europe.

Elena Omel'chenko is Director of the Sociological Research Centre 'Region' at Moscow State University (Ul'yanovsk branch). She has conducted research on a wide range of social, political and cultural phenenomena of contemporary Russian life, with special reference to their regional specificity. Her personal research interests are in Russian youth culture and subcultures.

Hilary Pilkington is Lecturer in Russian Politics and Society at the Centre for Russian and East European Studies, Birmingham University. Her research interests are in changing social and cultural identities in contemporary Russia and she is currently working on migrational processes between former republics of the Soviet Union and their implications for national identity formation.

Richard Sakwa is Reader in Russian and European Politics in the Department of Politics and International Relations at the University of Kent at Canterbury. His publications include *Soviet Politics* (1989), *Gorbachev and His Reforms* (1990) and *Russian Politics and Society* (1993), of which a second edition is in preparation. His recent articles have analysed the December 1993 Russian elections and the fate of Christian democracy in Russia.

Daphne Skillen studied at Sydney, Colorado and London universities. She is an honorary visiting fellow at the School of Slavonic and East European Studies, London University. Earlier she worked as a journalist and consultant on Soviet/Russian affairs for British television. At present she is Director of Media Programmes at the Open Society Institute (Soros Foundation) in Moscow.

Ian D. Thatcher lectures at the Institute of Russian and East European Studies, Glasgow University. He is joint editor of *Journal of Trotsky Studies* and *Studies in Marxism*, and is reviews editor of *Europe-Asia Studies*. The author of many articles, he also co-edited *Markets and Socialism* with Alec Nove (1994).

Stephen White is Professor and Head of the Department of Politics at Glasgow University and currently President of the British Association for Slavonic and East European Studies. His recent publications include *After Gorbachev* (1993), *The Politics of Transition* (with others, 1993), *Developments in Russian and Post-Soviet Politics* (with others, 1993) and *Russia Goes Dry: Alcohol, Society and the State* (1995).

Matthew Wyman is Lecturer in Russian Politics at Keele University. Previously, he was research associate on Glasgow University's project on Public Opinion and Democratic Consolidation in Russia and Eastern Europe. He has published articles on Russian political culture and elections, and is currently completing a book on Russian public opinion.

Acknowledgments

I have accumulated a number of intellectual and personal debts during the course of editing this book, and I should like to express my gratitude to all those who have helped me. Pauline Wickham of the Central European University Press patiently guided me through the procedures of editing a first book. Her enthusiasm for the project from its early stages, her good humour and professionalism all greatly contributed to bringing the final product to fruition. Liz Lowther provided greatly appreciated assistance during the production stage. In addition, two anonymous referees who read an earlier draft of the manuscript provided useful comments on chapters and the book's overall structure.

Thanks go to all the contributors for their willingness to participate in this project, and for their generosity in finding time in the midst of hectic schedules to produce insightful, original contributions. In particular, I wish to express my gratitude to Stephen White for suggesting that I undertake the project and for his faith in my ability to carry it through. Ian Thatcher and Troy McGrath provided valuable comments on earlier drafts of some of these chapters, from which I benefited greatly.

This project is linked to a research trip I made to observe the elections to the Russian Federal Assembly during the time I was lecturing in the Sociology Department of the Central European University, Prague, in 1993–4. I am grateful to the department for providing funds for travel and accommodation and for allowing me to rework my teaching schedule in order to experience this historic event. My thanks go in particular to department head Claire Wallace, former programme coordinator Lynn Hayes, research fellow Andrii Palianytsia, Professor Ernest Gellner, Vlasta Hirtova and Sukumar Periwal for their support and friendship during the 1993–4 academic year. I wish also to thank those students from the CEU's Prague

xii *Acknowledgments*

campus who enhanced my knowledge of Russian politics, communist and post-communist politics more generally: Vrej Atabekian, Serge Bazarya, Olha Buriak, Elena Chernyavskaya, Ivan Chorvat, Alexander Chvorostov, Saulesh Esenova, Magda Gera-Pakulska, Olexander Hryb, Olga Issoupouva, Irina Khmelko, Gennady Korzhov, Michal Kowalski, Krzysztof Olechnicki, Svetlana Oudouchlivaia, Oxana Schmulyar, Vladimir Shevchenko, Elena Sidorenko, Matyas Szabo, Levan Tahrnishvili, Gevork Ter-Gabrielian, Alexander Tulko, Luis Ulrich and Natasha Yakovleva. I am indebted to Jochen Lorentzen for his friendship and professionalism, and for putting me in touch with the CEU Press. Keitha Fine encouraged me to keep writing, work hard and stay young. Finally, I am grateful to Sid Pes, Shannon Schraub and Donna Starr for their friendship and support.

In Moscow I greatly benefited from the kindness of Andrei Edemsky, who arranged my visit as a guest of the Russian Academy of Science's Institute of Slavonic and Balkan Studies. My gratitude is also extended to Marina Grafova, Natasha Kuzminnykh, Liudmilla Selivanova and Svetlana Yaroshenko.

Sue Blackburn, Marnie Boyce, Andy Butfoy, John Dalton, Alastair Davidson, Pauline Dwyer, Robyn Eckersley, Nick Economou, Hugh Emy, Grace Giannini, Hyam Gold, David Goldsworthy, Paul James, Mike Janover, Bruce Lindsay, Paul Muldoon, Margaret Nash, Brian Nelson, Ray Nichols, Carolyn O'Brien, Marko Pavlyshyn, Heather Rae, Chris Reus-Smit, Gillian Robinson, Roger Spegele, Effi Tomaras, Lesley Whitelaw, Steve Wright, David Wright-Neville and Chris Ziguras have eased me into the new environment of Monash University. I appreciate the assistance of Marion Merkel, who kindly transferred several chapters of this book onto disk.

Extra special thanks go to my parents and sister for their love and inspiration.

Finally, I wish to extend my heartfelt gratitude to Kylie Huang, who helped me realize that a world exists beyond the academic and whose support, encouragement and affection greatly eased the tensions of completing this project. It is to her that this book is dedicated.

Peter Lentini
St Kilda, Victoria
April 1995

1 *Introduction*

PETER LENTINI

Historically, elections to representative bodies throughout the territory of Russia and the former Soviet Union have yielded relatively impotent assemblies, largely subordinate to and obscured by first the tsar and then, until more recently, the Communist Party of the Soviet Union (CPSU). As Stephen White suggests, 'elections have not traditionally been an important form of linkage between regime and public in the USSR, or indeed its tsarist predecessor'.[1] Elections have, nevertheless, had a role to play in the country's history over the last century. However, rather than serving as mechanisms through which citizens could change their rulers, as potential means for influencing policy-making and redirecting government priorities, elections as practised in tsarist Russia, the USSR and the present-day Russian Federation were and are largely reflections of the power relations within their respective systems. To paraphrase Samuel P. Huntington, Russian and Soviet elections clearly indicate the 'degree of government'[2] that the tsarist order, the CPSU and, more recently, Russian President Boris Yeltsin exercised within their respective systems. Evident in all cases are highly manipulative, politically interventionist institutions and individuals motivated more by a wish to preserve the status quo than by a desire for popular participation and democratic change. Neither contemporary Russia nor its tsarist or Soviet predecessors have ever experienced an exercise of franchise to a leading institution without some degree of higher-level interference in its proceedings or electoral design. This is certainly revealed in the main focus of this volume, the 1993 elections to the Russian Federal Assembly – Russia's first post-Soviet multiparty elections. Therefore, the evidence suggests that it is possible to argue that Russia has never held a 'free or fair' election.

Elections in which two or more political parties compete for seats in a parliament or for a country's presidency (classical or free elections) are generally regarded as centrepieces of democratic political systems, satisfying specific criteria and serving several distinct purposes. Martin Harrop and William L. Miller point to Robert A. Dahl's criteria of comprehensive eligibility, equality of information, universal adult suffrage, equally weighted votes, installation of winners in their offices and the fulfilment of campaign promises as being among the characteristics that ensure free elections in an 'ideally perfect society'.[3] They also regard David Butler, Howard Penniman and Austin Ranney's criteria of the 'democratic general election' (i.e. universal suffrage, regularly scheduled elections, opportunities for significant groups to form parties and run candidates, contested seats, no interference with voters and candidates, a secret ballot, honest vote tabulation and the installation of the rightful winners) as the 'concrete characteristics of elections we consider free and competitive'.[4] Among the infrastructural requisites for free elections, Harrop and Miller cite W.J.M. Mackenzie's formula of a free and independent judiciary to interpret electoral legislation, an honest, non-partisan administration to conduct the elections, and a well-developed system of political parties, organized enough to put forward their policies, traditions and candidates as alternatives from which voters may choose. Also included in this categorization is an acceptance of the rules of the game, by which the participants realize that if the rules are not followed 'the game itself will disappear amid the wreckage of the whole system'.[5]

Elections serve particular functions for a polity. David Butler, for instance, suggests that because 'fear of the next election is a constant in politics . . . elections offer the final sanction against governments'.[6] Thus, elections serve as a popular check for the electorate to hold on its leaders. Butler claims further that elections can be considered 'ideological consensuses of voters' and 'devices to choose viable governments and give them legitimacy', but also warns that they can be 'a mirror of what the electorate felt on one particular polling day'.[7] Mackenzie sees elections as creating popular consent and participation in public affairs despite governmental complexities, and as providing mechanisms for the direct orderly succession of governments and for the peaceful transfer of authority.[8] Anthony King argues that elections 'frequently settle major constitutional issues; they influence, even determine the structure of party systems; they can force changes of government; their results have a far greater impact on the content of public policy than is often supposed'.[9] Ideally, elections serve as a link between the governors and governed, in which an underlying compact is implied: fulfilment of the electorate's wishes helps to increase a party's or politician's prospects for continuance in office; failure to do so decreases these prospects.

While elections are core components of democratic political systems, not all countries including elections as part of their institutional framework are democratic. Butler, Penniman and Ranney claim that in categorizing countries from non-democratic to democratic it is true that states that do not hold elections would be included at the non-democratic end of the scale; however:

one notch nearer the democratic end of the scale come the ... nations in which elections are regularly held but only one candidate is allowed for office and these candidates are all chosen by the nation's sole or 'hegemonic' political party.[10]

The CPSU dominated the USSR; its monopoly status as the country's leading political organization was codified in Article 6 of the USSR's Constitution from 1977 to 1990.[11] It exercised its power by controlling and censoring the media and educational curricula; sanctioning social organizations; forming and directing party groups in work places, the military, state and educational institutions; supervising the economy; restricting employment and education opportunities; controlling political appointments to key bureaucratic, state and party posts or to the *nomenklatura* system; overseeing the electoral process and selecting and approving candidates. The CPSU determined the major direction of the country's internal and external development.[12] Therefore, any impetus for *official* political change had to meet with party authorization and was party-initiated. Moreover, it was the party which set the parameters within which any changes would occur. That the electoral system functioned non-competitively until the late 1980s is directly related to the CPSU's desires; that changes were eventually implemented can also be attributed to the party's will.

Soviet elections suffered from several serious deficiencies and thus fell far short of the aforementioned criteria for free and fair elections. For instance, although no law expressly prohibited more than one candidate from standing for each seat, it was the invariable practice from 1937 until the late 1980s that the number of candidates was equal to the number of seats. This occurred 'notwithstanding Stalin's observation, in an interview with an American journalist, that he expected a "very lively electoral struggle"'[13] in the elections to the First Convocation of the USSR Supreme Soviet, and despite the fact that Stalin and the party appeared to make considerable efforts to prepare for these elections on a multicandidate basis.[14] All contestants to these and subsequent elections were meticulously chosen by the party to satisfy specific *demographic* criteria – not because they possessed exceptional political skills. Few deputies had real decision-making powers, and only an elite corps were re-elected. This is despite the fact that at local levels, for instance, well over two million deputies were elected to any convocation of the soviets. True power and influence were held by high-ranking party officials who were frequently re-elected. Soviet representative institutions existed to 'rubber-stamp' previously made CPSU decisions and give them an air of popular legitimacy. Although provisions existed in which Soviet voters could be linked to their deputies and have some input over their own lives through their elected representatives, such as voters' mandates which bound deputies to fulfil voters' demands, elections were not true means of selecting a government.[15]

Serious students of Soviet politics were brazenly critical of the USSR's elections because of party control over their procedures and the absence of competition in them. Frederick C. Barghoorn scathingly asserts that 'applying the term "election" to this procedure does semantic violence to the word as defined in the Western democratic lexicon.'[16] According to the aforementioned criteria, Soviet elections were never free or democratic. In the period 1937–87 voting in the USSR followed the pattern that Mackenzie labelled 'elections by acclamation'; these were not elections *per se*, but an 'electoral pathology'. According to Mackenzie, in acclamatory elections:

No one believes in the secrecy of the ballot, the fate of known opponents of the regime is terrible, the whole population is mustered to the poll, and its votes can be depended upon – it is probably unnecessary to fake the count, though this is of course within the power of the totalitarian regime. The result is that an election ceases to be a public act of choice and becomes a public act of acclamation. Zealous servants of the regime push voting statistics to unheard of levels – 99 per cent of the votes in favour of the government; such figures condemn themselves in the sight of anyone who knows anything about electoral administration. There remains something which is called an election, and which possesses the trappings of an election, such as electoral cards, polling booths and voting papers: but which belongs in substance to the category not of elections, but of public demonstrations such as May Day processions and Nuremberg rallies. To quote (at secondhand) from an East German official: 'The actual voting is of no importance. It has all the inevitability of a marriage ceremony. The courting of the bride has been done.'[17]

Therefore, Harrop and Miller correctly ascertain that 'elections are about freedom and choice; [but] they are also about control and constraint'.[18] Indeed, control and constraint were central elements of the pre-revolutionary and Soviet political systems in general, and in particular were present in their manner of conducting elections. Moreover, they are also part of contemporary Russian politics. Our research analyses the interplay and conflict between freedom and choice, and control and constraint in elections in pre-revolutionary Russian, Soviet and contemporary Russian politics and seeks to address the levels and nature of continuity and contradiction between them.

Against these political and historical realities students of Russian politics have to question the degree of importance and impact that the December 1993 elections had in reflecting contemporary power relationships and in creating a post-Soviet political order. On the one hand, the country's long tradition of autocratic and totalitarian rule means that Russia's first post-Soviet multiparty elections should be viewed as historically and politically significant in their own right. But one of the major questions raised by this volume is to what extent these elections have broken away from the Soviet tendencies of limiting competition or, as Michael Urban suggests, creating 'democracy by design'. Moreover, to what extent do these elections conform to established criteria for free and fair elections? Did these elections perform the usual electoral functions? Have these elections brought legitimacy to the Russian political establishment in the wake of Yeltsin's forcible dissolution of the Russian parliament in September–October 1993? What are the results of these elections for Russian politics and society more generally?

As the contributors to this volume suggest, the elections produced outcomes which, although they should not be viewed overenthusiastically, could be interpreted positively for Russia's democratic development. First, as a result of a constitutional plebiscite held on the same day as the elections, Russia has a new constitution which has established the new 'rules of the game' (despite legal controversy surrounding the actual number of Russians who voted in its favour). Second, the election of the first post-Soviet parliament theoretically provides that institution with a degree of political legitimacy that its recently dissolved predecessor may have lacked in the period following the collapse of the USSR. Third, parties and political organizations now have the opportunity to be represented in a legislature and to create links with an electorate. Fourth, through their representatives, voters may now (potentially) exert greater influence over their governors than in the past. With these elections, Russia has taken the equivalent of one step in what will be a political marathon of institutional development and the foundation of an interest-based civil society. Russia also needs to develop and embrace values and attitudes conducive for democratic consolidation, such as tolerance of divergent points of view and trust in the new system and its institutions – although these institutions must demonstrate that they are trustworthy. In many respects old habits and ways of thinking still exist. Political and social forces openly antagonistic to further reform measures have grown in popularity in the post-election period. The Russian president's hegemony in the political sphere and the influence of his personal advisers overshadow those lesser powers allocated to the Federal Assembly. Events like the Chechen débâcle draw images of another 'Politburo' emerging, reducing Russia's policy-making institutions from an amalgam of three constitutionally empowered branches (albeit weighted grossly disproportionately in the president's favour) to, as Aleksandr Solzhenitsyn has accused, an oligarchy consisting of Yeltsin and the Security Council. Therefore, in this respect, it is necessary to consider whether or not the parliamentary elections actually made a difference in contemporary Russia.

The editor considers the political order referred to in the title of this volume to have two meanings. In the first instance it encompasses the set of political arrangements and institutions surrounding the elections. The chapters in this book reflect how the interrelationships between the non-ruling and ruling actors during the pre-revolutionary, Soviet and contemporary periods have affected the way in which electoral politics have been conducted in Russia and, subsequently, explain their results.

Secondly, the editor considers that in contemporary Russia (borrowing Samuel Huntington's phraseology) 'political order is a goal, not a reality'; political order in this instance being a process whereby institutions have become firmly rooted in the country's political practices, function according to their constitutionally defined roles and have acquired popular consensus and legitimacy. Indeed, Russia's path of development away from Communist Party rule is changing rapidly and the country has had little time to form new governing institutions and establish clear definitions of their duties, relationships and responsibilities, or a corresponding set of values which understands and supports the new rules of the political game. A wide array of social forces are competing for power. Numerous economic, political and societal problems must be surmounted before any serious forms of political institutionalization and democratic consolidation can become firmly entrenched in the country.[19] Moreover, the present author does not wish to engage in 'fortune telling'. This, however, does not mean that an analysis of Russia's first post-Soviet multiparty elections to its parliament, the Russian Federal Assembly of December 1993, should be ignored. In this respect, therefore, the elections are looked at in relation to their *degree* of contribution to the processes of institutionalization and consolidation. In this volume the contributors address several key questions: Did the 1993 elections to the Russian Federal Assembly bring forth new political institutions that may gain legitimacy and stability in the near future? Are there competing institutions or social forces which could potentially or actually impede the institutions brought about by the elections? Do these political interactions and relationships have the potential to contribute to the goals of political order or to its anathema: political decay and violence?

Part I of the volume is historical in focus, concentrating on the patterns and roles of the hustings in pre-revolutionary Russian and Soviet politics. Ian D. Thatcher concentrates on elections in Russia from the late nineteenth century until the adoption of the 1936 Stalin Constitution, providing ample evidence of civic activism and participation and political cognition among the pre-revolutionary population, challenging conventional notions of Russia's historical lack of 'civil society' and demonstrating that elections to local-level assemblies, because they affected the affairs of Russians most directly, may have been of more practical importance than is commonly acknowledged. The editor presents an analysis of the Soviet electoral reform in the Gorbachev era, viewing it as a 'half-hearted liberalization' that, paradoxically, the CPSU was unable to regulate entirely, and which subsequently affected the nature of post-Soviet politics, promoting demands for competition and equality of individuals and substantive groups to participate in the elections.

Parts II and III of this volume centre on the 1993 elections and feature case studies of various facets of the contest. The editor's chapter on the election campaign focuses on the contest itself, its major events and the campaign techniques of the electoral associations and Yeltsin administration. Daphne Skillen analyses the performance of the media in the 1993 elections, concentrating primarily on the role of television as the campaign's main – albeit somewhat deficient – medium of communication. Matthew Wyman, Bill Miller, Stephen White and Paul Heywood present a groundbreaking study on party-oriented voting, demonstrating that during the campaign the electoral associations successfully appealed to specific demographic groups. Their contribution challenges claims that Russian parties lack social support bases. Elena Omel'chenko and Hilary Pilkington's regional case study of the elections in Ul'yanovsk demonstrates the significance of local elites in contemporary Russian politics, showing how candidates with proven track records in representing the population appealed more to the electorate than parties with unsubstantiated promises, and how the elections were unable to resolve the political tensions between the centre and the periphery.

The final part of this book is concerned with the institutions, organizations and processes currently influencing the post-Soviet political arrangements. Richard Sakwa focuses on the development of the Russian party system, contending that political parties in Russia have been ineffective in providing a link between civil and political society and that the creation of an effective party system has been hampered by the provenance of parties as part of the 'insurgency' against the Soviet system, by current regime patterns of politics and governance, a fractured and amorphous society and an international trend in decline in party support. Despite these factors, Russian parties have not been entirely unsuccessful in attempting to participate in post-Soviet political life. Stephen White analyses the presidency, tracing the roots of the personalization of power in Russian and Soviet history and explaining how, under present conditions, an overly powerful executive in Russia may be a potential hindrance to the consolidation of a stable democracy. Troy McGrath undertakes an analysis of the Leninist legacy in contemporary Russian politics, arguing that Soviet political practices and attitudes have inevitably survived, with decision-makers either members of the former *nomenklatura* or conditioned by their experience of living in the Soviet 'anti-democracy'. Because these and other negative historical and socio-economic factors are paradoxically being used in an attempt to create a stable democracy, Russia's post-Soviet construction is destined to be haphazard and contradictory. The editor's Conclusion examines executive-legislative relations and post-1993 electoral developments.

An Appendix compiled by the editor contains basic information on the 13 electoral associations that competed in the campaign, including their leading candidates, programme content and committee dominance.

Finally, I would like to add a brief note on the conventions employed in this collection. The transliteration system follows a modified version of the *Europe-Asia Studies* guide. Hence the noted Russian newspaper is spelled *Izvestiya*. Diacritical marks have been removed from the names of the most prominent Russian politicians and in some cases their surnames have been anglicized. Therefore, the Russian president's name is spelled *Yeltsin*, not *El'tsin*, and the Yabloko faction leader's surname appears as *Yavlinsky*. The original Russian names of the political parties and organizations, together with the abbreviations employed in this volume, are given in the Appendix.

Notes

1. Stephen White, 'The Soviet Elections of 1989: From Acclamation to Limited Choice', *Coexistence*, vol. 28, no. 4 (December 1991), pp. 513–39, at p. 513.
2. Samuel P. Huntington, *Political Order in Changing Societies* (New Haven, CT: Yale University Press, 1968), p. 1.
3. Robert A. Dahl, *A Preface to a Democratic Theory* (Chicago and London: University of Chicago Press, 1956), pp. 56–71, cited in Martin Harrop and William L. Miller, *Elections and Voters: A Comparative Introduction* (London: Macmillan, 1987), pp. 5–6.
4. David Butler, Howard R. Penniman and Austin Ranney, 'Introduction: Democratic and Nondemocratic Elections', in David Butler, Howard R. Penniman and Austin Ranney (eds), *Democracy at the Polls: A Comparative Study of Competitive Elections* (Washington, DC, and London: American Enterprise Institute for Policy Research, 1981), pp. 1–6, at p. 4, cited in Harrop and Miller, *Elections and Voters*, p. 6.
5. W.J.M. Mackenzie, *Free Elections: An Introductory Textbook* (London: George Allen and Unwin Ltd, 1958), p. 14, cited in Harrop and Miller, *Elections and Voters*, p. 7.
6. David Butler, 'Electoral Systems', in Butler, Penniman and Ranney, *Democracy at the Polls*, pp. 7–25, at p. 22.
7. ibid., pp. 22–3.
8. Mackenzie, *Free Elections*, pp. 13–14.
9. Anthony King, 'What Do Elections Decide?', in Butler, Penniman and Ranney, *Democracy at the Polls*, pp. 293–324, at p. 322.
10. David Butler, Howard R. Penniman and Austin Ranney, 'Introduction: Democratic and Nondemocratic Elections', in ibid., pp. 1–6, at p. 4.
11. *Konstitutsiya (Osnovnoi Zakon) Soyuza Sovetskikh Sotsialisticheskikh Respublik* (Moscow: Politizdat, 1978).
12. For general discussions of the CPSU see Leonard Schapiro, *The Communist Party of the Soviet Union* (London: Methuen, 1963) and Ronald J. Hill and Peter Frank, *The Soviet Communist Party*, 3rd edition (Boston: Unwin Hyman, 1987).
13. Stephen White, 'Reforming the Electoral System', *Journal of Communist Studies*, vol. 4, no. 4 (December 1988), pp. 1–16, at p. 1.
14. J. Arch Getty, 'State and Society Under Stalin: Constitutions and Elections in the 1930s', *Slavic Review*, vol. 50, no. 1 (Spring 1990), pp. 18–35.
15. For discussions on the procedures and functions of elections and re-election in the Soviet period and the effectiveness of Soviet deputies in their legislative institutions see Victor Zaslavsky and Robert J. Brym, 'The Functions of Elections in the USSR', *Soviet Studies*, vol. XXX, no. 3 (1978), pp. 362–71; Everett Jacobs, 'Soviet Local Elections: What They Are and What They Are Not', *Soviet Studies*, vol. XXII, no. 1 (1970), pp. 61–76; Theodore Friedgut, *Political Participation in the USSR* (Princeton,

NJ: Princeton University Press, 1979), chapter 2; Jeffrey W. Hahn, *Soviet Grassroots: Citizen Participation in Local Soviet Government* (London: I.B. Tauris, 1988); Stephen White, 'Noncompetitive Elections and National Politics: The USSR Supreme Soviet Elections of 1984', *Electoral Studies*, vol. 4, no. 3 (1985); Ronald J. Hill, 'Continuity and Change in USSR Supreme Soviet Elections', *British Journal of Political Science*, vol. 2, no. 1 (1972), pp. 47–68; idem, *Soviet Politics, Political Science and Reform* (London: Martin Robertson, 1980), chapter 2. Statistical data on Soviet representation can be found in *Sostav deputatov, ispolnitel'nykh komitetov, postoyannykh komissii i rezervnykh deputatov mestnykh sovetov 1987 g. (statisticheskii sbornik)* (Moscow: Izvestiya, 1987).

16 Frederick C. Barghoorn, *Politics in the USSR* (Boston: Little, Brown & Co., 1972), p. 246.
17 Mackenzie, *Free Elections*, p. 172.
18 Harrop and Miller, *Elections and Voters*, p. 1.
19 For theoretical discussions on political order, institutionalization and consolidation see, for instance, Huntington, *Political Order*, esp. chapter 1, and John A. Hall, 'Consolidations of Democracy', in David Held (ed.), *Prospects for Democracy: North, South, East, West* (Cambridge: Polity Press, 1993), pp. 271–90, at pp. 277–83.

PART I

Elections in Russia and the USSR: A Historical Overview

2 Elections in Russian and Early Soviet History

IAN D. THATCHER

The lack of a democratic political culture under the tsars is often referred to in accounts seeking to explain how the Soviet Communist Party managed to establish its dictatorship. Alec Nove, for one, sees Stalin's Russia as the heir to a long tradition of dominance by the state.[1] For Leon Trotsky, pre-revolutionary Russian society lacked the social underpinnings, in the form of a strong, indigenous middle class, for a bourgeois democracy; political change in Russia would leap from autocracy to a dictatorship of the proletariat.[2] However, if one examines voting in pre-revolutionary Russia in its widest sense, i.e. not restricting one's focus to elections for a central authority, a more active, democratically inclined picture of civil society emerges.

The commune

Tsarist Russia was a predominantly agrarian society and the predominant form of peasant organization was the commune.[3] Peasant households were collectively responsible for the payment of taxes through the commune, which issued its decisions by communal decrees. The decrees affected many aspects of the peasants' lives, from how much land they would receive to when they could plough it, and when and under what conditions they could leave the village. Communal decrees were not the will of one man, but were decided upon by a meeting of heads of households, mainly but not exclusively male, in the village assembly. The assembly would gather in the open air, on days when its members had time to attend (Sundays and holidays), and often witnessed lively debates. It elected office holders, including the village elder and the communal tax collector. When the majority view was in doubt, the elder would call for a vote; all peasants submitted themselves to its outcome.

Richard Pipes is rather dismissive of the political significance of the village assembly. According to one of his most recent works, the elder was chosen and removed by state bureaucrats; the assembly had no permanent organization, and it contributed nothing to the (non-existent) political culture of its members: peasants expected and responded best to repeated orders from a strong regime.[4] However, a contemporary observer of peasant life remarked:

let not the reader be astonished overmuch ... he is about to receive a still more startling bit of information – a statement that should be heralded in by a flourish of trumpets. In 'the great stronghold of Caesarian despotism and centralized bureaucracy' these village communes ... are capital specimens of representative constitutional government of the extreme democratic type![5]

At minimum peasants seemed able to meet, discuss, resolve issues of common concern, and abide by the authority of the assembly.

Municipal government

Russian males who satisfied certain age, property, or tax and estate requirements were given the opportunity to vote in elections to local authorities by the Zemstvo Statutes of January 1864 and the Municipal Statute of June 1870.[6] These bodies were responsible for the organization and maintenance of roads, and for health care, poor relief and so on. They were not introduced into the Western Provinces until 1911–13, subsequently had additional restrictions placed upon them, and could be suspended by state officials. The electoral principle did, though, run throughout their hierarchical structure: members of the *uezd zemstvo* assembly were elected by a mixture of landed proprietors, urban and village communities; the *uezd zemstvo* executive board was, in part, elected by members of the *zemstvo* assembly.

Pipes argues that elections to the *zemstvo* were of no great significance. The peasants' choice, he states, 'was narrowly circumscribed by bureaucrats and government-appointed officials'.[7] Indeed, the suffrage restrictions imposed by the New Statute concerning Town Government of June 1892,[8] for example, reduced the size of the St Petersburg Duma electorate to a mere twelve thousand;[9] this out of one million inhabitants.[10]

However, elections to local authorities were not abolished outright, and at a later date they were of enough importance for the Prague conference of the Russian Social Democratic Labour Party (RSDRP) of January 1912 to call for 'Social Democratic agitation during elections to the organs of municipal government'.[11] In the long term, municipal elections acted as barometers of the prevalent political mood of the country. In 1909, for example, a Kadet victory over an Octobrist in Moscow's municipal elections convinced the Social Democrats that 'the situation in the country was changing, the bourgeoisie was "moving to the left"'.[12] In 1917, it was precisely at the level of local government that elections were, for the first time in Russian history, universal, direct, secret and equal. Local elections were held across the country from 27 May onwards. They were run on the principle of proportional representation, in which parties and groups put forward lists of candidates. Information regarding the local elections is sadly incomplete. However, on the basis of existing work, useful indicators of levels of party support, and how this support varied over time and by district, are available. In the main, the elections were fair and competitive; public interest, especially in the early campaigns, was high. In contrast to the case in some modern elections, soldiers in barracks also had the franchise. Minor political groups, such as the 'League for Female Equality', in some areas fielded candidates alongside those of more 'established' parties – Kadets, Social Democrats and Socialist Revolutionaries (SRs). One analyst of the local elections of 1917 concludes his report thus: 'By October, Russia's municipal electorate was politically aware. Absenteeism in the later votes suggests frustration with local politics, not political immaturity.'[13]

In the shorter term, it was local government politicians who were to play an important role in the movement which, against a background of wider social upheaval and defeat in war, succeeded in wresting the October manifesto of 1905 from the tsar. This document promised civil liberties and elections to a national state assembly, the Duma.[14]

The Duma

Four Dumas were to meet before this institution was replaced by others created during the revolutions of 1917. To date, there is no single work which compares and contrasts the national elections of 1906, 1907 (two) and 1912.[15] The Law of 11 December 1905, which governed the first two elections, established a complicated electoral process. The 524 deputies to the Duma were to be elected by electoral colleges at the provincial and city levels. The provincial electoral college was made up of persons elected by meetings of five curia, representing the town, landowners, peasants, cossacks and workers. Elections to the curia were not direct, except in the case of the landowners' curia, to which large landowners had a direct vote. The 1,952 members of the landowners' curia were also in part chosen by preliminary curia elected by small landowners. The 1,372 electors in the town curia were chosen by town district assemblies; the 2,659 electors in the peasants' and cossacks' curia had already faced two elections, one at the household level (one representative per ten householders) and the other at the *volost'* or village election. The 150 members of the workers' curia had been elected by a meeting of workers' representatives, themselves elected on the basis of one representative from each factory employing between 50 and 1,000 men. The largest factories elected one additional representative for each extra thousand employees.[16] The different curia did not have equal representation in the provincial electoral college; peasants formed the largest share of electors (42 per cent), and workers the smallest (2.5 per cent). The city electoral college was drawn from cities with separate representation, whose individual deputy was selected by electors representing city districts. Apart from the requirements mentioned above, possession of the franchise depended upon either ownership of land or payment of taxes. Those with multiple ownership could receive more than one vote. Excluded were, among others, women, three and a half million servants, one million construction workers, and workers in small enterprises.

The elections to the First and Second Dumas are notable in several respects. Interest in them was high; in European Russia, for example, over 50 per cent of those eligible to vote cast ballots.[17] Although political parties other than those considered in a favourable light by the government (the Union of October 17, the Union of Russian People, and the Party of Peaceful Restoration) were not legalized, the Kadets, in particular, managed to construct a party organization, although it was limited to the two capitals plus the major towns and cities. Opposition groups depended more upon large contributions from wealthy well-wishers than on individual subscriptions, but their resources proved sufficient to publish campaign literature and newspapers, including the big political daily *Rech'* (Speech). Since a simple majority sufficed in provincial assemblies which could not elect deputies on a majority vote after three days of deliberations, horse trading between groups was engaged in to secure election. Sometimes this meant Octobrists and Kadets colluding to block candidates from the extreme right. In these negotiations peasant electors, mainly literate, showed themselves well able to distinguish those candidates who best suited their interests; in the majority of cases deals were struck with Kadets, although agreements were reached with Octobrists who made plain their abandonment of the party's land policy. The Social Democrats, with the odd exception but including the Social Democracy of the Kingdom of Poland and Lithuania, boycotted the first elections.[18] In the second campaign, despite differences between the Mensheviks and the Bolsheviks, the former being in favour and the latter against electoral agreements with the Kadets, Social Democrats stood on independent platforms.[19]

In both elections, but particularly the second, the government tried to influence the outcome. Those with a claim to multiple votes but who at the same time were likely to vote against the government were denied a second vote. Thus, a peasant who had purchased land through the Land Bank was not allowed to vote in the landowners' curia. The police would arbitrarily strike off peasants and workers from the franchise list; sometimes this involved several thousand voters. Head bureaucrats would instruct subordinates for whom to cast their votes, and priests were enlisted to encourage their flock to support pro-regime candidates. Opposition group meetings were likely to be banned or have special restrictions placed upon them (the parties themselves were, after all, illegal); parties favoured by the government would receive 'perks', including considerable amounts of money to cover campaign costs. In short, considerable effort was expended to obtain a docile, pro-status quo Duma. The attempt failed. Voters proved themselves unimpressed by the government's actions, perhaps, as suggested by Alfred Levin, viewing them as an additional form of repression.

The First Duma was too radical for the regime's liking: 170 Kadets, 90 Trudoviks and only 16 Octobrists. It was dissolved after a mere two months' existence. Its successor was younger and less well-educated in composition. It was also more radical: 123 Kadets, 97 Trudoviks, 83 Social Democrats and Social Revolutionaries, and only 18 extra Octobrists. A disappointed government resolved, first, on another early dissolution and, second, on a change to the electoral law.

Elections to the Third and Fourth Dumas were held according to the subsequent new electoral law, announced on the day of the dissolution of the Second Duma, 3 June 1907. The law's intention was to produce a more 'responsible' Duma, one that more accurately reflected the best interests of the people and one that was more 'Russian in spirit'.[20] Whole areas of the empire were to be disenfranchised, including the Turgai, Yakutsk and Ural *oblasti*, and the Turkestan and Steppe regions. The Duma was scaled down in size from 542 to 442 deputies. A certain number of deputies from the Polish and Transcaucasian delegations had to be Russian, and areas of predominantly Russian population received a disproportionately high number of deputies. No longer would peasants form the largest number of electors in the provincial electoral college. That privilege now fell to the landowners, with 49.6 per cent, followed by the urban population (26.2 per cent); peasants formed only 21.7 per cent and industrial workers a mere 2.3 per cent. For contemporaries and, the odd exception notwithstanding, subsequent historians, 3 June 1907 was a *coup d'état*.[21] Matters were not left there. As if in search of extra insurance that the bias of the new rules would pay dividends, additional obstacles were placed upon the registration of 'unstable types' still holding the franchise. Alfred Levin has provided a convenient summary of these 'irregularities' as they operated in the run-up to the elections to the Third Duma.[22] Among other things, they included the provision that non-taxpaying apartment renters and state pensioners had to present written statements of intention to enrol on the electoral register. These groups had to provide evidence of their status in the form of confirmation from the police or the relevant state body. Often the necessary certification would be denied. Several thousand voters were disenfranchised in Kremenchug for this reason. The liberal press attempted to provide help and information for would-be voters perceived as vital to the Kadets' constituency. However, the rates of urban participation dropped considerably from the previous national elections: a contemporary report covering 67 cities in European Russia noted a 55 per cent turnout of eligible urban voters in the first election of 1907 falling to 19.1 per cent in the second. A similar picture emerges from the rural areas, in which small landowners were notable victims of the regime's exclusionary drive. In Poltava Country, for instance, 16,000 voters in the elections to the First Duma had dwindled to a mere 575 participants in those to the Third. Government interference continued after electors had been chosen. This could take the form of raising doubts about an elector's property qualification: the prominent Kadet professors Milyukov and Gessen had their status as electors questioned because of doubts over whether they actually lived in their flats or not. They survived, but numerous other opposition hopefuls did not. One contestant who stood on the right, Shmid, had objections raised to his candidacy on the grounds that he had been convicted of treason in 1891. In the interim the tsar had pardoned him, and his election was confirmed as legitimate.

Faced with so many problems, it is hardly surprising that large sections of the population looked at the elections to the Third Duma through apathetic eyes. The results revealed that the government, by fair means and foul, had at least secured its immediate objective. In social composition the Third Duma was dominated by the landowning nobility, who accounted for 40 per cent of all deputies. Politically, the leading force was the Octobrists (150 seats). At the other end of the spectrum the Kadets lost over half of their deputies, the Social Democrats even more.

Despite the 'success' of 1907, tsarism never managed to insulate itself from the workings of a democratic spirit. Even the Octobrists expected further liberal reforms and, when these were not forthcoming, their alliance with the government ended.[23] In the 1912 elections to the Fourth Duma the government found itself with a new task: securing a majority of candidates to the right of the Octobrists. It resorted to familiar tactics,[24] but failed to produce the desired result. One study of peasant attitudes in the elections to the Fourth Duma reveals a group of agricultural labourers with a commitment not only to land reform, but also to civil liberties, local government autonomy, and religious and cultural freedoms.[25] Some electors voted for opposition candidates out of annoyance at government interference.[26] The Octobrists emerged with 60 deputies less than in 1907, but they remained the largest single grouping in the new Duma. On top of this, groups to the left, as well as to the right, made gains at the Octobrists' expense. All shades of the political spectrum found representation in the Fourth Duma, which was much less stable from the government's point of view than its predecessor.

The Fourth Duma was to be Russia's last. It survived the declaration of Russia's entry into the World War, but not the February revolution of 1917, although it played a role in bringing about the latter. It was from the floor of the Fourth Duma that Milyukov made his famous speech of November 1916, in which he accused the government of treason.[27] During the war itself Russian 'civil society' revealed its liveliness in demands for a role in the war effort. The government even made provisions for limited elections, for example among the workers who were to elect workers' representatives to the War Industries Committees.[28] It was only after the fall of tsarism, however, that Russia was presented with an opportunity to hold national elections on the four-tail suffrage. This opportunity was taken advantage of in November 1917 when the elections to the Constituent Assembly took place.

The Constituent Assembly

More than thirty parties competed for the 44 million votes cast by men and women aged 20 years and over in November 1917. At a general level, the results themselves were clear enough. The Socialist Revolutionaries topped the polls (40 per cent), followed by the Bolsheviks (23.9 per cent), the Kadets (4.7 per cent) and the Mensheviks (2.3 per cent). Some forms of intimidation during the campaigns undoubtedly took place. In some cases, radical soldiers might threaten waverers with violence if they did not vote Bolshevik; in another incident, a schoolmistress in the Samara province took Bolshevik lists out of the locals' hands, in this way preventing votes being cast for Lenin's party.[29] However, these cases in no way amounted to the sort of concerted campaign which the tsar's government had been able to wage; nor did they have the same impact on the result. Interest in the elections was high, and turnout figures good: 70 per cent in the major cities and from 80 per cent to 97 per cent in the villages. In only one case did the district electoral commission consider holding a re-election because of 'irregularities'. Most electoral observers agreed that the elections were fair and proper. It is true that administrative problems meant that some electoral commissions gave no results of returns. However, in November 1917 the Russian people proved themselves able to conduct democratic elections. Some far-reaching consequences have been extrapolated from the outcome of these elections, including the claim that they reveal the main battle lines of the future Russian civil war.[30] The questions of greatest importance to the current analysis are whether the people knew what they were doing and, therefore, whether one can say that the Russians in 1917 were 'conscious democrats'.

Doubts about the political maturity of the Russian people have been raised from several perspectives, including the lack of voter stability between the various elections – municipal and national – held in close succession, the way in which peasant voters could be swayed by agitators, and, finally, the fact that whole villages were noted to vote as one mass. Do these factors not reveal a politically unsophisticated electorate and, in some cases, an inert peasant mass willing to be led through the polls in unison? There are good reasons for refuting this.

First, given the revolutionary upheavals taking place in Russia in 1917, one could expect nothing other than voter volatility. With regard to the countryside, it is hardly surprising that peasants took into account what information they had at hand. If, for example, political parties had been able to penetrate further into the countryside, peasants would have relied less upon returning soldiers and workmen for information about the general political situation. One cannot say that the peasants lacked the ability to listen to conflicting arguments and make their own decisions simply because the circumstances themselves were sometimes lacking. Finally, peasants voting as one should not be taken as a sign of political immaturity. This occurred because peasants would decide at a meeting of the village assembly, by way of debate and a vote, which party they were going to support at the polls – a method which actually reinforced the democratic process!

One should not point to the lack of open resistance to the dispersal of the Constituent Assembly by the Bolsheviks in January 1918 as an indicator of the weakness of a democratic culture in Russia. This case has been put most forcibly by William Chamberlain in his influential history of the Russian revolution,[31] and repeated by other equally influential historians since.[32] Chamberlain argues that only the numerically small radical and liberal intelligentsia were worried by the dissolution of the Constituent Assembly. The vast majority were indifferent since, according to Chamberlain, there 'was the absence in Russia of any parliamentary tradition, of any widespread understanding, among the masses, of the significance of universal suffrage, free parliamentary debate, civil liberties and other things which, in Western countries, were the fruits of centuries of a process of struggle and evolution which had no parallel in Russia'.[33] Chamberlain makes a final claim that Russia's deficiency of a democratic political culture was such that the alternative to Bolshevism, even on a free election, was a military dictator *à la* Kolchak or Denikin. One can challenge this account for several reasons.

Chamberlain's argument ignores the fact that the Russians did not elect a dictator in November 1917. Furthermore, they rejected the alternative offered by Denikin and Kolchak by not supporting them in the civil war. This does not mean that the Russians preferred a dictatorship of the Bolshevik variety. The Reds were given only qualified approval in the civil war, expressed, for instance, in the slogan 'Bolsheviks not Communists'. Preventing further sessions of the Constituent Assembly did not mark the end of the establishment of Bolshevik one-party rule. This process was still in its early stages, and calls for the reconvening of the Constituent Assembly were to be heard for several years to come. Chamberlain probably underestimates the amount of pro-Constituent Assembly feeling among the workers. Committees in defence of the Constituent Assembly were formed. That armed detachments were not used to resist the dispersal order was due more to a crisis among the leadership than a lack of concern from below.[34] Thousands of Petrograd's workers, particularly in the south-eastern, Nevsky and Vyborg districts, made plain their dissatisfaction at the fate of the Constituent Assembly.[35] The absence of wider protest should not lead one to be too pessimistic about the level of political culture in Russia. Indeed, wide sections of Russian society had been displaying their democratic credentials through another important institution of the Russian revolution, the soviets.

The soviets

Soviets (councils) first appeared in the turmoil of 1905 and reappeared after the February revolution of 1917, forming the backbone of the USSR's state structure and outliving the Soviet system until Yeltsin disbanded them in late 1993. They were composed of workers' representatives elected at the factory. Once gathered, the workers' representatives could, in turn, elect an executive committee and various office holders of the soviet. It was possible for a soviet to represent only a handful of factories situated in a particular district, sometimes connected by trade or craft, while other soviets operated on a city-wide basis. The functions of the soviet varied according to whether it was district- or city-based, and according to the circumstances in which it operated. At a minimum a soviet was a coordinator of strike activity and the workers' negotiator with the factory owners; at a maximum it could demand wider political change and even assume the tasks of local government. Whatever the scale, soviets provided workers with further experience of the electoral process and are an important indicator of the extent to which pre-revolutionary Russian society was democratized.

Representation in the soviet was based upon the size of the factory or garrison concerned, the general rule being one delegate for each four to five hundred workers or, in the case of the Petrograd soviet of 1917, one delegate for each thousand. The elections to the soviets were an ongoing process, with more and more factories sending representatives; there was no provision for

26 *Ian D. Thatcher*

elections on a city-wide basis to be held on one particular day. Once elected a deputy would face re-election every few months, or could be recalled if a sufficient amount of the electorate (one-quarter) so desired. Electoral commissions, elected by the district soviet, ensured fair play at the elections. Of course, there is much debate about the definition and significance of the soviets. However, in his study of St Petersburg during 1905, Surgh notes that 'Petersburg workers participated actively and enthusiastically in the election of their own deputies',[36] and Israel Getzler, writing about the soviets in Saratov, Krasnoyarsk, Tiflis and Kronstadt during 1917, found that:

> it was the multiparty soviets that provided the forum for, and consolidated, that free and open debating society . . . it was the soviets that, by working overtime on the elective principle, turned Russia into a society of voters *par excellence*.[37]

Such democratic institutions would be an obstacle to any force wishing to establish one-party rule. The two issues are so closely interconnected because after the October revolution it was precisely the soviets that formed the new system of government. According to the constitutions of 1918 and 1924, supreme legislative authority lay with the Congress of Soviets of the USSR and, between Congresses, with its Central Executive Committee, while responsibility for local government lay with the town and rural soviets. Following the dispersal of the Constituent Assembly, the town and rural soviets remained as the only institutions through which voters could directly elect their representatives in government. The Central Executive Committee of the Congress of Soviets was to be elected by the Congress's deputies. These in turn were elected by deputies of the town and rural soviets on the basis of one Congress deputy for each 25,000 electors in the towns and one deputy for every 125,000 inhabitants in the villages.[38] Elections to the town and rural soviets were to be called by the soviets themselves, whose executive committees would appoint electoral commissions for overseeing the elections.[39] Enfranchised were all those over 18 who depended upon labour for the satisfaction of their wants, workers' housewives, members of the army and navy, and all those in these categories who through sickness had lost the ability to work. All holders of the franchise could also stand for election. Disenfranchised were those who hired labour or lived off unearned income, professional priests, members of the tsar's security forces, criminals and the clinically insane.[40] The electoral commission would publish names of the disenfranchised, who then had three days to lodge a complaint. This electoral system was defended by the Bolsheviks as protecting the interests of the workers, and compared favourably with bourgeois constitutions which granted the franchise on a property basis to uphold the dictatorship of the bourgeoisie.[41]

Whatever Bolshevik intent, the electors used their votes to show their displeasure with current Bolshevik policies. Indeed, in the spring of 1918 opposition candidates – Menshevik, Socialist Revolutionary and non-party – won majorities in elections to local soviets across Russia. Although regional differences were evident, voters in, for example, the central industrial region, the Black Earth and upper Volga-Urals regions expressed a shared concern on several issues, including Bolshevik economic policy, corruption, authoritarianism, and negotiations for a separate peace with Germany.[42] The Bolsheviks attempted to control the elections to produce results favourable to them. Opponents were arrested, the rules governing the elections were changed, seats were reserved in the soviets' executive committees for 'revolutionary organizations', and in some cases the elections themselves were suspended. However, like the tsarist regime before them, the Bolsheviks ran into several difficulties when trying to channel the popular will. Workers resented the attempts to rig elections and continued to vote for non-Bolshevik candidates. In the famous case of Yaroslavl' the Bolsheviks had to concede to elections, which they subsequently lost, after they had tried to avoid them by arresting the local Mensheviks.

The vitality of multiparty politics in the soviets in 1918 reveals that Russia was not doomed to suffer a dictatorship. Such a system had to be imposed, and electoral politics crushed in the process. It was this that the Bolsheviks chose to do. They responded to their losses in the elections by intensifying repression. Demonstrations were banned, opposition newspapers closed down, curfews announced; in short, martial law was imposed. It was in this way that the conditions for holding multiparty elections were removed. The only answer to this level of repression was all-out war. The politics of the civil war, however, were not simply between antidemocratic Bolsheviks and pro-democratic parties. Equally antidemocratic Whites complicated the picture, and democratic socialists such as the Mensheviks ended by supporting what they thought of as the 'lesser evil', i.e. the Bolsheviks. Some non-Bolsheviks continued to be tolerated in soviets until the early 1920s, but they had no real power. It was not the case that pluralistic politics in the soviets failed because of the poverty of Russian political culture. Rather, the Bolsheviks had to be brutal to subvert the level of pluralism in existence. One of the most famous incidents of this struggle was, of course, the bloody suppression in March 1921 of the Kronstadt rebellion, which called for, among other things, the restoration of multiparty elections to the soviets.[43] By 1922, the Bolsheviks had succeeded in controlling the selection of candidates for election to the soviets. Seats were essentially uncontested and, in these circumstances, it is hardly surprising that interest in voting among the electorate dropped. In the 1922 elections to the soviets, for example, slightly above one in five voters turned out, while in elections to village soviets, in which almost all candidates were male, only one in seven women voters bothered to do so.[44]

In stifling pluralism in the soviets, the Bolsheviks did not extinguish all avenues for democrats to voice their concerns. Pro-democratic forces continued to seek an outlet for expression whenever the opportunity arose, including within the Bolshevik Party itself.

Elections in the Bolshevik Party

Although affecting only a tiny proportion of Russia's population (party membership was some 700,000 by 1921), elections within the Bolshevik Party are worth studying. Given that the party dominated the soviets, it was from within the party that the leading government figures would emerge. Hence, plurality of candidates and freedom of discussion in elections to party posts would be one way in which differing political programmes could compete for dominance. In turn, these programmes would be subject to (admittedly limited) popular approval in the elections to the local soviets. According to its rules the Bolshevik Party made provisions for elections at several levels of its organization. At the bottom of its structure were the party cells; above them county and district conferences and committees; above them regional conferences and committees; and above them the All-Russian Congress and its Central Committee. The All-Russian Congress was the party's highest organ and delegates to it were elected by local organizations. The officials of the local organizations themselves were elected by local party members.

In the first year of Bolshevik rule debates on the leading issues of the day were conducted throughout the party, its sections changing sides according to the developing situation and the persuasiveness of arguments. This was especially true over the issues of peace with Germany and economic policy, in which the Left-Communist proponents of a revolutionary war with Germany and of workers' control of industry managed to win over many regional party congresses and committees and to issue their own journal, *Kommunist*".[45] However, the Seventh Party Congress of March 1918, at which the Left Communists were defeated, was the last Congress to resolve an important (state) policy issue by a majority vote. Moreover, from 1919 the party's higher echelons increasingly came to control the party's structure, sending instructions down without prior consultation. It was at the Eighth Party Congress of 1919, for instance, that the Politburo, Orgburo and Secretariat were formed. The first was to decide policy on urgent matters, the latter two were to monitor the party's rank and file, and soon took to the practice of appointing local party officials.

Various groups emerged to protest against the elimination of the electoral principle within the party, including the Workers' Opposition and the Democratic Centralists, both of which found representation at the Tenth Party Congress of March 1921. Elections to this Congress were still relatively free and open,[46] and Aleksandra Kollontai was able to distribute her pamphlet *The Workers' Opposition*, which criticized the bureaucratic nature of the Soviet state.[47] However, it was precisely the Tenth Congress which sanctioned the demise of both free debate and the possibility for competitive elections within the party by banning the formation of fractions. Henceforth, party members could not coalesce around a platform independent of the Central Committee's. It was with reference to this resolution that all subsequent calls for intra-party democratization were crushed. In the light of the upper echelon's increasingly tight grip over the party (from the Eleventh Congress onwards, for example, the Central Committee could authorize the provincial committees to select delegates to the All-Russian Congress by means other than elections) the amount of support given to future calls for intra-party democratization was impressive. In his study of the officially sanctioned Party Discussion of 1923–4, for example, Darron Hincks found that at least one quarter of Moscow's workers' cells backed Trotsky's campaign for a return to a regime of intra-party democracy.[48] Such campaigns were to fail for a number of reasons, but partly because the Secretariat had control over who would attend congresses and who could publish what and where. With the party under the control of the Central Committee, opposition to the leader within the Central Committee subdued and party control of the soviets secure, the circumstances were favourable for the Bolshevik leadership to 'liberalize' elections to the soviets. This it did in the new constitution of 1936.

The 1936 Constitution

When the party leadership under Stalin felt safe from criticism within the party, and from the emergence of political forces within society, it decided to change the rules governing the elections to the soviets. The 1936 Constitution made the party's domination of the governmental system and of society explicit. It also sought to overcome the embarrassing situation in which sections of the population were explicitly disenfranchised. In contrast to those of 1918 and 1924, the 1936 Constitution made elections to all soviets – provincial, national and all-union – universal, equal and direct by secret ballot. The vote was given to all citizens over 18 years of age, including those in the armed forces. The right to stand as a candidate was open to all citizens aged 23 years and over. Candidates could be nominated by social organizations, including those of the Communist Party, trade unions, cooperatives, youth organizations and cultural societies.[49] Appointed electoral commissions were to ensure that all nominations were lawful and that the elections conformed to electoral procedures. Electors to the Supreme Soviet were to vote for deputies to the Council of Union (one deputy for each 300,000 inhabitants) and the Council of

Nationalities (twenty-five deputies from each Union republic, eleven from each autonomous republic, five from each autonomous region, and one from each national circuit). Thus, electors would vote twice, unless they also lived in an autonomous region within a republic, in which case they would vote three times. Polling would take place on a Sunday between 6 a.m. and midnight in electoral districts of between two and three thousand. Once elected a deputy could be recalled at any time if a majority of electors demanded this. If not, elections would be held once every four years. In the regulations for the first Supreme Soviet elections of 1937 provision was made for multicandidate elections: voters were told to cross out all names apart from the one candidate they wished to vote for. In the event, despite Stalin's assertion to a foreign journalist that the elections would be lively and contested,[50] only one candidate was offered to electors in each constituency.[51]

The Communist Party could be well pleased with the results of the first elections to the Supreme Soviet of 1937. Almost 97 per cent of the electorate turned out to vote, with 97 per cent of those voting in favour of the official candidate. The pattern for subsequent elections to local and national soviets had been set. The purpose of these elections was to show the legitimacy of Communist Party rule as a reflection of the popular will. The low turnout figures of the 1922 elections could not be allowed to continue. In future elections as many as 99.7 per cent (1954), 99.97 per cent (1958) and 99.99 per cent (1984) of the electorate would vote in elections to the USSR Supreme Soviet. In turn, those elected were a microcosm of Soviet society itself; a sign, it was hoped, of the representative nature of the Soviet electoral process.

The fact that Stalin changed the constitution in the way that he did showed that the Communist Party now felt able to achieve what Nicholas II and the Bolshevik regime of the early 1920s had not: a successful manipulation of the electorate. This was not a testimony to the political immaturity of the Russian and Soviet people, but a sign of the extent to which the Communist Party had imposed itself on society. On the surface, at least, elections to the soviets were conducted in the 'acclamatory' fashion described in the Introduction to this volume, managing to keep alive procedures associated with free elections – regularity, polling booths, equality of franchise. Therefore, Gorbachev's reforms realized more fully – albeit not completely – the electoral potential that was present for more than half a century under both the Stalin and the Brezhnev Constitutions.

Conclusion

In this chapter, a historical contribution to a book on Russia's modern elections, I have chosen to emphasize the extent to which voting was prevalent in the late nineteenth and early twentieth centuries. If one recognizes the strength of the emerging democratic culture of the time, and sees how much Russian citizens understood about elections, and what they expected from them, it is not difficult to understand why dictatorial Bolshevism, and later Stalinism, had to shed so much blood in order to establish themselves on Russian soil. Elections and popular expressions of voters' intentions, together with pluralism within the party itself, were unacceptable obstacles in the way of the party's complete domination of the political and social spheres.

The examples raised in this chapter point to significant continuities in the country's turbulent political culture: the overwhelmingly powerful central institution or personality willing to manipulate and intervene in the electoral process in order to maintain its dominant position, and an electorate which, when given the opportunity to do so, will use their votes to express their dissatisfaction with the status quo. These factors were evident in the elections conducted under Gorbachev and, more recently, in Russia's first post-communist, multiparty contest. Supporters of democratic change in the USSR had grounds for rejoicing when, in 1989, the electorate cast their ballots for (an albeit small corps of) reform-minded candidates who successfully unseated unresponsive, unpopular party-sponsored candidates, often despite CPSU interference. The fact that, in 1993, nearly one-quarter of all Russian voters cast their ballots for the national list of Vladimir Zhirinovsky's ultra-nationalist Liberal Democratic Party of Russia demonstrates even more clearly the extent to which Russian voters can be pushed when they perceive that their government is not taking their interests into consideration when formulating policy. The lessons to be learned from this development are self-evident.

Notes

1 See, for example, Alec Nove, *Stalinism and After* (London, 1975), p. 13.
2 For an exposition of Trotsky's view on the course of the Russian revolution see Ian D. Thatcher, 'Uneven and Combined Development', *Revolutionary Russia*, 2 (1991), pp. 235–58.
3 According to Mackenzie Wallace, about five-sixths of the Russian population lived in rural communes. See D. Mackenzie Wallace, *Russia* (London, 1877), p. 126.
4 Richard Pipes, *The Russian Revolution 1899–1919* (London, 1990), chapter 3.
5 Mackenzie Wallace, *Russia*, p. 126.
6 For an abridged version of these statutes see George Vernadsky et al., *A Source Book for Russian History From Early Times to 1917*, vol. III: *Alexander II to the February Revolution* (New Haven, 1972), pp. 613–14, 621–2.
7 Pipes, *The Russian Revolution*, p. 111. In an account of his visits to the sessions of the *zemstvo* assembly, however, Mackenzie Wallace noted the presence of peasant delegates, how they were listened to, and how the workings of the *zemstva* (pl.) were 'not only unmistakably parliamentary but extremely democratic'. Mackenzie Wallace, *Russia*, pp. 213–28.
8 Vernadsky et al., *A Source Book*, pp. 689–90. For the suffrage restrictions imposed by the New Zemstva Statute of June 1890 see ibid., pp. 688–9.
9 Robert B. McKean, *St Petersburg Between the Revolutions* (New Haven, 1990), p. 39.
10 Gerald D. Surgh, *1905 in St Petersburg* (Stanford, 1989), p. 11.
11 Ralph Carter Elwood (ed.), *Resolutions and Decisions of the Communist Party of the Soviet Union*, vol. I: *The Russian Social Democratic Labour Party 1898–October 1917* (Toronto, 1974), p. 150.
12 G.R. Swain, 'Bolsheviks and Metal Workers on the Eve of the First World War', *Journal of Contemporary History*, vol. 16 (1981), p. 279.
13 William G. Rosenberg, 'The Russian Municipal Duma Elections of 1917: A Preliminary Computation of Returns', *Soviet Studies*, vol. XXI (1969), p. 163. Information about these elections is drawn from Rosenberg's excellent paper.
14 Vernadsky et al., *A Source Book*, p. 705.
15 The information in this section is derived from several works, most notably Abraham Ascher, *The Revolution of 1905: Authority Restored* (Stanford, 1992); Terence Emmons, *The Formation of Political Parties and the First National Elections in Russia* (Cambridge, MA, 1983); David Lane, *The Roots of Russian Communism* (Assen, 1969), and Alfred Levin, *The Second Duma* (Hamden, 1966).
16 This principle of electing factory representatives had already been employed by the tsarist regime when it requested workers to elect representatives to the Shidlovsky Commission. For a contemporary's account of these elections

see Solomon Schwarz, *The Russian Revolution of 1905: The Workers' Movement and the Formation of Bolshevism and Menshevism* (Chicago, 1967), chapter 2. Provisions for elections among workers were also part of the social insurance legislation of 1912. For an English version of the legislation itself see Vernadsky et al., *A Source Book*, pp. 821–2. For an account of the elections see McKean, *St Petersburg*, chapter 7.
17 Ascher, *The Revolution of 1905*, p. 45.
18 For an account of Russian Social Democracy and the elections to the First Duma see J.L.H. Keep, 'Russian Social Democracy and the First State Duma', *Slavonic and East European Review*, vol. 34 (1955–6), pp. 180–99.
19 Levin cites an example of agreements between Moscow Bolsheviks and *Narodniki*, and between Moscow Mensheviks and Kadets, breaking down because of differences over the distribution of seats.
20 Vernadsky et al., *A Source Book*, p. 788.
21 For a contemporary view, see, for example, Trotsky's article (under the pseudonym Anon) in his journal *Bor'ba*, 1 (1914), pp. 7–13. Modern historians holding this opinion include Ascher, *The Revolution of 1905*, pp. 355–8, and, more recently, James D. White, *The Russian Revolution 1917–21: A Short History* (London, 1994), p. 35. A different view is held by, for example, Pipes, *The Russian Revolution*, pp. 180–2.
22 Alfred Levin, 'The Russian Voter in the Elections to the Third Duma', *Slavic Review* (1962), pp. 660–77.
23 For an analysis of Octobrist–government relations in the Third Duma see, for example, Ben-Cion Pinchuk, *The Octobrists in the Third Duma, 1907–1912* (Seattle, 1974).
24 See, for example, Geoffrey A. Hosking, *The Russian Constitutional Experiment, Government and Duma, 1907–1914* (Cambridge, 1973), pp. 183–4.
25 Eugene D. Vinogradoff, 'The Russian Peasantry and the Elections to the Fourth State Duma', in Leopold H. Haimson, *The Politics of Rural Russia 1905–1914* (Bloomington, IN, 1979), pp. 219–60.
26 White, *The Russian Revolution*, p. 39.
27 For an account of Milyukov's speech and its impact on the politics of the time see, for example, Pipes, *The Russian Revolution*, pp. 253–5.
28 For an exposition of the events surrounding the elections among workers to the War Industries Committees, see, for example, McKean, *St Petersburg*, p. 380*ff*.
29 For these examples see Oliver Henry Radkey, *The Election to the Russian Constituent Assembly of 1917* (Cambridge, MA, 1950), chapter 4.
30 William A. Dando, 'A Map of the Election to the Russian Constituent Assembly of 1917', *Slavic Review* (1962), pp. 314–19.
31 William Henry Chamberlain, *The Russian Revolution*, vol. I (Princeton, 1987).
32 See, for example, E.H. Carr, *The Bolshevik Revolution 1917–1923*, vol. I (London, 1950), p. 121.
33 Chamberlain, *The Russian Revolution*, p. 371.

34 Pipes, *The Russian Revolution*, p. 557.
35 Vera Broido, *Lenin and the Mensheviks* (Boulder, CO, 1987), pp. 25–6; William G. Rosenberg, 'Russian Labor and Bolshevik Power: Social Dimensions of Protest in Petrograd after October', in Daniel H. Kaiser (ed.), *The Workers' Revolution in Russia, 1917: The View From Below* (Cambridge, 1987), p. 117.
36 Surgh, *1905*, p. 328.
37 Israel Getzler, 'Soviets as Agents of Democratization', in E.R. Frankel, J. Frankel and B. Knei-Paz (eds), *Revolution in Russia: Reassessments of 1917* (Cambridge, 1992), p. 17.
38 B. Vinogradov, *Konstitutsii Soyuza SSR i RSFSR* (Moscow, 1933), p. 26.
39 P. Stuchka, *Uchenie o gosudarstve i o konstitutsii RSFSR* (Moscow, 1923), p. 212.
40 Vinogradov, *Konstitutsii*, pp. 35–6.
41 See, for example, Stuchka, *Uchenie*, pp. 202–13.
42 See, for example, the excellent article by Vladimir Brovkin, 'The Mensheviks' Political Comeback: The Elections to the Provincial City Soviets in Spring 1918', *Russian Review*, vol. 42, no. 1 (January 1983), pp. 1–50, from which much information for this section has been derived.
43 On Kronstadt see, for example, Paul Avrich, *Kronstadt 1921* (Princeton, 1970) and Israel Getzler, *Kronstadt 1917–1921: The Fate of a Soviet Democracy* (Cambridge, 1983).
44 Roger Pethybridge, *One Step Backwards Two Steps Forward* (Oxford, 1990), p. 158.
45 On the Left Communists see Ronald I. Kowalski, *The Bolshevik Party in Conflict: The Left-Communist Opposition of 1918* (Basingstoke, 1991).
46 R. Gregor, Introduction, in R. Gregor (ed.), *Resolutions and Decisions of the Communist Party of the Soviet Union*, vol. 2: *The Early Soviet Period 1917–1929* (Toronto, 1974), p. 11.
47 For an English translation of this text see *Alexandra Kollontai Selected Writings* (London, 1977), pp. 159–200.
48 Darron Hincks, 'Support for the Opposition in Moscow in the Party Discussion of 1923–1924', *Soviet Studies*, vol. 44, no. 1 (1992), pp. 137–51.
49 F.J.M. Feldbrugge, *The Constitutions of the USSR and the Union Republics: Analysis, Texts, Reports* (Alphen aan den Rijn, 1979), pp. 120–22.
50 Leonard Schapiro, *The Government and Politics of the Soviet Union* (London, 1972), p. 112.
51 For a very detailed discussion of the 1936 Constitution and the debate surrounding the holding of the 1937 elections see J. Arch Getty, 'State and Society Under Stalin: Constitutions and Elections in the 1930s', *Slavic Review*, vol. 50, no. 1 (Spring 1990), pp. 18–35.

3 Reforming the Soviet Electoral System

PETER LENTINI

This chapter outlines the major features of the Soviet electoral system, positing that throughout its existence the USSR – even under the Gorbachev leadership – never held 'free' or 'fair' elections in the conventionally understood sense. When one looks at the standard criteria for free elections and the functions elections serve in a polity, Soviet pre-reform (pre-1989) elections were relatively unimportant: they had no influence over the formation of governments and their policy-making; they did not initiate regime change. Rather than being free or classical elections, they were 'acclamatory' elections.

Despite increasing opportunities for Soviet voters to select from more than one candidate, who usually stood on different platforms, the Soviet electoral reform measures under Gorbachev are considered examples of *liberalization*, according to Elemer Hankiss's definition. This process includes 'only half-hearted and incomplete reforms, alternating them with anti-reform measures', owing largely to a 'duality of goals' on the part of the regime. Hankiss contends that:

> Liberalization is the opposite of democratization ... the latter is the creation of an institutional system based on real power, that guarantees rights stipulated in the constitution of a community. Liberalization, on the other hand, works without rights ... [and] make[s] people feel free ... without giving them rights.

He argues that liberalization is a form of paternalism. Liberalizing rulers are likened to 'enlightened despots': they desire to be loved but do not want the population to become too pushy. Liberalizers strive for their citizens to obey them through love rather than through coercion.[1] Under Gorbachev, reform measures opened a wider sphere of participation and new roles for citizens. However, they were intended to be a means of strengthening socialist society. The Communist Party of the Soviet Union (CPSU) was to remain the country's leading force. Electoral changes were implemented largely in order to disentrench opponents of reform measures, while retaining a CPSU monopoly in the political sphere.[2] Rights that were implemented under the changes were not new; rather they were reinterpreted or, more precisely, finally allowed to be fulfilled. This chapter concentrates predominantly on the 1989 elections to the USSR Congress of People's Deputies and their impact on future Soviet electoral development. Also addressed are post-1989 Soviet writings on electoral reform.

Pre-reform Soviet elections

The laws governing Soviet elections up to December 1988 resembled those of many countries considered to be liberal democracies.[3] Voting was a constitutional right.[4] All Soviet citizens aged 18 and over, unless declared legally insane, possessed active electoral rights (i.e. the right to vote). Those 21 and over could stand as USSR Supreme Soviet deputies (passive electoral rights). Elections were conducted frequently: elections to local soviets (from village to provincial and territorial – *oblast'* and *krai* – levels) were held every two and a half years; voters elected the USSR and republican Supreme Soviets every five years. Men and women had the same voting rights and every elector participated on an equal basis – one vote per citizen. Voting was to be conducted by secret ballot; and restricting a voter's exercise of this right was forbidden by law.

Despite their superficial conformity with exercises of franchise generally regarded as 'fair and free', Soviet elections were justifiably viewed critically by outside observers. First, although no law expressly limited the number of candidates who could stand as deputies in any given constituency, it was the invariable practice – under all leaders from Stalin to Chernenko – that only a single candidate was put forward. Second, nomination rights were restricted to a closed circle – among them the CPSU, trade unions and other officially sanctioned social organizations, meetings of labourers in work collectives and farms and servicemen in military districts. Attempts by other groups, such as Election 79, to propose candidates without CPSU sanction – in this case dissident historian Roy Medvedev – were unsuccessful.[5] Third, voting was a passive act. Electors were required to cross out the names of the candidates against whom they wished to vote. However, there was only one name on the ballot paper. Soviet citizens cast their votes by walking directly to the ballot boxes and dropping in their unmarked papers. In such conditions, the right to vote secretly was continually violated. Voting booths were set up away from the ballot boxes. Therefore, an elector who intended to vote against the officially approved candidate had to make a detour in full view of the public's gaze. V. Timofeev, a war and labour veteran, claimed:

You get your ballot – everyone is looking at you. You pull a pencil out of your pocket – everyone can guess your intentions. Young pioneers or poll attendants are standing by the polling booth. If you go into the booth, it's clear that you voted against the candidate. Those who don't want to vote against go straight to the ballot box. It's the same at plant trade union elections and party election conferences. You can't even go off into a corner by yourself before a curious eye is peering over your shoulder.[6]

The manner of conducting elections was deficient, and the quality of representatives was equally inadequate. Deputyships were allocated in conjunction with party leadership positions, as rewards for exemplary work records, or were handed out to cultural figures. Whether or not a particular deputy would be competent in his or her duties as a legislator was not important. Party officials took great pains to construct a reasonable demographic equivalent of the administrative unit in its representative organs.[7] As a result, there were higher numbers of young people, pensioners, manual industrial and agricultural workers, recipients of secondary education and women in Soviet representative institutions than in their Western counterparts.[8] It is indeed justified to state that most deputies who served in the soviets owed their positions to *who they were* not to *what they could do*. Deputy turnover was sufficiently high, however, that a corps of representatives – high-ranking male officials in the party/state/trade union/Komsomol hierarchy – was generally guaranteed to be re-elected.[9] According to Jeffrey W. Hahn:

from 1937 to 1988 all decisions by the 1,500 member Supreme Soviet were made unanimously in two sessions a year, each lasting only a few days. Obviously, one had to look for real political power elsewhere; it certainly did not belong to the soviets.[10]

True political power was held by the CPSU. Elected legislatures provided the party with a veneer that it could use to demonstrate to the outside world its popular legitimacy and right to rule.

Turnout figures were ridiculously high: official statistics reported that over 99 per cent of the electorate voted in the elections, casting nearly the same percentage of ballots in favour of the candidates.[11] Party officials went to great lengths to make voting almost unavoidable. Elections were scheduled on Sundays, a traditional day off from work, in order to maximize turnout. A corps of agitators went out and literally coerced voters to turn up to polling stations to participate in the façade; they, in turn, were hassled by the party to make sure the voters on their lists showed up. Conventions such as certificates to vote elsewhere removed electors from the rolls, effectively making it appear that more people than was actually the case had cast their ballots.[12]

Soviet elections performed a variety of functions, as a means of political participation and socialization, incorporation, mobilization and legitimation of CPSU rule.[13] Voters could, for instance, reject candidates, but this occurred very rarely, and usually only at village or city levels.[14] They could also air their grievances and refuse to vote if issues crucial to their locality were not rectified, such as street repairs and housing problems.[15] When one examines the functions of elections discussed in the Introduction to this volume, Soviet exercises of franchise more closely resembled the forms of 'coercion and control'[16] described by Harrop and Miller than, for instance, what David Butler considered a 'final sanction against government' or 'a device to choose a viable government and give it legitimacy'.[17] In this sense, they were clearly examples of what Mackenzie labels 'elections by acclamation'.[18]

Electoral reform under Gorbachev

Several factors prompted Gorbachev to initiate electoral reform measures to change the Soviet electoral process from an 'acclamatory' system to a 'limited-choice' variant like those that existed in Eastern Europe;[19] none, however, was intended to weaken the party's control over society or to reduce its hegemony in the political system. First, Gorbachev's reform programme was centred initially around economic reform. Political reforms followed as mechanisms to achieve the former. The electoral changes could be interpreted as measures to remove conservative members of the bureaucracy from positions of power. This in turn would open the way for (theoretically) reformist politicians to implement further changes and assist in achieving the general secretary's goals. Second, and closely related to the first point, Gorbachev sought to bring forth a new corps of deputies who possessed the technical competence to serve as effective legislators. Consequently, they would participate actively in sessions of the soviets and initiate measures necessary for societal reconstruction. Third, Gorbachev sought to renew the party's relations with society. The CPSU, he claimed, had to prove that it was worthy of leading society. Therefore, party secretaries would no longer be guaranteed seats in corresponding-level soviets. They would have to compete against other candidates and prove their mettle. Should the official fail to win a seat in the legislature his or her position within the CPSU would then come into question. In this sense, it is evident that Gorbachev sought to introduce some forms of popular checks over the party. Nevertheless, it is indeed plausible that Gorbachev intended to mobilize the human factor against his potential opponents in this manner.

Indeed electability was an important component of Gorbachev's overall programme. From 1987, competitive elections were to be conducted for positions within trade union and Komsomol organizations.[20] More significantly, places within the CPSU were to be determined by competitive, direct, secret voting. The centrepiece of the economic reform programme, the 1987 Law on State Enterprise, included provisions for workers to elect their managers. It was hoped that this mechanism would give workers more of a say in their own affairs and make them feel more like masters of their own destiny. Despite the good intentions behind attempts to introduce competitive elections for these positions, the reforms ultimately failed. Either *nomenklatura* officials interfered in the electoral proceedings of these organizations or elections were not conducted at all. Stephen White notes that elections in the party did not come to full fruition because of a lack of implementation at higher levels:

Over 1,000 local party secretaries had been chosen on a competitive basis [by 1989]. This, however, was only 8.6 per cent of the total; at higher levels the proportions were even less impressive – only seven provincial secretaries, for example, had been elected on a competitive basis, which [was] just 1 per cent of the total.[21]

Local officials influenced the proceedings of management elections and workers often voted for candidates who were 'easy-going' and proposed lower production targets and higher prices for their goods.[22] Former Politburo member Yegor Ligachev noted other drawbacks of management elections:

How much damage was caused by the pseudo-democratic principle of electing economic leaders? Not a single country in the world elects managers; they are appointed. But here too, we found ourselves ahead of the whole planet, demonstrating the immaturity of our democracy. Many excellent managers were removed from their posts.[23]

Because of their ineffectiveness, management elections were withdrawn from a later variant of the law.

Elections in these organizations and among economic managers formed part of the liberalization of the electoral process. These examples demonstrate that legislation was produced which contained an extension of rights. However, these rights were not allowed to be implemented in practice. The CPSU, by either interfering in the elections themselves or failing to implement them, obstructed further political changes.

Gorbachev also introduced an 'experimental' election to local councils in June 1987, in which 1 per cent of the USSR's constituencies were condensed to create multimember districts. Voters could select from among a number of candidates. The one receiving the greatest share of votes, exceeding 50 per cent of those cast by the participating electorate, was declared the winner. Other candidates who received over 50 per cent became reserve deputies who would act as substitutes when the actual deputy was absent from the soviet. Overall only some 5 per cent of deputies were elected in this manner. However, there were some instances in which leading officials either did not obtain the confidence of more than half of the participating electorate or were reduced to the status of reserve deputies.[24]

In 1988, the USSR Supreme Soviet released for public discussion drafts of constitutional amendments which revamped the state structure,[25] together with a new draft electoral law.[26] These documents were adopted at the Twelfth Extraordinary Session of the USSR Supreme Soviet in December 1988. The revisions to the state institutions included the creation of a new supreme legislative organ, a USSR Congress of People's Deputies. This comprised 2,250 deputies: 750 deputies elected from each of three electoral divisions. First, 750 deputies would be elected from territorial districts, divided notionally according to population distribution. Second, 750 deputies would be elected from national-territorial districts, established on a set basis according to the type of territorial administrative unit. There were 32 deputies allocated to each republic, 11 to each autonomous republic, five to each autonomous *oblast'* and one to each autonomous district. The remaining 750 deputies were representatives of all-union social organizations such as the CPSU, trade unions, creative unions and other similar organizations. Seat allocation was determined by the electoral law.[27] In the constituencies registered voters elected their deputies directly, whereas only delegates to the social organizations' all-union gatherings – conferences, congresses and plenums – could elect the representatives from that electoral division.

Congress deputies would elect from among their members 450 deputies to serve in the USSR Supreme Soviet, which would function as the Soviet Union's permanently functioning legislative organ (deputies were to serve on a rotating basis) – a change which in effect marginalized the electorate. With deputies electing the permanently functioning legislative body, it can be argued that Soviet voters in reality only chose an electoral college. Moreover, because it was assumed that deputies would be predominantly CPSU members, electing the Supreme Soviet would be yet another means by which the party could implement a liberalizing tactic of increasing electoral choice but reducing its significance.

The social organizations' provision, which is criticized in greater detail elsewhere in this chapter, can certainly be considered an example of liberalization. The addition of the social organization seats was another potential control mechanism that party officials used to maintain dominance in the legislature. First, it was thought that the overwhelming majority of social organization deputies would be CPSU members. By dint of adherence to principles of democratic centralism, they would be forced to promote the party line in any vote. Second, not all Soviet citizens had the opportunity to stand for these seats: only members could put forth candidacies. Third, not every elector could cast a ballot for these deputies; only the delegates to the all-union gatherings could do so. Hence, these seats and the procedures for their election violated the principle of one person – one vote.

The draft electoral law suggested that, as a rule, there were to be more candidates than seats (Article 9). This provision, however, did not make it into the final version, which mandated that there may be 'any number of candidates'. While the overwhelming majority of seats were contested, it is apparent that competition was not universal. For instance, during the first round of elections (11–26 March 1989), there were 2,895 candidates registered in the 1,500 constituencies which included 1,449 in territorial districts and 1,446 in national-territorial districts. However, this included 384 districts in which a single candidate stood.[28] Following the series of run-off and repeat elections held in April–May some 5,074 candidates made it to the final ballot paper.[29] Nevertheless, 399 candidates were selected in the old manner of one candidate per seat.[30] Within the social organizations there were initially 880 candidates who contested for seats,[31] and after repeat and run-off elections there were 912 who participated in the campaign.[32] There was, however, significant variation in the levels of competitiveness within the social organizations. For instance, there were 100 candidates for the 100 seats that the CPSU was allocated; but not all of them received unanimous approval, including Gorbachev himself (12 votes against).[33] The Council of Collective Farms approved 58 candidates for its 58 seats in an open vote within half an hour,[34] whereas the Writers' Union had to whittle down its final list of 12 candidates from a field of 92 contestants.[35]

Other innovations that the law introduced were the provision that candidates had to present their electorates with programmes of their future activities, and the expansion of nomination rights to encompass meetings of 500 or more voters from one particular locality. Moreover, citizens could nominate themselves as candidates. These were certainly qualitative steps forward in Soviet electoral practices. In the first instance, voters would have some idea of what their deputies would stand for or against at the Congress. Subsequently, they could make well-informed choices, based on issues, as to whom to vote for or against. Nevertheless, there were no provisions which stated that contestants had to determine ways in which they could *achieve* their objectives. As a result, the Soviet electorate viewed these programmes sceptically.[36] Meetings and self-nominations possessed democratic potentials. However, it was very difficult for independents without CPSU backing to break through the requirement that more than half of the members of a quorate work collective or residential meeting support the candidates. It was very easy for the CPSU and other reactionary forces to manipulate or obstruct meetings' proceedings.[37]

The discussion thus far has focused on how the ruling elite promoted measures that on the surface looked as if they were expanding political privileges, but in the end retracted them. There were other, positive achievements of the electoral reform, which demonstrated either that the CPSU was willing to tolerate limited opposition, or that it was unable to prevent it. Moreover, the rights that Soviet citizens possessed from previous legislation were finally realized. For instance, secret ballot was now compulsory. Voting booths were set up before ballot boxes. Soviet voters, even in constituencies where one candidate was on the paper, had to go into a voting booth before casting their ballots. Additionally, voters could exercise freely the right not to vote. Agitation was reduced and canvassers only left the polling stations to take the ballot boxes to those who were unable to make the journey to vote. Nevertheless, the overall turnout was still relatively good; some 89.8 per cent nationwide with significant republican variations: Azerbaijan recorded a near 'good old days' 98.5 per cent participation rate, while earthquake-stricken yet defiant Armenia's turnout was the lowest at 71.9 per cent, declining over 28 per cent from 99.99 per cent in 1984 according to official statistics.[38] Not all candidates who made it onto the ballot paper were CPSU-approved; in fact some were anti-establishment figures and some were very successful. Boris

Yeltsin's candidacy in Moscow national-territorial district no. 1 is a good example. In 1989, Yeltsin, out of favour with the leadership, ran a successful campaign against party-sponsored ZiL automobile factory director Yevgenii Brakov, polling nearly 90 per cent of the votes in the contest. Although the party may have tried to manipulate election meetings and restrict candidates, citizens agitated for those individuals they thought best expressed their interests. The example of Zhitomir residents rallying to get journalist Alla Yaroshinskaya on the ballot paper illustrates the high degree of civic activism that some Soviets demonstrated during the electoral campaign.[39] In addition, groups of electors or informal groups supported candidates or opposed official contestants, thus introducing grass-roots political organizing into Soviet electioneering.[40]

The Congress and Supreme Soviet, although dominated by conservative deputies,[41] produced several significant legislative acts, including the monumental adoption of the amendment to Article 6. Moreover, the elections to the Congress produced Soviet history's first opposition, the Inter-regional Deputies' Group, which consisted of Boris Yeltsin, future St Petersburg mayor Anatolii Sobchak and (until his death in December 1989) Academician Andrei Sakharov. Nevertheless, its ranks were small and shrank considerably, from 273 deputies (if its supporters are included the figure would be 450) at the First Congress in May–June 1989 to about 159 by the Second Congress in December 1989.[42] Soviet voters also got their 'deputies who were capable of running the country during perestroika': parliamentarians were more likely than before to be from the professions. However, it should not come as a surprise that the majority of deputies elected were CPSU members; in fact their share increased from over 71 per cent in 1984 to nearly 87 per cent in 1989.[43]

Therefore, the elections to the Congress of People's Deputies demonstrated that the regime put forth measures which appeared to open up the system for more competition and popular participation. However, officials either never allowed these possibilities to be utilized to their full potential, created obstructions or simply ignored them. These patterns reflect the liberalizing tendencies of the Gorbachev regime, which sought to control political reform and channel the 'human factor' to suit its own purposes. Nevertheless, the examples discussed above indicate that the party was unable to control all aspects of the electoral process. Moreover, these experiences instilled in the electorate a sense that competitive elections were essential components of a properly functioning state. Therefore, Soviet citizens were quick to attempt to address the shortcomings of the 1989 campaign.

Choice is not enough: Soviet debates on electoral reform 1989-91

The competition among candidates first implemented on a broad scale during the 1989 elections to the USSR Congress of People's Deputies was a marked improvement on the manner in which the Soviet Union had previously conducted elections. An overwhelming majority of Soviet voters were presented with opportunities to select their representatives from among a plurality of contestants who competed against each other on the principles established in their programmes. Nomination rights were increased so that, in addition to the CPSU and approved social organizations, meetings of 500 or more voters from the same locality could now propose deputies. Individuals could also put themselves forward and have meetings approve or reject their candidacies. These measures were qualitative steps forward, advancing the administration and conduct of Soviet elections. However, in themselves they did not, for instance, alleviate CPSU control over electoral procedures or maximize the democratic potential contained within the electoral law. Moreover, as political reforms expanded during 1989-91, electoral legislation did not keep pace with other developments. This, in effect, further reinforces the argument that the electoral system was liberalized under Gorbachev, not entirely democratized.

Electoral shortcomings were quickly identified by Soviet scholars and political practitioners. Indeed, these individuals were among the first to indicate that, although bringing positive changes into Soviet politics, electoral reform measures needed further improvements to catch up with political realities. Moreover, the content of these criticisms reflects the political atmosphere during which they were written. For instance, writings appearing immediately after the 1989 elections to the Congress of People's Deputies were system-specific: they focused exclusively on how Soviet legislators could introduce innovations to improve the conduct of elections and on how to improve the electoral system in conditions of an 'enlightened' single-party rule. Following the introduction of new republican constitutions and electoral laws in 1989–90, Soviet writers concentrated on improving the mechanisms for conducting elections. However, they were also forced to take into consideration the new political forces which had previously existed informally but now, following the adoption of the amendment to Article 6 of the USSR Constitution, had the right to become accepted, legal contestants for power in their own right. Subsequent debates emphasized the tactics that candidates and political organizations could use to win elections; systemic improvements were of secondary importance. By this time, the CPSU had lost its credibility as a ruling party and accepted that it would become one among several competing for power as potential parliamentary parties. Therefore, these contributions were part of the foundation upon which the post-Soviet electoral administration was built.

Electoral geography and the principle of one person – one vote were among the first of the shortcomings that Soviet scholars and politicians felt needed immediate improvement. Latvian deputy Viktor Alksnis, speaking at the First USSR Congress of People's Deputies in May 1989, noted that in his republic there were grossly disproportionate numbers of voters in different districts.[44] For instance, in one rural national-territorial district there were 28,000 voters, while in an urban constituency there were 137,000.[45] This posed a particularly acute problem in the republic. The rural voters' ballots had greater weight than those of their urban counterparts. Ethnic Russians living in the republic were more abundant in urban areas (where 71 per cent of Latvia's population was based), whereas the majority of rural dwellers were ethnic Latvians.[46] According to legal specialist Suren Avak'yan this demographic imbalance reduced the chances of working-class and Russian candidates being elected. Moreover, he recounts that 10 of 11 National Front of Latvia deputies won seats from these constituencies.[47] Political geographers A.V. Berezkin, V.A. Kolosov, M.E. Pavlovskaya, N.V. Petrov and L.V. Smiryagin indicate that:

[if] electoral district boundaries were drawn based on the population count according to the 1979 census, then a transfer of 14 electoral districts

from certain republics to others would be necessary, and, according to the preliminary results of the 1989 census, 28 of the 750 [territorial] districts would need to be changed.[48]

The Russian authorities did not alleviate the huge gaps of voters in constituencies and the problem of some voters' ballots weighing more than others. Elsewhere in this volume, the present author shows how this problem also occurred during the 1993 elections to the Russian Federal Assembly.

The principle of one person – one vote was challenged by the introduction of social organization seats. According to the electoral law, not all voters were allowed to elect these deputies – rather they were chosen by delegates to all-union congresses, conferences and plenums. Although not all voters could elect these deputies, they could all participate in candidate discussions and nominations: proposals for candidacies were supposed to come from the lower levels and were approved at higher levels within the organization. Gorbachev shrugged off criticisms that a portion of the electorate would be effectively disenfranchised by the procedure for electing these deputies. Given the nature of the Soviet system, the majority of citizens belonged to trade unions and to other social organizations of some type. Therefore, they possessed the right to discuss the candidates. As a result, Gorbachev claimed that it was not important to discuss disenfranchisement; in reality, there were very few Soviet citizens who did not belong to any of these organizations.[49] In any event, these 750 deputies were elected by only about 16,000 people.[50]

Avak'yan, while accepting that members of an organization possessed the right to discuss these candidates, nevertheless found further faults connected with the social organization seats. Voters in these congresses, conferences and plenary meetings possessed an extra vote: like their fellow citizens they had one vote for a deputy in a territorial district, plus one for a national-territorial district. However:

both theoretically and practically, some [social organization seat electors] may have had even more votes, in so far as members of several leading organs (for example the CPSU Central Committee, the All-Union Central Council of Trade Unions, the Central Committee of the Komsomol, the governing board of a creative union, etc.) participated in the elections of a series of deputies.[51]

Unlike candidates who stood in constituencies, social organization seat contestants often did not have their own personal election programmes. Rather, they frequently adopted the manifesto of their social organization.[52] There were, however, some notable exceptions. For instance, candidates from the USSR Academy of Sciences,[53] some from the CPSU[54] and from the Soviet Women's Committee[55] drafted their own platforms.

The status of social organization seats was heavily debated by Soviet parliamentarians, and they were removed from the USSR Constitution at the Second Congress in December 1989; republics possessed the right to retain them in elections to their own supreme legislatures.[56] Only Belorussia and Kazakhstan chose this option.[57]

There were other criticisms of the electoral system that needed to be addressed further. Avak'yan viewed the structure and practices of the Congress of People's Deputies itself as faulty. For instance, the parliament was to meet infrequently (only twice per year), and was to undertake the formation of the Supreme Soviet and adopt major laws at these sessions. Avak'yan also claimed that most deputies, based on their performances at the First Congress, were not inclined to take so modest a role. In addition, he felt that the Congress was too large and queried how the legislature could function effectively with more than 2,000 deputies.[58]

Nomination rights were also vague and introduced inconsistencies and inequalities. The electoral law mandated that candidates could be proposed by no less than 500 workers at a meeting, but it was also formally permissible for work collectives of 7–11 (cooperatives, the courts, the procuracy), 15–20 (editorial boards of periodicals, food shops, hairstylists), or 30–40 (polyclinics and schools) to nominate candidates alongside factories, institutes and universities, where, for instance, the number of workers ranged from 15,000 to 50,000.[59] Another commentator noted that there were problems with workplace nomination meetings – the work collective also being the easiest place for the apparatus to manipulate the candidate selection.[60]

Nomination meetings and candidates' meetings with the electorate received further criticism both in the USSR and abroad. Stephen White has argued that these served as filters through which candidates had to pass; however, party officials packed the meetings with their supporters to ensure that their people would win nominations.[61] Giulietto Chiesa considered them 'one option among many for district leaders in protecting their position' and that they 'became the *apparat*'s weapon of choice in eliminating radical candidates'.[62] Indeed, Boris Yeltsin noted that they were 'carefully designed to sift out undesirable candidates'.[63] Aleksandr Ivanchenko, a member of the current Russian Federation's Central Electoral Commission (appointed by the State Duma),[64] writing in 1990, argued that putting deputies forward through work collectives and meetings of electors would not be the 'wave of the future', given that new political forces had emerged. However, he defended them, claiming that they would play a role in the 'making of a multiparty system' by expanding paths for candidate nominations and stimulating assistance for candidates during the final stages of the electoral struggle.[65]

Avak'yan saw other inequalities in the way pre-election meetings were conducted for candidates who stood in the constituencies and for those from social organizations. Some of the former had to speak 30–40 times – some even held 100 or more meetings – before different crowds in different auditoria. By contrast, candidates from the social organizations had, on average, 2–4 meetings per month and, moreover, these were meetings with colleagues, in environments where they were well-known and among people with whom they were close.[66] Subsequently, district meetings were removed from the electoral laws of 11 republics – Turkmenia, Uzbekistan, Kirgizia and Kazakhstan being the exceptions.[67]

The CPSU Central Committee's historic vote of February 1990 amending Article 6 of the USSR Constitution, thereby renouncing its political monopoly in Soviet society, allowed other political and social forces to contend for power. Although this was indeed a significant political development, the amendment came far too late for the political organizations which had been developing since the late 1980s to participate effectively against the CPSU in many republican elections in 1990. Moreover, it should be noted that the Law on Public Associations which governed the registration, operations and norms of these new public organizations did not go into effect until 1 January 1991. The timing of these measures reinforces the argument that the CPSU implemented liberalizing tactics in its reforms. Nevertheless, these embryonic parties, movements and clubs participated in the elections in different capacities. They and their supporters met with varying degrees of success.[68]

Parties and other organizations were formally accepted as components of the Soviet political system. However, electoral legislation did not adequately address their status in the new conditions. For instance, in a contribution to a round table on 'Problems of the Development of Electoral Legislation' sponsored by the parliamentary journal *Narodnyi deputat* (People's Deputy), director of the All-Union Scientific Research Institute of Soviet State Construction and Legislation, V. Vasil'ev, noted that the emergence of multiparty conditions created problems of equality in campaigning. Previously, the state had provided the sole means of financial support and allocation of media time and space. In the new circumstances, this would not be acceptable: the state could not afford these policies. Nevertheless, he contended, measures had to be implemented to ensure that parties, other social organizations and citizens would be able to undertake comprehensive support of candidates. At the same time, all should have equal rights to the feeding trough. Therefore, he proposed that the state should distribute finances to candidates and parties fairly equally and place a cap on non-state donations to electoral contestants.[69] In another round-table forum, head of the USSR Academy of Science's Institute of State and Law, V. Smirnov, noted the importance of regulating non-monetary sources of campaign support, such as equipment, media, printing and specialist services.[70]

Political parties and movements were not the only problematic issues challenging the development of electoral legislation. The situation in the USSR during 1990–91 also reflected the increasing significance of the shift in power relations from the centre to the republics. This was reflected in the differing electoral codes that the republics adopted. Some of these, such as those enacted in the Baltic states, conflicted with the rights of Soviet citizens.[71] There were also deficiencies in electoral legislation regarding deputy recall procedures and referendums, and a lack of systematized information on electoral laws which needed to be rectified.[72] Therefore, the electoral reform process, although providing for increased choice and participation, lacked many of the legal provisions which would guarantee free and fair elections as outlined in the Introduction.

While accepting that the ground rules (electoral laws) regulating the hustings are important, Soviet writers also realized that the objective of any election campaign is to win seats. Therefore, from 1991 writings addressed campaign strategy, tactics and the role of 'political marketing'. For instance, *Narodnyi deputat* and the CPSU Central Committee's Institute of Social Problems conducted a round-table discussion between American and Soviet specialists concerned with the study of electoral campaigns. The discussion revealed some notable differences between the ways in which the Americans and the Soviets approached electioneering.

Ralph Murphine, director of the Washington-based Institute for Practical Politics, for example, stressed how political consultants and pre-election research in a campaign benefited the *contestants*. He informed his Soviet colleagues that the political consultant is a specialist who assists candidates or parties by organizing support among the electorate, develops an electoral strategy and works for its realization. In addition, political consultants contribute to their clients' success by providing answers to the important questions: Who is our candidate? What is his/her character? What are the candidate's views, political position, experience or other qualities which may influence the voter's choice? Who is our opponent? What are his/her strong and weak points? What concerns our voters and what are their interests? How will the personality of the candidate, his/her slogans and arguments influence the electorate? Moreover, he emphasized how important it was to study surveys and demographic analyses and focus group interviews to help the candidate win office.[73]

Soviet commentators, however, tended to focus on how election-related research was useful to *official bodies*. For instance, A. Demidov of the USSR Academy of Science's Institute of Sociology noted that these materials could benefit the soviets and electoral commissions. He added, however, that they could also be useful to political parties and groups and their candidates by providing recommendations about the qualities the electorate preferred in a candidate. District soviet chairwoman O. Bektabekova noted that election-related research was important because it notified authorities of electors' orientations, what they knew about the elections and the candidates, whether they met with the candidates and whether they intended to vote.[74] Notwithstanding their differences with their American colleagues, Soviet specialists recognized the changing nature of their political environment and deduced that the old ways of conducting elections were no longer appropriate.

The best example of new thinking in Soviet electoral strategies was produced by Moscow State University sociologists Tat'yana Yurasova and Ol'ga Selivanova and published in the Tallinn journal *Politika* (formerly the Communist Party of the Estonian Soviet Socialist Republic's theoretical journal *Kommunist Estonii*). The authors viewed politics as a 'market': 'politics is a social sphere where supply (the number of candidates) is increasing and this will decrease demand (deputy mandates and various kinds of political vacancies)'.[75] Moreover, they argued, politics can be seen as a market because its 'commodities' are the 'possibilities of profits and privileges ... connected with any political decision'. Power holders can be considered 'salespersons' and the voters are likened to 'consumers'. In order for the former to present their product to their buyers, they must engage in 'political marketing', which encompasses:

the careful and comprehensive study of the political market, the interests and expectations of various social groups, and addresses the basic position of the candidate's pre-election programme. On the other hand, it is an active influence over public opinion, on the formation of interests and political preferences.[76]

To conduct this activity, it is necessary to construct some type of strategy. In drawing up the 'marketing plan', Yurasova and Selivanova argued, the arrangement of forces in the local and central powers had to be analysed. Because of the activities of the CPSU and its dominance within the Soviet political system, it was necessary to determine whether or not the bodies would remain neutral during the campaign, and, if not, to deduce whether they would show support for one candidate or assist the other. They also advised the study of the economic situation in particular areas, looking at, for example, employment structures, unemployment and its sources, average wage levels, supplies and prices in the region. All these factors, they argued, should be included in the plan, because the candidate's aim is to attract the consumer. Moreover, candidates must consider the parameters of the social groups they seek to influence, taking into account their income, age and professional structures, national features, traditions, etc. In this manner candidates should 'model an image of the typical representative of the ... group' and build a campaign to influence that person's vote.[77]

Yurasova and Selivanova put forward several important factors to consider when campaigning. First, candidates must devise a strategy of how to attract more votes than their opponents. Second, they must determine causes of voter abstention and seek to remedy these symptoms. Third, candidates must remember that what they say is felt by the electorate to be more important than what they actually know. Therefore, contestants must make their statements tactfully. Fourth, if candidates want to be covered extensively, they have to 'create a spectacle'. Finally, Yurasova and Selivanova recommended that competitors should not give their opponents any ideas which they could put to their own use.[78]

Conclusion

Under Gorbachev's leadership the Soviet electoral system was reformed from its acclamatory practices to a limited-choice variant, emulating the electoral systems which existed earlier in other communist countries. Although 'democratization' was a buzz-word of the Gorbachev era, the electoral system actually went through a process of liberalization. Nevertheless, alternative candidates occasionally won seats in legislative bodies. Evidence also suggests that electability grew in importance during the aftermath of the 1989 elections to the USSR Congress of People's Deputies. There was a serious commitment on the part of scholars to improve and systematize electoral procedures throughout the USSR's republics. The growing diversity among electoral approaches is evidence, however, of a further shift of power from Moscow to the republics during 1989–90. With the increasing importance of the new political organizations in the USSR and a break from the old Soviet practices of 'rubber-stamp' legislatures, potential contestants began to take elections more seriously, and there was a shift in the general literature on electoral reform away from how to improve the system towards how to win seats. These developments greatly influenced the way in which political actors would approach future elections and the nature of forthcoming electoral competitions.

Notes

1 Elemer Hankiss, *East European Alternatives* (Cambridge: Cambridge University Press, 1990), pp. 54, 56.
2 Christopher Young, 'The Strategy of Political Liberalization: A Comparative View of Gorbachev's Reforms', *World Politics*, vol. 45, no. 4 (October 1992), pp. 47–65.
3 *Zakon Soyuza Sovetskikh Sotsialisticheskikh Respublik o vyborakh v Verkhovnyi Sovet SSSR* (Moscow: Yuridicheskaya literatura, 1978).
4 *Konstitutsiya (Osnovnoi Zakon) Soyuza Sovetskikh Sotsialisticheskikh Respublik* (Moscow: Politizdat, 1978), Articles 95–102.
5 Roy A. Medvedev, *How I Ran For Election and How I Lost* (Nottingham: Bertrand Russell Peace Foundation, 1979). This piece first appeared in the American socialist newspaper, *In These Times*, 3 July 1979.
6 *Izvestiya*, 10 February 1987, cited in Stephen White, Graeme Gill and Darrell Slider, *The Politics of Transition: Shaping a Post-Soviet Future* (Cambridge: Cambridge University Press, 1993), p. 22.
7 Stephen White raises some examples in 'Reforming the Electoral System', *Journal of Communist Studies*, vol. 4, no. 4 (December 1988), pp. 1–16.
8 For discussions of the differences between sex, power and political status in Soviet elected organs see Mary Buckley, 'Female Workers by Hand and Male Workers by Brain: The Occupational Composition of the 1985 Azerbaidzhan Supreme Soviet', *Soviet Union/Union Sovietique*, vol. 14, no. 2 (1987), pp. 229–37, and Peter Lentini, 'Women and the 1989 Elections to the USSR Congress of People's Deputies', *Coexistence*, vol. 31, no. 1 (March 1994), pp. 1–28, esp. pp. 1–4 and the figures contained in note 4, p. 23. General demographic statistical material can be found in, for example, *Deputaty Verkhovnogo Soveta SSSR: odinnadtsatyi sozyv* (Moscow: Izvestiya, 1984), and *Sostav deputatov, ispolnitel'nykh komitetov, postoyannykh komissii i rezervnykh deputatov mestnykh sovetov 1987 g.: statisticheskii sbornik* (Moscow: Izvestiya, 1987).
9 Ronald J. Hill, 'Continuity and Change in USSR Supreme Soviet Elections', *British Journal of Political Science*, vol. 2, no. 1 (1972), pp. 47–68.
10 Jeffrey W. Hahn, 'State Institutions in Transition', in Stephen White, Alex Pravda and Zvi Gitelman (eds), *Developments in Soviet and Post-Soviet Politics* (London: Macmillan, 1992), pp. 88–106, at p. 91.
11 See, for example, 'Soobshchenie Tsentral'noi izbiratel'noi komissii ob itogakh vyborov v Verkhovnyi Sovet SSSR odinnadtsatogo sozyva, sostoyavshikhsya 4 marta 1984 goda', *Vedomosti Verkhovnogo Soveta SSSR*, 1984, no. 11 (14 March), item no. 2241, pp. 199–203.
12 See, for instance, Victor Zaslavsky and Robert J. Brym, 'The Functions of Elections in the USSR', *Soviet Studies*, vol. XXX, no. 3 (July 1978), pp. 362–71; Theodore Friedgut, *Political Participation in the USSR* (Princeton: Princeton University Press, 1979), chapter 2.

13 See references in note 12, plus Alex Pravda, 'Elections in Communist Party States', in Stephen White and Daniel N. Nelson (eds), *Communist Politics: A Reader* (London: Macmillan, 1986), pp. 27–54, and Everett M. Jacobs, 'Soviet Local Elections: What They Are and What They Are Not', *Soviet Studies*, vol. XXII, no. 1 (1970), pp. 61–76.
14 Georg Brunner, 'Legitimacy Doctrines and Legitimation Procedures in East European Systems', in T.H. Rigby and Ferenc Feher (eds), *Political Legitimation in Communist States* (London: Macmillan, 1982).
15 Author's personal communication with visiting Soviet academic, Glasgow, 26 March 1989.
16 See Introduction, source in note 19.
17 See Introduction, source in notes 7–8.
18 See Introduction, source in note 18.
19 See Alex Pravda, in White and Nelson (eds), *Communist Politics*, pp. 27–54; Stephen White, 'Economic Performance and Communist Legitimacy', *World Politics*, vol. 38, no. 3 (1986), pp. 462–82; Werner Hahn, 'Electoral Choice in the Soviet Bloc', *Problems of Communism*, vol. 36, no. 2 (1987), pp. 29–39, and Barnabas Racz, 'Political Participation and Developed Socialism: The Hungarian Elections of 1985', *Soviet Studies*, vol. XXXIX, no. 1 (1987), pp. 40–62.
20 Werner Hahn, 'Electoral Choice'.
21 Stephen White, 'Rethinking the CPSU', *Soviet Studies*, vol. 43, no. 3 (1991), pp. 405–28, at p. 408.
22 Stephen White, *After Gorbachev* (Cambridge: Cambridge University Press, 1993), p. 123.
23 Yegor Ligachev, *Inside Gorbachev's Kremlin*, translated by Catherine A. Fitzpatrick, Michele A. Berdy and Dobrochna Dyrcz-Freeman (New York: Pantheon, 1993), pp. 331–2.
24 Jeffrey W. Hahn, 'An Experiment in Competition: The 1987 Elections to the Local Soviets', *Slavic Review*, vol. 47, no. 2 (1988), pp. 434–48.
25 *Proekt Zakon Soyuza Sovetskikh Sotsialisticheskikh Respublik ob izmeneniyakh i dopolneniyakh Konstitutsii (Osnovnogo Zakona) SSSR* (Moscow: Izvestiya, 1988).
26 *Proekt Zakon Soyuza Sovetskikh Sotsialisticheskikh Respublik o vyborakh narodnykh deputatov SSSR* (Moscow: Izvestiya, 1988).
27 See *Zakon Soyuza Sovetskikh Sotsialisticheskikh Respublik o vyborakh narodnykh deputatov SSSR* (Moscow: Izvestiya, 1988), Article 18. A listing of seat distributions also appears in *Izvestiya*, 28 December 1998, p. 1. See also Peter Lentini, 'Reforming the Electoral System: The March 1989 Elections to the USSR Congress of People's Deputies', *Journal of Communist Studies*, vol. 7, no. 1 (March 1991), pp. 69–94, table 1, p. 74.
28 I. Karpenko, 'Nachalis' vybory narodnykh deputatov SSSR', *Izvestiya*, 11 March 1989, p. 1.
29 'Doklad Mandatnoi Komissii', *Pervyi s"ezd narodnykh deputatov SSSR, 25 maya – 9 iyunya 1989 g: Stenograficheskii otchet* (Moscow: Verkhovnyi Sovet, 1989), 6 vols, vol. I, pp. 41–5, at p. 41, and *Sostav narodnykh*

deputatov SSSR, Verkhovnogo Soveta SSSR, postoyannykh komissii palat i komitetov Verkhovnogo Soveta SSSR, Prezidiuma Verkhovnogo Soveta SSSR: statisticheskii sbornik (Moscow: Verkhovnyi Sovet/Izvestiya, 1989), p. 3.

30 ibid., and 'Doklad Mandatnoi Komissii'.
31 Karpenko, 'Nachalis' vybory'.
32 'Doklad Mandatnoi Komissii' and *Sostav narodnykh deputatov*.
33 'Soobshchenie izbiratel'noi komissii po vyboram narodnykh deputatov SSSR ot KPSS', *Izvestiya*, 19 March 1989, pp. 1–2.
34 *Pravda*, 17 January 1989, cited in White, Gill and Slider, *The Politics of Transition*, p. 25.
35 ibid., p. 26.
36 A. Nazimova and V. Sheinis, 'Vybory v zerkale sotsiologii', *Izvestiya*, 12 May 1989, p. 3.
37 See White, *After Gorbachev*, pp. 47–8; for examples of self-nominations and alternative candidate proposals see Lentini, 'Reforming the Electoral System', p. 76.
38 See 'Soobshchenie Tsentral'noi izbiratel'noi komissii . . . 4 marta 1984' and the electoral commission report in *Izvestiya*, 5 April 1989, p. 1.
39 'U kamennoi stenoi', *Literaturnaya gazeta*, 15 February 1989, p. 10.
40 See, for instance, Geoffrey A. Hosking, Jonathan Aves and Peter J.S. Duncan, *The Road to Post-Communism* (London: Pinter, 1992), and Rein Taagepera, 'A Note on the March 1989 Elections in Estonia', *Soviet Studies*, vol. 42, no. 2 (April 1990), pp. 329–39.
41 See Giulietto Chiesa, *Transition to Democracy in the USSR: Ending the Monopoly of Power and the Evolution of New Political Forces* (Washington, DC: Woodrow Wilson Center Occasional Papers, no. 237, 1990), and idem with Douglas Taylor Northrup, *Transition to Democracy: Political Change in the Soviet Union, 1989–1991* (Hanover, NH: University of New England Press, 1993), esp. pp. 211–91.
42 Data collected by Giulietto Chiesa and 'Spisok narodnykh deputatov SSSR, podpisavshikh Zayavlenie MDG', cited in Chiesa with Northrup, *Transition to Democracy*, pp. 124–5.
43 See figures in *Deputaty Verkhovnogo Soveta*, p. 3; *Sostav narodnykh deputatov*, p. 11, and V. Sheinis and A. Nazimova, 'Vybor sdelan', *Izvestiya*, 9 May 1989, p. 6.
44 *Pervyi s"ezd narodnykh deputatov SSSR*, vol. I, p. 51.
45 A.V. Berezkin, V.A. Kolosov, M.E. Pavlovskaya, N.V. Petrov and L.V. Smiryagin, 'The Geography of the 1989 Elections of People's Deputies of the USSR (Preliminary Results)', *Soviet Geography*, vol. XXX, no. 8 (October 1989), pp. 607–34, at p. 613.
46 ibid., and S.A. Avak'yan, 'Zakonodatel'stvo o vyborakh: opyt primeneniya voprosy sovershenstvovaniya', *Vestnik moskovskogo universiteta (seriya pravo)*, no. 6 (1989), pp. 9–19, p. 11.
47 ibid., p. 12.

48 Berezkin et al., 'The Geography of the 1989 Elections', p. 612. Further data on unequal numbers of voters in constituencies are contained in ibid., pp. 613–15.
49 Mikhail S. Gorbachev, 'To Give Full Power to the Soviets and Create a Socialist State Based on the Rule of Law: Report by Mikhail Gorbachev at the 12th Special Session of the Supreme Soviet of the USSR of the 11th Convocation, November 29, 1988', *12th Special Session of the Supreme Soviet of the USSR of the 11th Convocation: Documents and Materials* (Moscow: Novosti, 1988), pp. 3–33, at pp. 25–8.
50 'Doklad Mandatnoi Komissii' and *Sostav narodnykh deputatov*.
51 Avak'yan, 'Zakonodatel'stvo', p. 9.
52 ibid., p. 10.
53 *Vybory narodnykh deputatov SSSR ot AN SSSR: spravki-annotatsii na kandidatov i ikh predvybornye platformy* (Moscow, 1989).
54 See Zukhra Valeeva's platform, 'Esli menya izberut', *Izvestiya*, 9 March 1989, p. 1.
55 This is mentioned in 'Programma deistvii', *Krest'yanka*, no. 3 (1989), p. 6.
56 The amendment is contained in *Vedomosti S"ezda Narodnykh Deputatov SSSR i Verkhovnogo Soveta SSSR*, no. 29 (1989), item 540.
57 Aleksandr Ivanchenko, 'Izbiratel'naya kampaniya – uroki na zavtra', *Kommunist*, no. 11 (1990), pp. 83–93, at p. 84.
58 Avak'yan, 'Zakonodatel'stvo', p. 9.
59 ibid., p. 13.
60 Ivanchenko, 'Izbiratel'naya kampaniya', p. 87.
61 White, *After Gorbachev*, pp. 47–8.
62 Chiesa with Northrop, *Transition to Democracy*, pp. 27–8.
63 Boris Yeltsin, *Against the Grain*, translated by Michael Glenny (London: Jonathan Cape, 1990), p. 2.
64 Analytica Moscow, *Politica Weekly Press Summary. Electronic Mail Version*, vol. II, no. 10 (11–17 March 1995).
65 Ivanchenko, 'Izbiratel'naya kampaniya', pp. 88–9.
66 Avak'yan, 'Zakonodatel'stvo', p. 10.
67 Ivanchenko, 'Izbiratel'naya kampaniya', p. 84.
68 See Commission for Security and Cooperation in Europe, *Elections in the Baltic States and Soviet Republics: A Compendium of Reports* (Washington, DC: US Government Printing Office, 1990).
69 V. Polubinsky, 'Vybory v demokraticheskii izmerii (zametki s "kruglogo stola")', *Narodnyi deputat*, no. 14 (1991), pp. 16–22, at pp. 17–18.
70 V. Gubernatov, 'Politicheskoe konsultirovanie izbiratel'nykh kampanii: opyt, perspektivy', Narodnyi deputat, no. 7 (1991), pp. 92–9, p. 99.
71 ibid., p. 98.
72 See V. Korobeinikov's comments in ibid., p. 97; statements by Ivanchenko, G. Vasil'evich, V. Otnisenko, V. Volkov and B. Khangel'dyev in Polubinsky, 'Vybory', pp. 19–22.
73 Gubernatov, 'Politicheskoe konsultirovanie', pp. 93–4.
74 ibid., p. 95.

75 Tat'yana Yurasova and Ol'ga Selivanova, 'Predvybornaya bor'ba i politicheskii marketing', *Politika*, no. 10 (Tallinn, 1991), pp. 68–79, at p. 68.
76 ibid.
77 ibid., p. 70.
78 ibid., p. 79.

PART II
The 1993 Election Campaign

4 Overview of the Campaign

PETER LENTINI

Boris Yeltsin's Presidential Decree No. 1400 of 21 September 1993, disbanding the Russian parliament elected in 1990 and providing the supplementary legislation necessary to create the bicameral Russian Federal Assembly,[1] set the stage for Russia's first multi-party elections since those to the short-lived Constituent Assembly in 1917. As discussed in earlier chapters, Russian and Soviet elections have not in the past created institutions capable of effecting major political changes: both the elections themselves and the legislatures they produced were marginalized by the supremacy of the tsars and the Communist Party of the Soviet Union (CPSU). Criteria defining the essential qualities and components of democratic elections indicate that both pre-revolutionary Russian elections and Soviet elections possessed numerous deficiencies excluding them from this classification. Admittedly, electoral reform measures implemented during the Gorbachev years made a number of improvements: they increased the scope of citizen activity in elections; provided the electorate with choices among candidates for state offices who stood on specific programmes (although competing parties were not allowed); influenced the creation of more professionally qualified parliamentary elites; infused the USSR's legislative organs with a slightly higher degree of autonomy from the CPSU, and transformed them from their previous status of institutions whose purpose was to rubber-stamp decisions made earlier at party Central Committee plenums to elected assemblies more akin (but not entirely similar) to the 'working' legislatures reflecting voters' choices established in liberal democratic countries. Nevertheless, these modifications all occurred within the context of maintaining and improving the single-party system that had been in existence since Lenin's time. Notwithstanding the election of a number of notable reformers and anti-CPSU politicians to them, perestroika-era institutions such as the USSR Congress of People's Deputies and the RSFSR Congress of People's Deputies were dominated by CPSU members who were bound to pursue the party line. This in itself seriously limited the degree of political and economic change that could be implemented within their respective territories.

Russia was presented with new political, social and economic challenges and possibilities to improve its nascent democratic order following the collapse of the Soviet Union and the end of Communist Party rule. Ironically, after having jointly led and orchestrated the popular resistance that thwarted the attempted coup in August 1991, the Russian president and parliament quickly fell out over numerous divisive issues, particularly over the formation of government, the pace of economic reform and, possibly most contentious, over which institution – the legislative or the executive – would occupy the dominant position in the post-Soviet political arrangement.[2] The crisis contained a series of flashpoints and reached its peak during the April 1993 referendum on the future of economic reform, the presidency and the Russian parliament.[3] A majority of Russians indicated that they would prefer their leaders to remain in place and reforms to continue,[4] despite the harsh economic difficulties that confronted them and the hostility that the two branches of government demonstrated towards each other.

Leading students of Russian politics generally agree that Yeltsin squandered an opportunity to usher in a reform-oriented legislature by not disbanding the RSFSR Congress in the wake of the post-coup victory. They believe that the timing of the elections was crucial to establishing a more stable democratic order and that Russia's democratic forces could have ridden on Yeltsin's coat-tails in elections to a new legislature.[5] Instead, the institution remained, and president and parliament were locked into a conflict lasting well over a year and a half which climaxed in the bloody events of October 1993.

Russia's inheritance of institutions created during the Soviet period (including its parliament, presidency and constitution) may have impeded the growth of its own post-communist democratic institutions during 1991–3. However, did Yeltsin, by dissolving the parliament in the 'name of democracy' and providing legislation for new elections and a plebiscite for a new post-Soviet constitution, lay the foundations for a legitimate democratic order? Or were Russians deprived yet again of a political order in which they could influence the state's agenda through their elected representatives? If so, who hijacked these possibilities for them: Yeltsin, old elites or the Russian people themselves?

These are among the questions addressed in this volume. The purpose of the present chapter is to provide an overview of the 1993 elections to the Russian Federal Assembly and the constitutional plebiscite, to outline the general provisions, protagonists, organizational structures and outcomes of these events, and to place them within the context of the debate over whether or not they contributed to the development of a 'new', 'democratic' or 'other' type of political framework.

New institutions and the draft constitution

The Statute on Federal Organs of Power in the Transitional Period created a restructured Russian legislature, the Federal'noe Sobranie (Federal Assembly), a bicameral institution consisting of an upper house, the Federation Council, and a lower house, the State Duma.[6] The Federation Council was structured in such a manner as to allow regional interests, which had been growing in significance since the late 1980s, to be represented. Each of Russia's 89 'subjects' would be represented by two members, one from the representative organs, the other from the executive bodies of authority. The chamber would be empowered to implement border changes between subjects of the Federation, as well as presidential decrees on martial law and states of emergency; to decide on the use of Russian armed forces outside the Russian Federation's borders; to set presidential elections; to affirm the appointment of federal judges and the Russian Procurator General, and to decide on the president's removal from office (Article 8).

The Statute mandated that legal voters – anyone over the age of 18 who had not been declared legally insane – would elect representatives to the Federation Council and to the 450-member State

Duma (whose deputies had to be at least 21 years of age).[7] The latter chamber would function on a 'permanent basis' (Article 6) and would be empowered to approve the Chair of the Government of the Russian Federation (i.e. the Prime Minister), conduct votes of confidence in the Russian government and its members, appoint and release from office (with presidential approval) the Chair of the State Bank of the Russian Federation and the Human Rights Commissioner, and grant amnesties (Article 10).

In addition to benefiting from a restructured parliament, Russian voters participated in a controversial plebiscite on a draft Constitution for the Russian Federation. As Wyman, Miller, White and Heywood have indicated elsewhere, 'Yeltsin's decree described the vote as a "plebiscite" rather than a referendum, since the terms of the Russian Law on Referendums, promulgated in October 1990, required that constitutional changes gain the support of the majority of all registered voters.'[8] The draft of the constitution was published in major papers and in booklet form for public scrutiny. However, it appears that its dissemination and distribution schedule left little time for the electorate to become acquainted with the document and its provisions.[9] Stephen White's contribution to this volume shows that the document clearly bore Yeltsin's vision for the future restructuring of a Russian political order in which the president would be the dominant actor.

Despite its leanings towards presidential dominance, the draft was a radical departure from earlier constitutions. Moreover, its provisions ensured that it was not just a tool for another form of dictatorship and reflected the leadership's interest to fuse the move towards a market economy with some type of social safety net, creating *at minimum* a foundation for a social contract between the regime and the population. This theoretically established a means for further popular legitimation.

Whereas Chapter VII of the last Soviet constitution[10] listed the rights and duties of citizens which the regime could use for coercive purposes rather than for human fulfilment, the Yeltsin draft contained a section on human and citizens' rights and freedoms which had the person, not the state, as its focal point. For instance, under the 'Brezhnev Constitution', work was a right, but also a duty. Individuals were not allowed to 'live off the labour of others'; those who violated this principle were subject to prosecution under 'parasite' laws and deprived of their personal freedom. In conditions of 'full employment' and complete party control it was feasible to maintain such a policy.

The Yeltsin draft similarly included particular duties which Russian citizens had to perform or to which they would be subjected. Among them were temporary suspension of a citizen's rights and freedoms during states of emergency, payment of taxes and duties, maintenance of the environment and defence of the fatherland, including military service (Articles 56–9). In certain circumstances Russian citizens committing serious crimes would be subjected to the death penalty (Article 20). However, the draft also took into account the changing political, economic and social conditions in Russia. With the emergence of a competitive labour market, a switch from a state-centralized to a market economy and the increase of unemployment, work is naturally no longer considered a duty; it remains, nevertheless, a right and citizens are free to choose their preferred career paths (Article 37). Private property is protected by law and citizens and civic associations are allowed to hold private property in the form of land (Articles 35–6).

Draft provisions included elements of a social safety net for Russian citizens. Article 7, for instance, states that 'The Russian Federation is a social state'. Moreover, the same article mandates:

> In the Russian Federation, labour and the people's health shall be protected, a guaranteed minimum wage shall be established, state support of the family, maternity, fatherhood and childhood, invalids and elderly citizens shall be guaranteed, a system of social services shall be developed and state pensions, stipends and other guarantees of social defence shall be established.

Other social guarantees in the draft include the rights to choice of place of residence (Article 27), housing (Article 40) and education (Article 43).[11]

The contestants

Drafters of the Statute on Elections of State Duma Deputies selected an electoral formula which combined proportional and population-based representation for voters to choose their parliamentarians. In the former, political parties and other social organizations established on an all-Russia basis and whose rules were registered by the Russian Ministry of Justice were permitted to put forward lists of candidates for a federation-wide constituency. Those lists receiving more than 5 per cent of the votes would have their deputies represented in the Duma. Social organizations, parties and blocs had to collect at least 100,000 signatures with no more than 15 per cent from any of Russia's regions and submit these documents to the Central Electoral Commission by midnight on 6 November 1993 to be included on the ballot paper. Therefore, the electoral associations had a very limited time-period in which to organize their platforms and campaigns and coordinate electoral support bases. As Richard Sakwa notes in Chapter 8 of this volume, this provision should have favoured the older and more established political organizations. The regulations, however, forced a number of organizations to band together as diffuse blocs. As a result, many smaller, comparatively marginal political organizations were able to compete at the federal level. Therefore, the range of the participants along the Russian political spectrum was not reduced as efficiently as the drafters probably intended, and thus the potential for effective parties to participate in a parliament with strong coalition-building potential was lowered.[12]

The Central Electoral Commission released a list of some 91 all-Russian political and social organizations possessing the right to nominate candidates for the Duma.[13] Initially, the government attempted to prohibit three of them from participating in the elections and Russian political life because of their links with the opposition groups in October 1993: these were the Russian Communist Workers' Party, the People's Party of Free Russia and the Communist Party of the Russian Federation.[14] Subsequently, however, the Communist Party of the Russian Federation was allowed to continue its activities by the Russian Ministry of Justice.[15] In addition, members of the other banned parties contested in single-seat constituencies or as members of other electoral associations.

Twenty-one parties and blocs attempted to get on the ballot paper. However, the number of contenders was reduced to 13 after the document submission deadline. Although all 21 blocs and parties claimed to have obtained the required number of signatures, eight were banned initially due to various administrative barriers. These included the Russian All-People's Union, led by the former head of the Russian parliamentary fraction Russian Unity and staunch Yeltsin opponent, Sergei Baburin. According to Baburin, police raided the bloc's offices and stole documents containing 20,000–22,000 signatures.[16] In addition, he claimed that his phone, and those of his colleagues, had been cut and that he could only meet with foreign journalists in his home after receiving official permission from the authorities.[17] Nevertheless, Baburin contested the election, winning in Tsentral'nyi district no. 130, Omsk *oblast'*.[18] Other blocs initially excluded from the poll included Nikolai Lysenko's National Republican Party of Russia (although Lysenko contested and won a seat in Engel'skii district no. 158 in Saratov *oblast'*); Mikhail Astaf'ev's Constitutional Democratic Party–People's Freedom Party (however, one of its members, Anatolii Fedoseev, won a seat in the Federation Council from the Komi-Permyak Autonomous District); the New Russia bloc, headed by Tel'man Gdlyan, and the Avgust (August) bloc.[19] One of the latter's principal figures, Konstantin Borovoi, leader of the business-oriented Party of Economic Freedom also competed as an individual candidate.[20] His Avgust bloc received only 62,000 signatures.[21]

Thirteen electoral associations were included on the final ballot paper. These comprised what can be broadly categorized as four main camps: 'democrats', 'interest groups', 'centrists' and 'opposition'. The following ranks the blocs on a pro-/anti-reform axis (their programmatic information is included in this volume's Appendix). The 'democrats' included the most overtly pro-market and pro-Yeltsin coalition, Yegor Gaidar-led Russia's Choice; the Russian Movement for Democratic Reforms (RDDR), led by St Petersburg Mayor Anatolii Sobchak; the Yavlinsky-Boldyrev-Lukin bloc (Yabloko), headed by reform economist Grigorii Yavlinsky, Yurii Boldyrev and former ambassador to the US Vladimir Lukin, and the Party of Russian Unity and Accord (PRES), led by deputy chairman of the Russian Federation's Council of Ministers, Sergei Shakhrai.

'Interest groups' included Dignity and Charity (DiM), led by Konstantin Frolov, which advocated the rights of invalids, Chernobyl victims and those adversely affected by market reforms; the Constructive Ecological Movement of Russia (KEDR), led by the chairwoman of the Soldiers' Mothers of Russia Movement, Lyubov' Lymar, and Women of Russia (ZhR), led by former deputy chairwoman of the Soviet Women's Committee and CPSU Central Committee member Alevtina Fedulova. (Although this group seeks to advance a female voice in the parliament, their voting record shows them to be very closely allied with the Communist Party of the Russian Federation.)

The 'centrists' were comprised of Future of Russia – New Names (BRNI), led by Vyacheslav Lashchevsky, secretary of the Russian Union of Youth, which among its goals included promoting new, younger politicians into political life; Civic Union, led by Arkadii Vol'sky, which represented industrial interests, and Nikolai Travkin's Democratic Party of Russia (DPR). 'Opposition' coalitions included Mikhail Lapshin's Agrarian Party of Russia (APR), Gennadii Zyuganov's Communist Party of the Russian Federation (KPRF) and Vladimir Zhirinovsky's ultra-nationalist Liberal Democratic Party of Russia (LDPR).[22]

Voters elected the remaining 225 deputies in a first-past-the-post system from candidates who stood in single-seat constituencies notionally based on population: each district deputy would represent some 500,000 people.[23] Candidates needed only to win the highest number of votes in the constituency to claim their seats; a contrast from Soviet practices in which they needed the support of 50 per cent of the eligible electorate in the district plus one vote. Contestants could stand independently (as the majority did) or as representatives of electoral associations after collecting signatures of no less than 2 per cent of the voters in the district. The required turnout figure was reduced to 25 per cent from its 50 per cent Soviet predecessor, largely in anticipation of greater political apathy and disaffection.

Overall some 3,797 people competed for seats in the Federal Assembly, including 494 Federation Council candidates, 1,586 State Duma contestants in single-seat constituencies and 1,717 on party lists. About 40 per cent of the Federation Council candidates were heads of the executive branch, and 16 per cent were from representative organs. Out of all the candidates nearly a quarter were involved in economics and finance (e.g. as heads of large industrial enterprises, joint-stock companies, funds or commercial banks); nearly 8 per cent were employed in education at different levels, and only 1–3 per cent were either journalists, lawyers, workers in the agro-industrial complex, or had medical or other specialist training. A little more than 13 per cent were formerly Russian People's Deputies.[24]

To sum up, the elections of December 1993, together with the constitutional plebiscite, would set the groundwork for a new, post-Soviet political order. That President Yeltsin would have the dominant position in the new institutional arrangements is undebatable. Nevertheless, citizens would be able to select representatives to both houses of the Federal Assembly and to establish links with these politicians, who would have some degree of influence over certain areas of Russia's policy formation. Moreover, the draft constitution could be considered a form of social contract between Yeltsin and the population, in which the former would be granted a prominent role in the country's politics in return for guaranteeing civic, human and social rights and freedoms to the latter.

Electoral provisions

Electoral commissions coordinated the elections from the federal level down to each individual precinct. A Central Electoral Commission (Tsentrizbirkom), comprised of a chairperson, appointed from among Russian Supreme Court judges by the president, and twenty other members, oversaw the electoral procedures throughout the country. The chairman for the 1993 elections was Nikolai Ryabov. Half of the membership was drawn from legislators in the Russian Federation appointed by the president, and he selected the other ten from among the existing heads of administration. Therefore, the president had considerable influence over the Tsentrizbirkom's composition. In addition, all competing electoral organizations possessed the right to appoint one of their members to the Central Electoral Commission; they did not, however, possess full voting rights in it. Electoral commissions at all levels ensured compliance with the electoral statute, making sure that candidates and their campaign staffs (*doverennye litsa*) were registered, that lists of candidates and voters were available and distributed to the electorate, and that ballots and finances were dispersed properly.

The elections were financed by several means. There was still some measure of state support for the elections (previously the state had provided the only source). By the beginning of December 1993, it was estimated that the government had expended about 252 billion roubles on the election campaign.[25] In addition to state support, the European Union donated 100,000 ECUs ($US113,000) to the Tsentrizbirkom to purchase equipment such as copying and fax machines.[26]

Tsentrizbirkom contributions went to the various electoral commissions to enable them to conduct their duties. For instance, each Moscow polling station received almost 642,000 roubles to conduct the elections, and some could have received an additional 300,000 roubles. Included in the expenditure of the more than 3,000 Moscow electoral precincts[27] were about 30,000 roubles for preparing the stations for elections (assembling and dismantling equipment), 80,000 to print voters' lists, 15,000 for the costs of paper goods, 50,000 for hooking up phones, and about 12,000 for security.[28] In addition, the Tsentrizbirkom distributed 50 million roubles to each electoral organization for it to conduct its own campaign.

Both electoral associations and individual candidates had the right to create campaign accounts. These sources of support were derived from several means. First, candidates and blocs had the opportunity to include finances which were provided through the electoral commissions from the Russian State Budget. Second, the accounts could be comprised of the candidates' and blocs' own finances. Third, the associations nominating individual candidates in the districts could provide them with financial support. Fourth, election funds could include voluntary private donations from both individuals and other juridical persons. There were, however, certain limitations on funding: campaigns had to be financed solely by Russian sources.

The electoral associations clearly used a wide range of financial sources to pay for the 1993 contest. For instance, the KPRF paid for its campaign through membership dues and the 50 million roubles it received from the Tsentrizbirkom. Civic Union received 100 million roubles from different sponsors and some from a campaign concert held to attract younger voters. It used these funds to finance the publishing of leaflets and signs bearing bloc leader Arkadii Vol'sky's portrait. The Democratic Party of Russia (DPR) produced 3,000 leaflets, several tens of thousands of posters and 2 million calendars. The total cost of these items was 50 million roubles.[29]

Before the elections, very few candidates or blocs publicized their financial information. For instance, in St Petersburg, of the 95 candidates competing in nine electoral districts, only city council chairman Aleksandr Belyaev published a declaration of his income from the beginning of the year.[30] Deputy Prime Minister Sergei Shakhrai publicized that he earned only 332,000 roubles per annum and that at the end of October he had only 14,000 in a savings bank.[31] Yabloko was the only association which openly reported its financial information. According to its figures the bloc had 64,722,934 roubles in its account on 29 November 1993. Among their contributors was the firm Mossibinterservis, which donated 30 million roubles. Yabloko's expenditures from 23 to 29 November included 1,305,402 roubles for copying agitational materials; 2 million roubles for issuing and distributing special editions of newspapers and posters; 4.5 million roubles for issuing brochures of the pre-election platform; 47,320 roubles for sending telegrams and 2.2 million roubles for publishing agitational materials.[32] On 6 December 1993, the bloc had 222,573,967 roubles in its account, and it expended 87,317,967 of them on its campaign. The largest amount, 40 million roubles, went to the periodical, *Zhurnalist* (Journalist), for printing informational materials and publishing an interview which ran in thirty Russian regional newspapers. Among the contributors that week were the companies Viamond (30 million roubles), the influential Gruppa Most (100 million roubles), Optsion (10 million roubles), Investionnaya kompaniya Most-Investment (100 million roubles) and Torgovlya i Kredit (10 million roubles).[33]

In addition to providing for some type of equality for contestants with respect to their financial support in the poll, the electoral statute contained provisions designed to ensure fair play in agitation. First, state institutions were forbidden from conducting any form of agitation (either for or against any candidate or electoral organization). Rather, their function was to assist candidates and blocs in such matters as finding halls for meetings and the like. Second, the statute forbade any publication of election-related survey results during the last ten days before the elections (as suggested elsewhere in this book, this stipulation was a factor in the

Liberal Democratic Party of Russia's surprising performance). Third, the state ensured that all contestants would have access to the media, by giving each candidate the right to present one speech on both state radio and television (the time allotment for the speeches was not specified in the statute). In St Petersburg, for instance, every candidate received twenty minutes of state-financed air time.[34] Indeed, the St Petersburg channel programme, *Vybory: pryamoi efir* ('Elections: Direct Broadcast'), kept a timer on the candidates. Additional television presenters and programme staff monitored the time on other election broadcasts. However, it was difficult to maintain a strict control over time allotments. For instance, during one television broadcast, Russia's Choice leader Yegor Gaidar 'was occupied with his speech and . . . [the bloc] was on the air a minute and a half longer' than they were scheduled.[35] The statute also mandated that state television should allocate no less than one hour of air time per day to state-financed political broadcasts between 7 and 9 a.m. and 7 and 11 p.m. (taking into account regional differences) during the three weeks preceding the elections.

Electoral shortcomings

The new electoral provisions had a number of shortcomings, some of which even threatened the legitimacy of the deputies elected. One particularly controversial matter was that of ensuring equal weight to the electorate's votes. As Richard Sakwa has noted elsewhere, the reduced turnout level and first-past-the-post system 'would theoretically allow a candidate to win with only 6 per cent of the vote in a constituency where, for example, there were three candidates'.[36] In addition, the schema of each deputy representing about 500,000 people was not strictly adhered to and there were some seriously unequal distributions of voters among the 225 electoral districts, with the effect that the votes of part of the electorate were worth more than those elsewhere in the country. For example, Tsentrizbirkom's list of constituencies and the number of voters in them, published in *Izvestiya* on 13 and 14 October 1994, revealed that the deputy elected in Astrakhan district no. 62 represented some 737,800 electors,[37] while the deputy from Evenkii district no.

224 represented approximately 13,800 electors.[38] Therefore, as Wyman, Miller, White and Heywood correctly note: 'The voice of the Evenki in the State Duma would thus be 53 times louder than that of Astrakhan, leaving aside their two deputies to the upper house.'[39] The unequal number of voters in districts has been a serious point of contention that Soviet and post-Soviet elites have not been able to solve effectively. It can be traced back to the 1989 elections to the USSR Congress of People's Deputies. Speaking at the First Congress in May 1989, Latvian deputy Colonel Viktor Alksnis (who went on to found the conservative Soyuz faction in the parliament) was among the first to note that the votes of some of the electorate were worth more than others.[40] This principle was also a major point of criticism made by Soviet geographers and legal scholars concerning methods to improve further electoral legislation and procedures in the aftermath of the vote to the USSR's Congress.[41]

The eligibility requirements for candidates included a major reversal of one aspect of Soviet electoral legislation. Under the 1988 Electoral Law, USSR ministers were not allowed simultaneously to hold their posts and be USSR People's Deputies (Article 11).[42] This provision would theoretically reduce the possibilities for conflicts of interests for ministers, who would be serving not just their ministries, but as elected representatives of the people. Ministers would have to decide whether they wanted to serve the electorate or remain in their positions. Rather than suffering a loss of status, many ministers chose to remain in their positions (the notable exception being Yeltsin, who resigned as the chairman of the State Construction Committee to take his seat in the Congress). This provision, therefore, had the effect of strengthening Gorbachev's position in the parliament vis-à-vis the state apparatus.

The Statute mandated that Duma deputies could not be members of the Federation Council, representative organs or organs of local self-government at the same time (Article 3). However, as written in a concluding section of the draft constitution, members of the government of the Russian Federation could simultaneously be members of the Duma of the first convocation (Point 9). This is a factor which, theoretically, could have worked to the advantage of the 'pro-reform' forces. Moreover, this had the potential to strengthen further Yeltsin's power base in the lower house. Prime Minister Viktor Chernomyrdin did not seek election to the parliament (although he is reputed to have supported Sergei Shakhrai's Russian Party of Unity and Accord).[43] Other members of government, however, actively sought seats in the Federal Assembly. Standing on the Russia's Choice list were, for instance, First Deputy Prime Minister Yegor Gaidar, Minister for Social Defence of the Population Ella Pamfilova, Deputy Prime Minister Anatolii Chubais, Foreign Minister Andrei Kozyrev, Finance Minister Boris Fedorov, Environment Minister Viktor Danilov-Danil'yan, Deputy Chair of the Council of Ministers Yurii Yarov, Deputy Finance Minister Aleksandr Pochinok, Science Minister Boris Saltykov and Culture Minister Yegvenii Sidorov. The Party of Russian Unity and Accord's candidates included deputy chairs of the Russian Federation's Council of Ministers Sergei Shakhrai and Aleksandr Shokhin, Justice Minister Yurii Kalmykov and Labour Minister Gennadii Melik'yan. Deputy Chairman of the Russian Federation's Council of Ministers Aleksandr Zaveryukha stood as a candidate for the opposition Agrarian Party of Russia.[44]

The prominence of government officials among Russia's Choice candidates and their activities in the campaign led Michael Urban to suggest that the December elections demonstrated some continuity with Soviet electoral practices. He considers this '"democracy by design", whereby those in control of the state machinery attempt to shape the institutions and procedures of a competitive election in ways that ensure an outcome favourable to the designers themselves'.[45] Russia's Choice, considered by Urban to be a 'party of power', had its candidates in key positions: Mikhail Poltoranin headed the Federal Information Centre and 'others in the bloc holding the top posts in state broadcasting would have a free hand to shape the images and messages of the election transmitted to mass audiences via television and the radio'.[46] Urban also claims that Russia's Choice had control over the 'primary rules', i.e. 'the established offices for which parties and independent candidates compete', and the 'secondary rules', i.e. 'the procedures and regulations that govern this competition', of the campaign.[47] His evidence for the former includes examples such as the manner in which the constitution was drafted (by a 'narrow political clique' rather than a constitutional convention): ministers were able to be members of the Duma, and criticism of the draft constitution was prohibited. Moreover, the committee overseeing the conducting of the plebiscite was headed by Russia's Choice candidate Vladimir Shumeiko.

Included in Urban's second category is the constituency gerrymandering from the former RSFSR Congress, which represented 1,068 districts, to the 225-district Duma, and the resulting grossly unequal numbers of voters per constituency. He also notes the speed with which the campaign was conducted and the manner and time frame in which electoral associations had to scramble for signatures, which hurt blocs other than Russia's Choice. Because Russia's Choice had the largest number of candidates competing for seats, the Tsentrizbirkom's directive to keep the political affiliations of the candidates off the ballot paper worked more to Gaidar's bloc's benefit and disadvantaged others. Moreover, Urban claims that media coverage was heavily in favour of Russia's Choice.[48] Indeed, as Daphne Skillen argues later in this collection, the fact that Russia's Choice's candidates included so many members of government and prominent personalities ensured greater exposure for the coalition in the run-up to 12 December.

Campaigning for the Federal Assembly

The media's importance in shaping the former Soviet Union's electoral politics is a recent development. The first election-related television broadcasts, for instance, began during the 1989 elections to the USSR Congress of People's Deputies. Programmes like *Vlast' sovetam* ('Power to the Soviets') and *Navstrechu vyboram* ('Meeting the Elections') informed the Soviet electorate of selected issues and candidates involved in the poll. Local programmes like Moscow's *Dobryi vecher Moskva* ('Good Evening Moscow') presented debates between contestants for the seats.[49] Subsequently, television took a more prominent role as the political system opened further. Television was the most widely used form of media agitation in the 1993 campaign.[50] As Daphne Skillen undertakes in much greater detail in the following chapter, television was an extremely expensive campaign medium. For instance, it was reported in *Izvestiya* that for one minute of air time on the Ostankino state television channel a party or bloc had to pay 707,000 roubles, and it cost 632,095 roubles for the same time allotment on the Rossiya channel.[51]

Party political broadcasts began in late November,[52] providing voters with details on programmes and personalities in the campaign.[53] Thus the term *agitvecher* (agitational evening) entered the Russian political lexicon.[54] As Daphne Skillen notes, these telecasts were important in influencing voters. However, not all of the viewing public watched them enthusiastically. Many voters preferred to watch imported soap operas such as the Mexican *Prosto Mariya* ('Simply Maria') or the American favourite 'Santa Barbara' while the party political broadcasts were shown.[55] Former Constitutional Court Chairman Valerii Zorkin noted the intrusiveness and abundance of political broadcasts when he claimed 'I eat in the morning – they tell me to "Vote for Russia's Choice". I eat in the evening and it is the same.'[56]

St Petersburg television's *Vybory: pryamoi efir* provided candidates competing in the city's single-seat constituencies with opportunities to speak about their programmes and their intentions. Candidates used different methods to convey their election messages. For instance, on one show broadcast on 1 December 1993 at 9:45 p.m. (Moscow time), Vitalii Kalinin, a PRES candidate, presented a speech to promote his platform, while Russia's Choice candidate, advocate Aleksei Aleksandrov, used a video to present his personal and programmatic information to the St Petersburg electorate.[57]

Electoral associations, candidates and their assistants used a variety of campaigning techniques to bring their platforms to the electorate. These included producing political advertisements, leafleting and carrying out mail-box drops, getting involved in photo opportunities and conducting rallies.[58] Electoral associations sponsored rock concerts specifically to attract the support of younger voters. Russia's Choice, for instance, promoted a major rock concert at the Palace of Congresses in Moscow on 3–5 December. Their advertisement was a take-off (one could even say rip-off) of the Pepsi Cola advertising slogan '*novoe pokolenie vybiraet*' ('the choice of the new generation'). This event was televised on Ostankino at 3 p.m. on 5 December 1993. The RDDR held a concert sponsored by the Fund for Support of the Russian Movement for Democratic Reforms on 5 December 1993 in St

Petersburg. Entitled 'Stars of the Stage in Support of the RDDR', this event was scheduled to be televised on the St Petersburg station between 2 and 3 p.m. (Moscow time). However, the broadcast was cut short by a hockey game between SKA St Petersburg and Dynamo Moscow. Undeterred, the RDDR even managed to capitalize on this change in programming. Whether for personal or political motives, Sobchak and other members of the RDDR arrived at the game during the second period, and were depicted by the cameras amid the cheers of the crowd. In this way, the RDDR gained extra, unpaid publicity.

Candidates and electoral associations were not the only actors interested in presenting information to the electorate. The Russian government used the media to achieve different goals. First, the government had to get voters to the ballot boxes; second, they had to persuade them to vote in favour of the draft constitution. There were several ways in which the state promoted and publicized the elections and the plebiscite. The government sponsored several public service announcements advising citizens on when to vote, the institutions they would be choosing and the proper methods for casting their ballots.

Under the new rules, voters would have to cast their ballots differently from when they elected deputies to Soviet institutions. Therefore, the government was responsible for informing voters on this subject. Earlier, voters had been instructed to cross out the name(s) of the person(s) *against* whom they wished to vote. The new provisions mandated that voters put a cross or some other mark in the box next to the electoral association or person(s) *for* whom they wished to vote in the elections for deputies on the party lists or in the constituencies. However, they were instructed to cross out – as they had been instructed before – the opposite response to their acceptance or rejection of the draft constitution.[59]

Several government-sponsored public service announcements dealt with election and plebiscite procedures. The Rossiya channel broadcast one such informational programme on 1 December at 4:20 p.m. (Moscow time). This particular advertisement informed Russian voters that the polling stations would be open from 8 a.m. to 10 p.m. on 12 December. In order to vote citizens would have to bring their passports; voting by non-citizens was prohibited. Actors in the broadcast demonstrated the correct voting procedures as described by the announcer. The government sponsored another procedural broadcast pertaining to the elections at about 9:50 p.m. (Moscow time) on 6 December on the Rossiya channel. On this public service announcement Tsentrizbirkom chair Nikolai Ryabov went through the different numbered ballot papers and demonstrated how to mark them validly. First, Ryabov noted that voters would be given four ballot papers (although in some of Russia's regions and major cities there would be more, as elections to other institutions were to be held at the same time).[60] The first ballot paper contained the list of names of Federation Council candidates. The second was the list of parties and blocs competing for the State Duma. The third contained the names of the candidates competing for the State Duma in the single-candidate districts. The final ballot paper was for the draft constitution. As well as such televised announcements, newspapers also carried information on election and referendum procedures and issues.[61]

The constitution itself occupied a primary place in the election campaign and affected the way in which the electoral associations' candidates canvassed. Vice-Premier Vladimir Shumeiko, in charge of the government commission which oversaw the conducting of the nationwide plebiscite, tried to ban the activities of four electoral blocs and parties – Civic Union, the Agrarian Party, BRNI and Yabloko – for expressing critical opinions about the constitution in their pre-election broadcasts.[62] However, there was a public outcry against this proposal. Noted scholar and Civic Union candidate Aleksandr Tsipko opposed Shumeiko's stance, declaring that if the Tsentrizbirkom barred the dissenting electoral associations from participating in the elections, all candidates would have a 'moral question' placed in front of them about whether to continue participating in the 'vulgar style' of the election campaign.[63] In fact, neither the Tsentrizbirkom nor the Arbitration Tribunal supported Shumeiko's proposal.[64]

Finally, in order to clear confusion about the issue (and possibly to distance himself from Shumeiko in the eyes of the electorate), Yeltsin himself issued a statement declaring that constructive criticism is a 'natural manifestation of the original position of the different parties, population groups and political leaders', but that 'indiscriminate, negative [criticism] from a position of narrow party egoism and political revenge' was unacceptable.[65] This confusion was certainly damaging even to constructive debate on the constitution, although parties and blocs did, nevertheless, continue to express their opinions.[66] Former Constitutional Court chairman Valerii Zor'kin summed up the issue as follows:

The relationship to the constitution is the basis of [the electoral associations'] pre-election platforms. It is forbidden to criticize the draft constitution – this, in effect, violates free elections, violates a free Russia. This means that one must do nothing but praise if one hopes to gain access to 'the feeding trough'. But, excuse me, then this is the same as Orwell.[67]

The voting process: observations and violations

On 12 December voters proceeded to their local polling stations to cast their ballots. After arriving at their respective precincts,[68] in accordance with the Statute, they presented their passports to electoral commission workers. Having inspected the documents, the commission workers struck the voters' names off the electors' list to indicate that they had participated. The voters then proceeded to another table to receive their ballot papers. Again, they presented their passports. The attendants inspected them, signed or initialled the ballot papers and passed the documents back to the voters. The voters then took their ballot papers across the room to the voting booths, entered the booths, closing the curtains behind them, and made their selections in secret. They then exited the booths, folded their ballot papers, walked directly to the voting urns and dropped the papers into the secured ballot boxes, thus completing the voting procedure. The voting was largely unceremonious, in stark contrast to the picture of Soviet elections that Theodore Friedgut painted in his classic *Political Participation in the USSR*, in which he described polling stations adorned with flowers, young pioneers guarding the ballot boxes and election day a national holiday.[69] Nevertheless, it was noted that in some Russian areas the old traditions continued. For instance, in Volgograd the voters treated the elections like a holiday, and in Tula first-time voters continued to receive flowers or books as initiation presents for performing their civic duties.[70]

The entire election campaign was the subject of external scrutiny.

On 9 December 1993, the Tsentrizbirkom accredited more than 800 foreign observers from more than 50 countries and 20 international, parliamentary, social, legal and research organizations who were working in more than 100 Russian cities and other population centres.[71] There was general agreement among the observers that the contest was held fairly and without widespread violations of voters' or candidates' rights. For instance, Adzum Sedze, Japanese First Deputy Minister of Foreign Affairs, heading the Japanese observers' team, Magdelena Hoff, in charge of the observer team from the European Parliament and the EC and head of the Group of the European Parliament for ties with the CIS, and Michael Emerson, the official representative of the EC in Moscow, noted that the elections were 'the first honest elections in Russia in the last 75 years'.[72] Dane Ole Espersen and Austrian Fritz Probst, observers from the Parliamentary Assembly of the Council of Europe, after visiting eight electoral precincts, stated that 'there were no serious violations of voting procedures nor was there evidence of any influence over voters.'[73] Japanese observers, focusing their activities in Moscow and Khabarovsk *krai*, felt that during the preparatory stages of the elections all blocs were given free access to the media. Representatives of the European Parliament, however, after concentrating their efforts in 37 regions, felt that Russia's Choice exercised power over the media.[74]

Despite her generally positive evaluation of the poll, Hoff complained that the right of secret ballot had been violated in some instances and that the electorate was ill-informed on matters such as candidates' party or bloc affiliations. She noted that there were no bloc representatives to provide further information to voters at polling stations. Moreover, she felt that voters did not have enough time to become acquainted with the draft constitution. Hoff also stressed that the wording of the document and the referendum itself were presidentially directed.[75] Michael Urban's previously mentioned observations support Hoff's claims.

Incidents of foul play also occurred during the campaign. In one instance, *Izvestiya* reported that entrepreneur Ivan Degtyarev, a candidate for the Democratic Party of Russia standing in Arkhangel'sk *oblast'*, had committed a criminal act when he illegally sold fish from boats of the Arkhangel'sk trawler fleet in Norway. The Arkhangel'sk tax inspector estimated from the losses and damages caused by Degtyarev that he would face penalties amounting to 32 billion roubles. The *oblast'* procurator issued a warrant to arrest Degtyarev and his assistant, and the latter was in fact arrested.[76] This report prompted a strong reaction from the Tsentrizbirkom, who stated that the editors of *Izvestiya* had violated a portion of the election statute prohibiting the dissemination of materials which could weaken the honour and dignity of a candidate to the State Duma. As a penalty, the paper would have to publish the Tsentrizbirkom's Decree on Mass Information without any cuts, editorial headlines or commentaries, before 10 December 1993.[77] The newspaper complied, and the decree appeared in its 8 December 1993 issue.[78] As a reaction to this incident, the PRES adopted a decision to remove from its list any candidate who did not have a clean past.[79]

In another case of alleged foul play, Gavriil Popov complained that Russia's Choice had privileges that other blocs did not, asserting that Gaidar had visited a military unit, whereas none of the other bloc leaders had received the opportunity to speak to the army.[80] In addition, he argued that the bloc used Yeltsin's image on their signs, which in effect made him a supporter solely of that bloc.[81] There were also some more sinister incidents: Bagavutdin Gadzhiev, a Federation Council candidate and chairman of the council of the Dagestan commercial-investment corporation, was killed (along with two others) by submachine-gun fire while leaving work in the city centre of Makhachkaliya.[82]

Evaluating the results

The results (see Tables 4.1 and 4.2) became the subject of criticism within hours of the polls closing. Emulating the traditions of both American and British political broadcasting, the Russians attempted to hold an all-night television special devoted to reporting the official results as they were tabulated. Although the adoption of the draft constitution was reported quite early on in the programme, actual voting tabulations kept being delayed. Because of the failure of the show's presenters to provide accurate and prompt electoral information, the Tsentrizbirkom issued a statement claiming that it was not involved in the delays in any way.[83]

Table 4.1 Seat allocation in the State Duma

Party/Bloc	PR seats	Constituency seats	Total (seats)	Total (%)
Russia's Choice	40	30	70	15.6
LDPR	59	5	64	14.2
KPRF	32	16	48	10.7
APR	21	12	33	7.3
Yabloko	20	3	23	5.1
ZhR	21	2	23	5.1
PRES	18	1	19	4.2
DPR	14	0	14	3.1
RDDR	0	4	4	0.9
DiM	0	2	2	0.4
Civic Union	0	1	1	0.2
Other parties	–	14	14	3.1
Independents	–	129	129	28.7

Note: At the time of election six seats were unfilled.
Source: Adapted from 'The Final Tally', *The Economist*, 8 January 1994, p. 30.

Table 4.2 Seat allocation in the Federation Council

Party/Bloc	Number of seats
KPRF	11
Russia's Choice	6
APR	1
PRES	1
RDDR	1
Civic Union	0
DPR	0
LDPR	0
Yabloko	0
ZhR	0
Other communist parties and organizations	4
Other democratic parties and blocs	4
Independents	144

Source: Adapted from Terry D. Clark, 'The Russian Elections: Back to Square One?', *PS: Political Science and Politics*, vol. XXVII, no. 3 (September 1994), pp. 520–24, at p. 524.

The elections were scrutinized closely during the months that followed, particularly with regard to their validity. For instance, Aleksandr Minkin writing in *Moskovskii komsomolets* noted that there were substantial differences among the reportages in a number of newspapers and that the constitution had been approved by what amounted to 31 per cent of the electorate.[84] Therefore, the legal status of the constitution is indeed questionable. In February 1994, the human rights activist Kronid Lyubarsky noted that as late as two months after the elections no one really knew how many electors had voted and there was still no final district-by-district list published.[85] (However, several preliminary reports did exist.)[86] Moreover, in May 1994 *Izvestiya* published an article which disclosed that nearly 3.5 million votes had been falsified at precinct level and that about 5.7 million had been tampered with at the constituency level.[87] Thus, the elections remain the subject of serious disrepute. At the time of writing, no changes had yet been made to rectify the electoral violations.

Conclusions

Several evaluations can be made from the final election results. The first conclusion that can be reached is that the Russian population elected candidates who represented diverse political tendencies. This reduced the coalition-building potential of the parliament and enhanced the prospects for interfractional conflict. Parliamentary fragmentation further strengthened Yeltsin's position within the Russian political system. As the data indicate, no party or bloc won an absolute majority in the lower house. In fact the largest proportion of elected deputies stood as independents (129 or 28.7 per cent). Among electoral associations Russia's Choice had the largest number of deputies in the parliament, with 70 (15.6 per cent of all seats). However, nearly one-third of the parliament could be deemed hostile to Yeltsin and 'democratic reforms': the Liberal Democrats gained the largest share of the party-list votes with 59 seats (22.8 per cent of the votes in this category); the KPRF controlled 10.7 per cent of the seats, and the APR 7.3 per cent.

Richard Sakwa makes several key observations about the elections. First, he notes that the vote 'revealed the profound divisions in Russian society and the absence of consensus over many issues'. He points to the baffling situation that arose as a result of the choice of electoral system: had the deputies been elected solely according to a system of proportional representation the LDPR would have been the country's leading party, whereas under a first-past-the-post formula they would hardly have mattered. In adopting the constitution and electing an anti-reform lower house, the electorate sent forth 'two mutually exclusive signals: in accepting the constitution they were voting for stability; but in voting for the opposition, they were rejecting the existing basis for order.' The results underlined the significance of regional variations in Russia (a theme traced more fully in this volume by Elena Omel'chenko and Hilary Pilkington). Rather than consolidating Russian politics, the results indicated its degree of fragmentation. The elections could also be placed within the wider European context of disenchantment with traditional parties, or could be seen as a protest vote against IMF-directed reform. Sakwa suggests that the elections marked the beginning of 'a new Russian politics' in which the previous bipolarity of 'communist' versus 'democrat' was replaced by a tripolar arrangement, consisting of the former two groups together with a 'semi-fascist movement of the leadership type'.[88]

Other authors have suggested different interpretations. Stephen Whitefield and Geoffrey Evans write that on the one hand the elections could be seen as a 'predictable reaffirmation of traditional Russian political culture', blending values of 'orthodoxy, autocracy and nationality' with 'support for state control of the economy and egalitarianism'. On the other hand, the elections could be interpreted as a 'protest vote by an electorate whose political culture had changed significantly during the last forty years'.[89] Terry D. Clark suggests that the communists scored a 'remarkable victory', re-emerging at the centre of the anti-reform movement. They would, however, not be assured of control over the political agenda.[90] Stephen Sestanovich, for his part, suggests that the elections were 'a communist setback'.[91]

While other chapters contain much fuller discussions on the implications of the elections, a few general observations can serve as a conclusion to this analysis of the campaign itself. First, the elections to the Federal Assembly marked a greater movement towards fulfilling the criteria for free and fair elections, though still falling far short of this goal. Moreover, the campaign had many of the attributes common to campaigns established in liberal democratic countries which consistently employ free elections as a means of changing the government. Alternative parties and coalitions competed against each other to win seats. They publicized their objectives broadly through the media and made a serious attempt to reach a wide array of supporters using various campaign techniques. It must be noted, however, that Russia's Choice had advantages over the other contestants in certain aspects of the campaign, thus calling into question the fairness of the poll.

The outcome affected policy-making and the composition of the government. Aspects of the former could be seen in the Yeltsin administration's more hawkish attitude towards Serbia and NATO's eastward expansion; in its controversial foray into Chechnya and in an initial backtracking on economic reform. The composition of the government was affected by the voting. The high vote for the opposition reflected a deep dissatisfaction with the pace of economic reform, whereas a Russia's Choice victory could have signalled the reverse. Had Russia's Choice performed better, it is probable that Yegor Gaidar would have replaced Chernomyrdin as prime minister and that this would have had an impact on the pace of the reform process. However, as the vote stood, Chernomyrdin remained.

The 1993 campaign reflected historical trends. There was still some interference hindering the accurate reflection of candidates' and voters' attitudes. Cases of censorship, government interference, vote falsification, scanty information and restrictions on candidates and electoral associations certainly support Michael Urban's thesis that the elections replicated early Soviet practices.

There are further points of continuity between 1989 and 1993 which it may also be important to consider. In both instances there was an institution which attempted to prevent those contestants which it considered threatening from winning seats in the parliament. However, in both cases, significant victories were scored precisely by those who were supposed to be kept out of seats. In this respect, the preference of the electorate overruled that of the CPSU and the Yeltsin administration. While it is inconceivable that popular power could come close to matching either CPSU or presidential power, the voters showed that they at least have the ability to influence their leaders in some way and to make known their satisfaction or disaffection with particular policies and with the government in general.

Notes

1 'Polozhenie o federal'nykh organakh vlasti na perekhodnyi period', *Izvestiya*, 24 September 1993, p. 3.
2 For a discussion of the conflict between Yeltsin and the parliament see Richard Sakwa, *Russian Politics and Society* (London: Routledge, 1993), chapter 2. Reflections on the power distribution in post-communist Russia by the principal figures in the struggle can be found in Boris Yeltsin, *The View From the Kremlin* (London and Glasgow: Harper Collins, 1994) and Ruslan Khasbulatov, *The Struggle for Russia: Power and Change in the Democratic Revolution*, edited by Richard Sakwa (London: Routledge, 1993), esp. part III. On the problems of drafting a post-Soviet constitution see Edward W. Walker, 'The New Russian Constitution and the Future of the Russian Federation', *The Harriman Institute Forum*, vol. 5, no. 10 (June 1992).
3 See Stephen White, *After Gorbachev* (Cambridge: Cambridge University Press, 1993), chapter 8.
4 Russian Academy of Sciences, 'Vserossiiskii referendum 25 aprelya 1993 goda' (mimeograph). I am grateful to Hugh Jenkins, CREES, Birmingham University, for this document. Results also appear in *Rossiiskaya gazeta*, 6 May 1993, and Sakwa, *Russian Politics and Society*, p. 428.
5 Michael McFaul, *Post-Communist Politics: Democratic Prospects in Russia and Eastern Europe* (Washington, DC: Center for Strategic and International Studies, 1993).
6 'Polozhenie o federal'nykh organakh vlasti na perekhodnyi period'.
7 It should be noted here that the Statute on Elections of State Duma Deputies initially mandated that the lower house would consist of 400 deputies: 270 to be elected in single-mandate electoral districts and 130 to be chosen on the basis of proportional representation from federation-wide party lists. See 'Polozhenie o vyborakh deputatov Gosudarstvennoi Dumy', in *Izvestiya*, 24 September 1993, pp. 3-5.
8 Matthew Wyman, Bill Miller, Stephen White and Paul Heywood, 'The Russian Elections of December 1993', *Electoral Studies*, vol. 13, no. 3 (September 1994), pp. 254-71, at p. 255.
9 See, for instance, 'Konstitutsiya Rossiiskoi Federatsii (proekt)', *Argumenty i fakty*, no. 45 (1993), pp. 7-12. The state-published text, *Konstitutsiya Rossiiskoi Federatsii (proekt)* (Moscow: Yuridicheskaya literatura, 1993),

was available from street vendors for about 1,000 roubles, or slightly less than 1 US dollar.
10 *Konstitutsiya (Osnovnoi Zakon) Soyuza Sovetskikh Sotsialisticheskikh Respublik* (Moscow: Yuridicheskaya literatura, 1978).
11 In addition to the variants of the draft constitution cited above, discussions of its main features were published in *Izvestiya*, 9 December 1993, p. 7.
12 For a discussion of what constitutes effective parties see James McGregor, 'How Electoral Laws Shape Eastern Europe's Parliaments', *RFE/RL Research Report*, vol. 2, no. 4 (22 January 1993), pp. 11–18.
13 See Interfax report, 'Kto budet borot'sya za mandaty v Gosudarstvennuyu Dumu', *Rossiiskaya gazeta*, 14 October 1993, p. 2.
14 Postfaktum report, 'Bitva za izbiratelei nachalas'', *Izvestiya*, 14 October 1993, p. 4.
15 Jonathan Steele, 'Yeltsin's Beauties Line Up', *Guardian*, 23 October 1993, p. 14.
16 See, for instance, John Lloyd, 'A Constitution For Yeltsin's Time', *Financial Times*, 11 November 1993, p. 3, and David Hearst, 'Moscow Bars a Third of Parties from Poll', *Guardian*, 11 November 1993, p. 4.
17 John Lloyd, 'Yeltsin Accused of Impeding Fair Russian Election', *Financial Times*, 5 November 1993, p. 1.
18 'Spisok Gosudarstvennoi Dumy Federal'nogo Sobraniya Rossiiskoi Federatsii, izbrannykh po odnomandatnym izbiratel'nym okrugam', *Rossiiskaya gazeta*, 28 December 1993, pp. 3–5, at p. 4.
19 Information on winning candidates is from ibid. and 'Spisok deputatov Soveta Federatsii Federal'nogo Sobraniya Rossiiskoi Federatsii, izbrannykh po dvukhmandatnym izbiratel'nym okrugam', ibid., pp. 5–6, at p. 6. A listing of the political organizations prohibited from putting lists forward is in Hearst, 'Moscow Bars'.
20 ibid.
21 Georgii Ivanov-Smolensky, 'Vybornuyu gonku prodolzhayut 21 blok i partiya', *Izvestiya*, 9 November 1993, p. 2.
22 Ranking based on arrangement in Yana Meteleva, Dmitrii Orlov and Lyubov' Tsukanova, 'Izbiratel'nye bloki: kto est' kto', *Rossiiskie vesti*, 11 December 1993, p. 2.
23 See 'Kak budem golosovat'' column, *Argumenty i fakty*, no. 42 (1993), p. 2.
24 N. Ryabov, 'Nam est' iz kogo vybirat'', *Rossiiskaya gazeta*, 11 December 1993, p. 1.
25 Ivan Rodin, 'Repressivnaya propaganda konstitutsii', *Nezavisimaya gazeta*, 2 December 1993, p. 1. During the first ten days of December, the government was to provide 76 billion roubles for bread subsidies for the lowest stratum of the population and 65 billion roubles for pension subsidies, whereas 85 billion roubles were to be spent on the elections and referendum. This point is raised in 'Pravitel'stvo-maloimushchim: idte vy na referendum', *Megapolis Express*, no. 48 (8 December 1993), p. 3.

26 'Evropeiskii soyuz podaril Tsentrizbirkomu orgtekhniki', *Rossiiskaya gazeta*, 7 December 1993, p. 2.
27 Roza Sergazieva has suggested that there were 3,473 electoral precincts in Moscow. See for instance her article 'U oblasti svoya Duma', *Moskva* (supplement to *Argumenty i fakty*), no. 24 (1993), p. 1. It was published elsewhere that there were 3,199 precincts in the city, e.g. in A. K., 'Moskva gotova k 12 dekabrya', *Nezavisimaya gazeta*, 9 December 1993, p. 1.
28 Roza Sergazieva, 'Po "limono"-izbirkomu', *Moskva*, no. 24 (1993), p. 1.
29 'Vlast' stoit dorogo', *Moskovskie novosti*, no. 49 (1 December 1993), p. A9.
30 Sergei Slyusarenko, '70 peterskikh bomzhei gotovi k golosovaniyu', *Kommersant" daily*, 10 December 1993, p. 4.
31 John Lloyd, 'Russian Deputy PM Milks Poverty Ticket', *Financial Times*, 30/31 October 1993, p. 2.
32 'Vlast' stoit dorogo'.
33 'Kto zakazyvaet muzyku?', *Moskovskie novosti*, no. 50 (8 December 1993), p. A9.
34 Slyusarenko, '70 peterskikh bomzhei'.
35 Rodion Ivanov, '"Vybor Rossii" pereshel v nastuplenie', *Nezavisimaya gazeta*, 2 December 1993, p. 1.
36 Richard Sakwa, 'The Russian Elections of December 1993 and the New Russian Politics' (unpublished manuscript, 1994).
37 'Odnomandatnye okruga po vyboram v Gosudarstvennuyu Dumu v 1993 godu', *Izvestiya*, 13 October 1993, p. 4.
38 ibid., 14 October 1993, p. 4.
39 Wyman, Miller, White and Heywood, 'The Russian Elections of December 1993', p. 255.
40 *Pervyi s"ezd narodnykh deputatov SSSR, 25 maya – 9 iyunya 1989 g: Stenograficheskii otchet* (Moscow: Verkhovnyi Sovet/Izvestiya, 1989), 6 vols, vol. 1, p. 51.
41 See, for instance, A.V. Berezkin, V.A. Kolosov, M.E. Pavlovskaya, N.V. Petrov and L.V. Smiryagin, 'The Geography of the 1989 Elections of People's Deputies of the USSR (Preliminary Results)', *Soviet Geography*, vol. XXX, no. 8 (October 1989), pp. 607–34, esp. pp. 612–16, and S.A. Avak'yan, 'Zakonodatel'stvo o vyborakh: opyt primeneniya voprosy sovershenstvovaniya', *Vestnik moskovskogo universiteta (seriya pravo)*, no. 6 (1989), pp. 9–19.
42 *Zakon Soyuza Sovetskikh Sotsialisticheskikh Respublik o vyborakh narodnykh deputatov SSSR* (Moscow: Izvestiya, 1988).
43 'Kto pretenduet na mesta v novom parlamente', *Izvestiya*, 28 October 1993, p. 4.
44 Meteleva, Orlov and Tsukanova, 'Izbiratel'nye bloki'.
45 Michael Urban, 'December 1993 as a Replication of Late-Soviet Electoral Practices', *Post-Soviet Affairs*, vol. 10, no. 2, pp. 127–58, p. 128.
46 ibid., p. 131.
47 ibid., p. 132.
48 ibid., pp. 133–9.

49 These broadcasts are discussed in Peter Lentini, 'Reforming the Electoral System: The 1989 Elections to the USSR Congress of People's Deputies', *Journal of Communist Studies*, vol. 7, no. 1 (March 1994), pp. 69–94; Brendan Kiernan and Joseph Aistrup, 'The 1989 Elections to the Congress of People's Deputies in Moscow', *Soviet Studies*, vol. 43, no. 6, pp. 109–64, and Stephen White, 'The Soviet Elections of 1989: From Acclamation to Limited Choice', *Coexistence*, vol. 28, no. 4 (December 1991), pp. 513–39.

50 For discussions of the media and the elections see James Hughes, 'The "Americanization" of Russian Politics: Russia's First Television Elections, December 1993', *Journal of Communist Studies and Transition Politics*, vol. 10, no. 2 (June 1994), pp. 125–50.

51 'Za skol'ko politiki pokupali efir', *Izvestiya*, 10 December 1993, p. 4.

52 For discussions of the content of the Liberal Democratic Party of Russia's 30 November 1993 party political broadcast see, for example, Peter Lentini and Troy McGrath, 'The Rise of the Liberal Democratic Party and the 1993 Elections', *The Harriman Institute Forum*, vol. 6, no. 6 (February 1994), p. 8, and Peter Lentini, 'Elections and Political Order in Russia: The 1993 Elections to the Russian State Duma', *Journal of Communist Studies and Transition Politics*, vol. 10, no. 2 (June 1994), pp. 151–92, at pp. 161–2.

53 For a description of these broadcasts, see David Hearst, 'Party Political Broadcast Wakes up Russian Viewers', *Guardian*, 22 November 1993, p. 4.

54 This term was employed by *Kommersant" daily* journalist Maksim Sokolov in his column during the campaign 'TV vybor'.

55 See, for instance, 'Vybor Rossii – Prosto Mariya', *Moskovskie novosti*, no. 49 (1 December 1993), p. A9. See also Helen Womack, 'Politicians Soft-Soap Russian Viewers', *Independent*, 24 November 1993, p. 13.

56 Radik Batyrshin, 'Svobodnykh vyborov ne budet', *Nezavisimaya gazeta*, 1 December 1993, pp. 1 and 3, at p. 3.

57 *Vybory: pryamoi efir*, broadcast on the St Petersburg channel on 1 December 1993, at 9:45 p.m. (Moscow time).

58 For examples see Lentini, 'Elections and Political Order in Russia', pp. 163–8.

59 The ballot paper was worded in the following manner:

Do you accept the Constitution of the Russian Federation?
        YES   NO

If you vote for the adoption of the Constitution of the Russian Federation, cross out the word 'NO'.

If you vote against the adoption of the Constitution of the Russian Federation, cross out the word 'YES'.

See *Vsenarodnoe golosovanie po proektu Konstitutsii Rossiiskoe Federatsii 12 dekabrya 1993 goda byulleten' dlya golosovaniya*. Official ballot paper.

60 On these other elections see Sergazieva, 'U oblasti svoya Duma'; 'V Rossii eshche odin prezident', *Nezavisimaya gazeta*, 14 December 1993, p. 1;

Vladislav Dorofeev, 'V Federal'noe sobranie proshlo mnogo gubernatov', *Kommersant" daily*, 14 December 1993, p. 3.
61 See respectively the advertisements 'Nashe budushchee zavisit ot nas!', *Izvestiya*, 7 December 1993, p. 7, and '12 dekabrya 1993 goda vsenarodnoe golosovanie po proektu Konstitutsii Rossiiskoi Federatsii', *Izvestiya*, 9 December 1993, p. 7. See also, 'Raz"yasneniye o poryadke zapolneniya izbiratel'nykh byulletenei dlya golosovaniya po vyboram deputatov Soveta Federatsii i Gosudarstvennoi Dumy Federal'nogo Sobraniya Rossiiskoi Federatsii i byulleten' dlya vsenarodnogo golosovaniya po proektu Konstitutsii Rossiiskoi Federatsii', *Rossiiskie vesti*, 11 December 1993, p. 3. A similar version of the same item appeared in *Rossiiskaya gazeta*, 3 December 1993, p. 5.
62 Ivan Rodin, 'Repressivnaya propaganda konstitutsii'.
63 Ol'ga Odintsova, 'Trebuyut otstranit' "Vybor Rossii"', *Kommersant" daily*, 2 December 1993, p. 2.
64 See, for instance, the reports by Interfaks, 'Tsentrizbirkom ne udovletvoril trebovanie Shumeiko', *Izvestiya*, 3 December 1993, and ITAR-TASS, 'Treteiskii sud ob obrashchenie Shumeiko', *Izvestiya*, 2 December 1993, p. 2.
65 ITAR-TASS, 'Prezident PR schitaet, chto proekt Konstitutsii kritike podlezhit', *Izvestiya*, p. 1.
66 See, for instance, 'Konstitutsiya: "za" i "protiv"', *Moskovskie novosti*, no. 49 (1993), p. A10.
67 Batyrshin, 'Svobodnykh vyborov ne budet'.
68 The following examples recount the experiences I had observing the voting at electoral precinct 2411 located in Moscow's single-member district 204 (Yugo-Zapadnyi) on 12 December 1993.
69 Theodore Friedgut, *Political Participation in the USSR* (Princeton, NJ: Princeton University Press, 1979), p. 110.
70 Vitalii Cherkasov, 'Volgograd', *Rossiiskaya gazeta*, 14 December 1993, p. 1, and Nikolai Kireev, 'Tula', ibid., p. 2.
71 N. Ryabov, 'Nam est' iz kogo vybirat".
72 Aleksandr Koretsky and Valeriya Sycheva, 'Sereznykh narushenii zamechno ne bylo', *Kommersant" daily*, 14 December 1993, p. 3.
73 'Nablyudateli: narushenie ne bylo', *Rossiiskaya gazeta*, 14 December 1993, p. 2.
74 Koretsky and Sycheva, 'Sereznykh narushenii'. For another example of foreign observers' positive evaluations of the poll see Aleksei Portansky, 'Vybory byli svobodnym', *Izvestiya*, 14 December 1993, p. 2.
75 All examples are derived from ibid.
76 Viktor Fridman, 'Kriminalnyi ottenok v izbiratel'noi kampanii: ot partii Travkina ballotiruetsya kandidat, kotorogo rasskazyvayut norvezhskie i rossiiskie syshchiki', *Izvestiya*, 7 December 1993, p. 4.
77 'O publikatsii "Kriminalnyi ottenok v izbiratel'noi kampanii" v gazete *Izvestiya* ot 7 dekabrya 1993 goda', *Rossiiskaya gazeta*, 10 December 1993, p. 1.

78 'Tsentrizbirkom preduprezhdayut', *Izvestiya*, 8 December 1993, p. 2.
79 *Nezavisimaya gazeta*, 7 December 1993, p. 2; 'PRES peresmatrivaet spiski svoikh kandidatov', *Izvestiya*, 7 December 1993, p. 4.
80 Indira Duraeva, 'RDDR zhaluetsya na "Vybor Rossii"', *Nezavisimaya gazeta*, 10 December 1993, p. 2.
81 ibid.
82 'Ubit kandidat v deputat', *Rossiiskaya gazeta*, 8 December 1993, p. 1.
83 'Zayavlenie Tsentral'noi izbiratel'noi komissii po vyboram v Sovet Federatsii i po vyboram v Gosudarstvennuyu Dumu Federal'nogo Sobraniya Rossiiskoi Federatsii', no. 139 (13 December 1993). This appears in *Rossiiskaya gazeta*, 14 December 1993, p. 1.
84 Aleksandr Minkin, 'Opyat' "dvoika"?', *Moskovskii komsomolets*, 11 January 1994, p. 1.
85 Kronid Lyubarsky, 'Fal'sifikatsiya', *Novoe vremya*, no. 7 (1994), pp. 8–12, and, by the same author, 'Fal'sifikatsiya – 2', *Novoe vremya*, no. 9 (1994), pp. 10–13. See also his interview conducted by Georgii Tselms, 'Taina tainykh vyborov', *Ogonek*, 1994, no. 6–7 (February), pp. 6–7.
86 See the series of reports prepared by Organizatsionnyi otdel, Tsentr operativnoi informatsii, Upravlenie po rabote s territoriyami i predstavitelyami Prezidenta Administratsii Prezidenta RF, Otdel regional'noi politiki, Otdel vzaimodeistviyu s federal'nymi organami predstavitel'noi vlasti i obshchestvennymi organizatsiyami Soveta Ministrov – Pravitel'stva RF. These include 'Predvaritel'nye rezul'taty golosovaniya po obshchefederal'nomu okrugu' (this report includes the district-by-district support levels of each electoral association and contains data from 14 December 1993); 'Vybory Sovet Federatsii RF' and 'Vybory v Gosudarstvennuyu Dumu po odnomandatnym okrugam' (these reports include constituency results for the top three and two candidates respectively and contain information from 21 December 1993), and 'Vybory v Gosudarstvennuyu Dumu RF po obshchefederal'nomu okrugu' (this report includes data on support for the electoral associations according to Russia's subjects from 21 December 1993). I am grateful to Hugh Jenkins, CREES, Birmingham University, for these documents.
87 Valerii Vyzhutovich, 'Tsentrizbirkom prevrashchaetsya v politicheskoe vedomstvo', *Izvestiya*, 4 May 1994, p. 4.
88 Richard Sakwa, 'The Russian Elections of December 1993', *Europe-Asia Studies*, vol. 47, no. 2 (March 1995), pp. 195–227, at pp. 220–22.
89 Stephen Whitefield and Geoffrey Evans, 'The Russian Election of 1993: Public Opinion and the Transition Experience', *Post-Soviet Affairs*, vol. 10, no. 1 (1994), pp. 38–60, at p. 39.
90 Terry D. Clark, 'The Russian Elections: Back to Square One?', *PS: Political Science and Politics*, vol. XXVII, no. 3 (September 1994), pp. 520–24, at p. 523.
91 Stephen Sestanovich, 'A Communist Setback', in 'Symposium: Is Russian Democracy Doomed?', *Journal of Democracy*, vol. 5, no. 2 (April 1994), pp. 4–41, at pp. 23–7.

PART III

Influences and Trends of the 1993 Campaign

5 *Media Coverage in the Elections*

DAPHNE SKILLEN

> One voice! Who needs it?
> A lone voice is fainter than a squeak.
> Who will hear it?
>
> *V. Mayakovsky*

Television, potentially, is bound up with democracy as the medium that informs and responds to the largest possible audience. It can, of course, be manipulated to elicit the resounding unanimity that characterized the Soviet totalitarian system. In new Russia's first multiparty elections the role of television in providing objective electoral coverage was seen, therefore, as crucial in proving the country's democratic credentials. There is no doubt that a concerted effort was made to provide the necessary conditions on television to enable free and fair elections to take place, but it is arguable whether these conditions were either wise or fair. The role of television was ambivalent and contradictory; the mistakes made were foreseeable and avoidable. Old habits die hard and, on the one hand, Soviet ways of thinking persisted; on the other hand public officials bent backwards to such an extent to be 'neutral' that they largely contributed to the unexpected success of the right-wing nationalist Liberal Democratic Party of Russia (LDPR), led by Vladimir Zhirinovsky.

This result came as a shock not only to political observers but also to the pro-Yeltsin broadcasting executives, especially those of

Ostankino TV, who had organized a television extravaganza on the night of the polls to celebrate victory, only to be forced to reflect soberly on the campaign they had run. A number of new factors have emerged from the elections about the power of television in Russian society today. In the first place the influence of television on the electorate surpassed all expectations, showing for the first time in Russia how politicians on the screen could radically change public opinion and affect voting patterns in a short space of time. In the second place it can be argued that television did not adequately perform its social and political functions, allowing politicians to use it for their own propagandistic purposes rather than for the elucidation of the electorate. Thirdly, the results demonstrated that 'hype' had come to Russian politics and that it was possible for such telegenic politicians as Zhirinovsky, previously considered more of a buffoon than a political threat, to create overnight a pop-star image that attracted about 23 per cent of the electorate.[1]

It was clear from the start that the election campaign would be fought out on television. In a country as vast as Russia, with poor roads, fuel shortages and unpredictable delays in travel, campaigning on television made for more efficient use of time than having direct human contact with voters, especially in the short time-span which allowed five weeks in all to polling day on 12 December 1993. Many candidates remained in the capital throughout the electoral campaign without ever visiting their constituencies. Mikhail Reznikov, campaign manager for Russia's Choice, confirmed that being on television was the best way of getting publicity. 'The most important thing is not so much meeting with local activists and supporters, but the coverage in the local and national media,' he said. 'Whenever we make a trip, we send a group of television people and then they prepare a TV clip about the visit.'[2]

Moreover, as in most countries, television is the main source of news and information in the Russian Federation: it is watched by 86 per cent of the population while, by comparison, only 43 per cent listen to the radio news and 28 per cent read newspapers. Research carried out by the All-Russian Centre for the Study of Public Opinion (VTsIOM) shows that the population can be divided roughly into three sections according to the degree to which it expresses confidence in the media as an accurate source of information: 35 per cent trust the media, 37 per cent do not trust the media, and 27 per cent do not know either way. In the group that trusts the media, far more are supporters of Yeltsin and the reform parties, young people and people with higher education, while communists, national-patriots and rural inhabitants harbour more suspicious attitudes towards the media. Those who voted for Zhirinovsky were more likely to come from rural areas and have lower than average education, and were mainly women and older people – that is, those who tend to be wary of the media.[3] Wyman, Miller, White and Heywood pursue this theme in far greater detail in Chapter 6 of this volume. The questions to ask, then, are how television affected the 'sceptics' in swinging votes in favour of Zhirinovsky, and how it influenced the electorate away from those parties and coalitions which showed substantial leads in the early pre-election public opinion polls.

The Central Electoral Commission's Regulations 'On Information Guarantees in the Election Campaign' comprised the fundamental document regulating media coverage. Approved by Yeltsin's decree of 29 October 1993, this document set out to provide equal opportunities for all parties, blocs and candidates taking part in the elections. Under the regulations an arbitration court was set up to hear complaints and resolve issues of discrimination. Apart from regulating general media coverage, the document laid out guidelines for an official campaign to allow parties and blocs to promote their political programmes on four state-owned airwaves – Ostankino TV, Russian TV, St Petersburg TV and Radio Russia. Privately owned television and radio companies, as well as cable TV, were not subject to these restrictions. In all, as an official document the regulations went some way to be reasonable and fair but, as is the case with most legal documents, what is more important is how the regulations were interpreted and what ways were devised of getting around them.

Early on in the media campaign the biggest fear of parties (blocs) opposed to the government was that the two main state-owned nationwide television channels – Ostankino and Russian TV – would be biased in favour of the 'democrats' (loosely comprised of former deputy prime minister Yegor Gaidar's Russia's Choice bloc; Yabloko, led by economist Grigorii Yavlinsky, former USSR people's deputy Yurii Boldyrev and former ambassador to the US Vladimir Lukin; the Russian Movement for Democratic Reforms, led by St Petersburg mayor Anatolii Sobchak, and the Russian Party of Unity and Accord, headed by deputy premier Sergei Shakhrai). This concerned news coverage which, according to the regulations, required that election items be placed at the beginning of news bulletins, that they be identified as separate items from the rest of the news, and that they be reported straight as information without comment – a safeguard against the inclination of newsreaders to make personal remarks. The fear of bias was not without grounds. Arkadii Vol'sky, the industrialist leader of Civic Union, complained at a press conference on 3 November 1993 that the media had organized an 'information blockade' of opposition parties and were giving preference to Russia's Choice. He claimed that Ostankino TV owed him eleven hours of air time based on the amount of coverage received by Russia's Choice.[4] The high visibility of Russia's Choice candidates was indisputable and was made possible under the transitional provisions of the elections, which allowed members of the current government to run for the new parliament. Thus the democrats enjoyed considerable air time by virtue of their government posts, making the most of frequent press conferences and travel, at the expense of the government, to get extra television exposure. During a trip to St Petersburg, Yegor Gaidar constantly switched hats between being deputy prime minister and leader of Russia's Choice, drawing justified accusations of hidden political advertising. Whether, in the end, this proved advantageous for the bloc's candidates is doubtful. In the first place they were burdened with all the ills identified with the government; in the second place an electoral regulation, which prevented opposing candidates from criticizing each other in the media, left candidates *qua* ministers exposed. Moreover, the feeling early on that Russia's Choice would beat the other blocs was harmful, as it put voters off guard about serious political rivals. Nevertheless, Russia's Choice received more than their fair share of air time until the arbitration court forced some of these political jaunts to be cancelled. The court also forestalled other inequities, one such example being its prohibition of the chairman of Ostankino TV, Vyacheslav Bragin, from standing as a Russia's Choice candidate while remaining TV chief, although Bragin's presumption does not seem as outrageous today in the light of media magnate Silvio Berlusconi's victory in the 1994 Italian elections.

According to the regulations, the official campaign on TV and radio, which began on 21 November 1993, three weeks before polling day, was divided into free and paid time for the blocs to air their political broadcasts and commercials. The organization of free time was straightforward and the regulations laid to rest any fear of inequality by guaranteeing all thirteen blocs campaigning in the elections equal access to state television and radio. One free hour of air time on each of the state-owned Ostankino, Russian and St Petersburg channels, as well as on Radio Russia, was allotted to each bloc. It was up to the blocs to divide up their air time as they saw fit. One condition, that candidates were not to use their free time to attack political rivals, was an attempt to prevent a replay of the endless bickering and abuse that characterized the last Russian Supreme Soviet.

There were serious reasons for regimenting the official media campaign, given the tense situation immediately after the disbanding of the Supreme Soviet and the tragic bloodshed of 3–4 October 1993. Moreover, inexperience in the workings of democracy had to be considered, as well as the low level of political culture and a strife-ridden media lacking that sense of social responsibility and objectivity characteristic of quality papers in the West, with their long tradition of working in conditions associated with a free press. The newly acquired freedoms in Russia were often taken to mean 'anything goes', with few effective laws to prevent ethical violations, sensationalism or the purveying of rumour as fact. The dire financial straits of the media and poor salaries for journalists encouraged bribery: news items could be bought, as could air time and print space, passing for objective information. Condemning this practice, Yeltsin stated: 'I cannot consider the press "free" if journalists receive money – sometimes exceeding their annual pay – for covert advertising, the favourable presentation of a party line or the hushing up of criticism.'[5]

In addition to equally distributed free time, the regulations enabled parties and blocs to buy time on all TV and radio channels without limit, so long as each party that wanted to pay was equally served. The role of money, as we shall see later, played a central part in the elections, enabling richer blocs to buy more air time and, inevitably, giving the pro-government bloc an advantage. The price of paid time was officially set: one minute of air time on Ostankino cost 707,000 roubles (at the time about $578) and on Russian TV 632,095 roubles (about $511); while the amount on independent channels was negotiable. When *Moskovskie novosti* (Moscow News) appealed to all parties to reveal their sources of financing during the campaign, only Yabloko complied (for a listing of Yabloko's contributors and their donations see Chapter 4) and up to the time of writing it has remained unclear how much each party or bloc's budget was and how much each paid for advertising in the media. What is known from the arbitration court is that some coalitions and parties received preferential treatment from television companies by being given credit, while others were forced to pay in advance. Zhirinovsky benefited from such favouritism, which may go some way to answering the intriguing questions that have been raised about who his sponsors were and whether German fascist parties were involved. It may well turn out that many of these sponsors were mythical, given the colossal debts the LDPR is known to have amassed as a result of its media campaign and which it has not yet managed to pay back.

Surprisingly, the nine-member arbitration court, which had been set up to resolve media disputes, worked successfully and was taken seriously by political candidates, although it had no real power to impose sanctions on those who violated the regulations. It was thought that a watchdog committee without an 'arbitration prison' could not be effective, but the court's standard threat that it reserved the right to pass on any violations to the future Federal Assembly's credentials commission, with a request that the correctness of a deputy's behaviour be examined once parliament opened, seemed to work. In all, 159 complaints were addressed to the court, of which eight referred to violations regarding free and paid air time, thirteen concerned charges by candidates and blocs that their 'honour and dignity' had been damaged; and five related to charges from journalists of interference in their work and of pressure from local officials.

The most publicized cases were those in which some of the better-known candidates hurled accusations and abuse at each other. The worst offenders were Zhirinovsky and the Democratic Party of Russia's (DPR) chairman Nikolai Travkin and film director Stanislav

Govorukhin, with long-standing enemies Zhirinovsky and Travkin exchanging a bout of insults which the arbitration court condemned as violating normal codes of conduct. Zhirinovsky accused Gaidar of causing him moral damage by calling him a Hitler, although many others, including Zhirinovsky himself, have made this association. The charge was thrown out on the fine point that Gaidar had compared Zhirinovsky to Hitler in 1929, which the arbitration court deemed to be acceptable as it referred to Hitler before he had stepped beyond the framework of the constitution, thus thwarting Zhirinovsky's hopes of taking the matter to the people's court and demanding 100 million roubles in damages. The case that caused the greatest furore, however, was the DPR's political commercial on 25 November in which Travkin and Govorukhin repeatedly referred to Gaidar as a 'crook' ('*zhulik*') and Russia's Choice as crooked and corrupt. Govorukhin broached two further topics which were particularly sensitive for the Yeltsin government: he criticized the constitution and revived allegations against the government over the events of 3–4 October.

In the latter case Govorukhin exploited rumours circulating in Moscow that the government had covered up its true role during the October unrest. The anti-government newspaper, *Nezavisimaya gazeta*, had already come out with one such rabble-rousing story on 30 October, printing on its front page an interview with an anonymous officer who alleged that some 1,500 corpses had been found inside the White House. Govorukhin's statements were equally lurid and unsubstantiated, claiming that government forces had been paid secret bonuses to attack the parliament and that hundreds more than the official figure of 143 had been killed. As a well-known film director, Govorukhin also included in the DPR's political commercial footage from his forthcoming documentary, showing a mêlée of street fighting and bloody scuffles from which it was quite unclear who was fighting whom, but which Govorukhin offered in lieu of proof. The arbitration court later condemned the commercial as no more than an attempt by Govorukhin to get free publicity for his film. The outcome of the DPR's broadcast was predictable, opening up old wounds and arousing feelings of anger and hostility. Former St Petersburg TV presenter and nationalist, Aleksandr Nevzorov, appeared on television calling Yeltsin a mass murderer, and other nationalists took up the call.

Yeltsin, who on the whole remained aloof throughout the electoral campaign, forestalling any accusations that he was showing a preference for the democrats, reacted immediately but with restraint, saying he would call together all party representatives the following day to 'remind them that they have been given time on television to set out their party political platforms and not to attack the constitution and the president'.[6] Instead Yeltsin's spokesman, Vyacheslav Kostikov, took up the cudgels, attacking parties for abusing their free television time in order to put out 'streams of lies, juggled facts, social demagogy and abuse' and for stirring up passions which could lead to civil war.[7] If there were reasonable grounds to fear that reviving the controversy over the October days could seriously undermine the elections and endanger the fragile stability which had been achieved, the official reaction to critics of the constitution and the attempt to ban any criticism of the constitution in the media did not hold the same moral or pragmatic legitimacy, especially as hardly anyone had even seen copies of the complete draft constitution before being told they could not criticize it.

Because a vote in favour of the constitution was seen as a vote of confidence in Yeltsin, it was considerably more important to the government than the unruly behaviour of would-be MPs, whose hostility to each other Yeltsin could even use to his advantage in controlling a future parliament. The heavy-handed attitude of the government, however, had all the hallmarks of Soviet *diktat*. An outburst of protest from most parties, including prominent members of Russia's Choice, greeted Vice-Premier and Minister of Press and Information Vladimir Shumeiko's demand that the Central Electoral Commission ban the DPR and the Communist Party for their criticism of the constitution. Moreover, Shumeiko's curious proposition that the decision of parties to run for parliament assumed an acceptance of the (as yet unread and unadopted) constitution, since the parliament would be founded on it, was a kind of catch-22 which left few people convinced. The government, however, felt sufficiently strongly about the issue to compromise the restrained chairman of the electoral commission, Nikolai Ryabov, whose methodical explanations to TV viewers about electoral procedure had introduced a calm and fatherly note to the proceedings on television. Overstepping all bounds of acceptability, Ryabov used a public service announcement to persuade viewers to make the 'right choice' and vote for the constitution. It was thought that the arbitration court would not be able to withstand such high pressure from above, especially since Shumeiko's complaint had been addressed not to the court but to the electoral commission. Nevertheless, the court's judgment that there was nothing in the laws on the electoral campaign or in the referendum that barred criticism of the constitution, so long as this criticism was constructive and did not call for violence or overturning the regime, succeeded, and the ban was lifted.

The most serious failing of the television campaign was that it was conducted without any objective journalistic analysis. Some 94 hours of television electoral coverage on three channels, both free and paid air time, were used for party political broadcasts and commercials. There were almost no debates where candidates had to confront each other or answer questions put by a panel of journalists. This curious state of affairs was partially, but not entirely, due to the Regulations on Information Guarantees. The regulations set out a sufficiently broad range of forms that broadcasts could take, naming options such as political commercials, speeches, press conferences, interviews, debates and round tables. Only the first two forms, however, were selected by blocs for their public broadcasts. The result was unremitting wall-to-wall party political monologues without any probing into the accuracy of statements or the validity of some of the more bizarre political promises made by candidates such as Zhirinovsky. An essential aspect of objective coverage – the role of the inquiring journalist – was missing. Yet the job of journalism, especially during electoral campaigns, is an educative one: to present the voter with a clear explanation of the issues, to examine the extent to which a candidate's statements correspond to the truth, to distinguish realistic party programmes and promises from pure demagogy. If the candidate has the right to be heard, the voter has the right to be provided with full and accurate information. Without the journalist's intermediary role, an essential function of the electoral process is lacking: to protect the voter from misinformation so that, having received as full a picture as possible, he or she can make a well-informed personal decision on whom to vote for. In this context it can be said that the TV campaign was essentially lopsided, favouring the candidate and not the voter.

The blocs' decision to avoid public debate can be explained by their fear of media partisanship, but much more it reflected a reversal to the comfortable certainties of one-sided Soviet rhetoric. A lack of experience in the cut and thrust of democratic politics had been amply evident in the Supreme Soviet, where political disagreement was immediately perceived as personal hostility, or in the Leninist tradition of 'those who are not with us are against us', almost as sacrilege. Given half a chance it was inevitable that parties and blocs would choose the 'authoritarian' form, something the electoral commission could easily have foreseen. Although TV executives made several attempts to persuade parties to accept different styles of debate they were not very successful. Justifying his position, the chairman of Russian TV, Oleg Poptsov, explained that as far as free time went 'it was their time and they could use it as they saw fit – that is a criterion of democracy'. As for paid time, Poptsov admitted the need for parties and blocs to learn to be more open with the electorate. 'It's said that the journalist should help in this, but tomorrow he would be accused of ruining and not making the candidate or party more open . . . Don't think we stood with our heads bowed. We were consulted, everything was explained and discussed, but there was more apprehension than trust. The Central Electoral Commission was scared of making a mistake and having to confront the parties.'[8]

The point is that both the electoral commission and TV executives were scared of being accused of bias, especially with the eyes of the world looking on to see whether what Clinton had called 'free and fair' elections would take place, and with some one thousand foreign observers ready to descend on Russia. In the circumstances it was perhaps pusillanimous, but less of a headache, to stand aside and let the parties and blocs have their way. In effect, however, this meant that TV broadcasters abandoned their responsibility of informing and enlightening the public. There was nothing to stop them from arranging debates and inviting those candidates prepared to take part, especially as this was an alternative suggested by the arbitration court.

A series of articles in the press critical of the TV campaign warned of the danger of leaving the voter defenceless in the face of political propaganda. One of the first articles in this vein, by sociologist Vsevolod Vil'chek, described the pre-election TV screen as playing the role of 'the opium of the people', guaranteed to prevent the populace from thinking. Moreover, although journalists played no 'objective' part in the TV campaign, it was not the case that they were totally absent from the screen. Loyal journalists were hired as programme 'frontmen', giving the appearance of objective interviews when what the viewer was really seeing was a party political broadcast. Clause 11 of the Regulations on Ways of Implementing the Media, of 1 October 1993, clearly stated that parties had the right to choose both the form of their broadcast and the candidates they wanted to participate in it 'with the exception of the presenter'.[9] Although TV broadcasters agonized over this 'exception', they never implemented it. Only in the last two days of the campaign were two free-time debates organized, and then only on the issue of the constitution. One of the presenters, Yurii Semenov, told me that he was so hemmed in by instructions to be rigidly fair that it was difficult for him to do anything when Zhirinovsky broke the previously agreed format and spoke louder and longer than anyone else.

A compromise solution that state-owned television never managed to reach with the parties was negotiated by the privately owned company NTV (Independent Television), which ran a series of interviews with candidates hosted by Matvei Ganapolsky. Although parties bought time from NTV, Ganapolsky was allowed a certain amount of freedom to be 'himself': a witty, aggressive presenter with a habit of interrupting his interviewee. A forty-minute interview was recorded and edited down to twenty minutes, removing items too obviously propagandistic, as well as remarks by Ganapolsky considered too probing. Significantly, Zhirinovsky declined an invitation to be on the show, preferring to avoid any dialogue over which he did not have total control. According to Oleg Poptsov, Zhirinovsky was among those candidates particularly opposed to debates when Russian TV was negotiating with the parties. The only time Zhirinovsky appeared in conversation was on 28 November on Dmitrii Dibrov's chat show on NTV, in which the smiling Dibrov allowed him free scope to perform and asked no serious questions. As hardly any other political candidates had been invited to the show, Dibrov was accused of bias or of fishing for good laughs and high ratings. Although it remains a mystery how much Zhirinovsky paid for this valuable piece of prime-time publicity on Moscow's most popular show, the Dibrov company is not known to underrate itself.

If in these first multiparty elections for 76 years inexperience in the running of the media campaign was understandable, we can assume all the more so that the voter would be inexperienced in decoding undiluted doses of propaganda, especially in a society where the concept of objective truth has little meaning. With facts hard to come by and a plenitude of rumours and conspiracy theories in existence to put any event under a cloud, it was unavoidable that, faced with little authoritative information, voters would tend to make irrational responses, based on emotion and mood rather than on argument or conviction. A dramatic change in public opinion ten days before the elections testifies to the spontaneity of voting responses. If we take Russia's Choice, which counts among its supporters many with higher education, practically everyone who voted for the bloc said they intended to do so early in the campaign, indicating a consistent corps of prodemocratic supporters and, equally, demonstrating that in terms of performance Russia's Choice did not attract new voters during the media campaign. The opposite is true of Zhirinovsky.

According to VTsIOM, at the start of the campaign the LDPR had only gathered 1.3 per cent of potential voters, but by the first week of December it was predicted that Zhirinovsky's party would get 15–17 per cent of the vote. The sudden change in voting responses among the electorate is also confirmed by the Public Opinion Foundation, whose research showed that 16 per cent decided they would vote a week before the elections and 10 per cent on the day of the elections. This late vote went in Zhirinovsky's favour. Of the 23 per cent of votes Zhirinovsky received at the polls, 40 per cent of those who voted for him decided to do so during the last few days. Almost one-fifth of those who made up their minds to vote for Zhirinovsky said they were influenced by television and the other media.[10] Given that the main propaganda vehicle was television (and not public meetings or door-to-door canvassing), the candidate with the most 'current' appeal on screen was likely to get the spontaneous vote. If we remember also that opinion polls were banned from being published ten days before the elections, the public was deprived not only of journalistic analysis but also of any warning from opinion pollsters during the last ten days of the sudden switch in popularity towards Zhirinovsky. His audacity and theatricality on television paid off.

What the public did not know about opinion poll results, the government did, and, in a last-minute gambit to deflect the Zhirinovsky vote, Ostankino TV broke the electoral regulation banning campaigning after midnight on 10 December and broadcast, one day before the polls, Pavel Chukhrai's documentary 'The Hawk' (*Yastreb*), an extremely damning but accurate portrait of Zhirinovsky. The film did not have its intended effect, either because it was too late or because the government's presumption acted as an irritant, spurring protest votes in Zhirinovsky's favour. We should look more closely, then, at exactly how television helped to influence votes to Zhirinovsky's advantage.

One way of reaching an answer is the quantitative approach, to see how much television exposure leaders and parties received. The amount of air time that parties bought on television gives an idea of this (see Table 5.1), although it should be noted that the statistics available are not always exact and that those between different organizations do not always coincide.

According to the figures of the Russian-American Press and Information Center, which monitored all three state-owned channels, Ostankino, Russian and St Petersburg TV, Russia's Choice bought the most advertising time, with more than five hours, followed by the pro-government Party of Russian Unity and Accord and the centrist Civic Union. The Communist Party bought no advertising time, relying on its stalwart supporters. If we take total time on all three channels comprising paid advertising, free time and news and current affairs, Russia's Choice comes out with the highest total of more than 23 hours. In all, the three pro-government blocs (Russia's Choice, Party of Russian Unity and Accord and Russian Movement for Democratic Reforms) received the largest segment of air time: more than 42 hours. Centrist parties and blocs totalled 25.5 hours, conservative groups almost 15 hours, and special interest groups 11 hours.[11]

In this scale of things, Zhirinovsky's Liberal Democratic Party of Russia came fifth in paid advertising with 2 hours and 44 minutes. The party's combined total of all air time was 7.5 hours, way below Russia's Choice. A crucial factor, however, lay in the exposure of its leaders. Russia's Choice, in addition to its leader, Gaidar, had a

Table 5.1 Paid air time on major state-owned channels in the run-up to the December 1993 elections

	Russian TV	Ostankino TV
Civic Union	88 min. 30 sec.	30 min.
Party of Russian Unity and Accord	88 min.	77 min.
Russia's Choice	87 min. 20 sec.	150 min.
Liberal Democratic Party of Russia	84 min.	90 min.
Future of Russia–New Names	73 min. 30 sec.	10 min.
Russian Movement for Democratic Reforms	44 min. 40 sec.	50 min.
Democratic Party of Russia	30 min. 45 sec.	30 min.
Women of Russia	4 min.	–
Agrarian Party of Russia	–	20 min.
Yavlinsky-Boldyrev-Lukin bloc	–	20 min.

Note: The figures for Russian TV do not include political video clips, usually between two and ten minutes long.

Source: Ostankino and Russian TV's own figures.

strong contingent of well-known and respected politicians, all of whom participated to some degree in its electoral campaign. With the LDPR almost the sole representative was Zhirinovsky himself. Thus, in terms of individual candidates, Zhirinovsky received more television exposure than any other electoral association leader, amassing a total of five hours. Gaidar came a close second with 4 hours 52 minutes, followed by Arkadii Vol'sky and Sergei Shakhrai, with about 3.5 hours each.

From these figures we can see that having the most air time was not in itself a guarantee of victory. Russia's Choice, with more exposure than any other party or bloc, failed to achieve a resounding victory, while Civic Union, which ranked next after Russia's Choice in paid advertising time, received under 2 per cent of the votes cast, and the Communists, who bought no advertising time, more than 12 per cent. A combination of air time and performance, then, was the heady cocktail that brought about Zhirinovsky's triumph. Of all the candidates Zhirinovsky made the most effective emotional use of television, exploiting nationalist sentiments and populist solutions and tapping into the well of economic resentment and social discontent. With nobody to challenge him, he was free to make outrageous promises and score easy emotional points. He would offer free vodka to everyone if he won, he would 'nuke' Japan if it tried to acquire the Kurile Islands, he would return Russia to its pre-1917 borders by annexing parts of Finland and Poland, virtually the whole of Ukraine and Alaska, and so on. Instead of the Western politicians' device of kissing babies, Zhirinovsky offered the orgasm. Bullishly looking into the screen in his neat burgundy jacket, he presented his sex/pol version of Soviet history, a mish-mash which would have amazed Wilhelm Reich, blithely introducing words such as 'masturbation' and 'orgasm' which had hardly ever been heard on television. It all seemed like a bad joke, except that there was shrewd psychological and political nous to this madness.

Whereas many politicians continued in the Soviet tradition of appealing to the 'people' (*'narod'*) as if it were 'one and indivisible', Zhirinovsky divided up his electorate into gender and interest groups, devoting short segments of air time to each. He singled out women and arranged to meet them later in a park without their husbands, talking about cooking and underwear and playing the role of agony aunt. He appealed separately to Cossacks, the army, the much-maligned legal profession, and in a brilliant gesture addressed the Islamic population in Turkic. His appearances on television were relatively brief and cleverly distributed, regularly appearing on the screen but never long enough to become a bore. All his appearances on state television were in the form of speeches, since he had rejected both the short video commercials and the longer documentaries that other parties used as well. It is interesting to compare the spread of these speeches, which he divided up into eight segments, with the five speeches made by different Russia's Choice leaders (see Table 5.2).

Although one would not wish the sound-bite on Russia, and Russians are perhaps too verbose for it to have an appeal, Zhirinovsky, whether instinctively or with the help of image-makers, made use of this strategy. A study by the St Petersburg psychologist, V. Vasil'ev, on audience feedback shows the changes that have occurred in TV tolerance. Today information is most effectively conveyed to Russians if it is short – only 5–7 per cent will watch a whole TV news item that lasts longer than ten minutes

Table 5.2 Comparison of televised speeches made by Zhirinovsky and Russia's Choice leaders, November–December 1993

LDPR (Zhirinovsky)			Russia's Choice (various leaders)		
November	19	15 minutes	November	18	7 minutes
	24	15 minutes		19	15 minutes
	26	12 minutes		25	6 minutes
	29	7 minutes			
	30	10 minutes			
December	2	10 minutes	December	1	28 minutes
	6	5 minutes		9	10 minutes
	9	10 minutes			

Source: RAU Press data.

– and if it is simple and demands little intellectual effort. The days of 1989–90 when people watched parliamentary sessions well into the night or spent three hours happily engrossed in the slow-moving cultural programme 'Fifth Wheel' have long gone.

The media frequently employed satire during the campaign. On television, with its stricter regulations against commentary, two short programmes bypassed the restrictions by ridiculing the electorate's gullibility. The programme 'Press-Express' in tandem with the newspaper *Komsomolskaya pravda* carried out an experiment on the streets in which they offered free beer to anyone who voted for their candidate, who changed from day to day with posters showing such famous faces as Chancellor Kohl, and proved that they could easily get votes. A documentary called 'Sub-Tropical Russia' revolved around a party whose aim was to canvass support for raising Russia's temperature, with a sly dig at Zhirinovsky's dream of Russia's conquering troops washing their boots in the Indian Ocean. In the press, one of the most stylish articles came from the pen of *Izvestiya*'s Sergei Mostovshchikov, who summed up the Zhirinovsky syndrome when he wrote: 'Pluralism is dear to the hearts of Russians, especially as the Great Medical Encyclopedia defines the term as group sex, in which no less than three citizens participate. It really is good of Vladimir Vol'fovich to promise to provide this quickly, in the course of the first three months of his rule. It's true that at first we will have to destroy 5,000 criminal gangs, halt supplies of anything and everything outside the borders of our Motherland, sell arms to India in return for food and clothing, take back all the debts we owe the world and pay nothing in return and get housed in cottages but then, oh then we'll have pluralism.'[12]

Given the growing element of boredom experienced by TV viewers, Zhirinovsky's exhibitionism and extravagance can be seen as an asset. At times aggressive and rude, at other times vulnerable, he in many ways exemplified the so-called 'new Russian', an entrepreneurial figure whose successful gambles depend on being brash, arrogant and somewhat crooked. Undoubtedly the phenomenon of Zhirinovsky rested on an emotional response coinciding with the mood of the moment which, looking at the current situation and his declining popularity today, may have been a temporary aberration, especially as the main rival for his votes, former Vice-President Aleksandr Rutskoi, was sitting in prison. But given that 23 per cent voted for a 'nutter' means that the element of volatility, or what Russians used to refer to as *stikhiinost'* (spontaneity) or '*Pugachevshchina*', which the early Bolsheviks took so much trouble trying to eliminate, is still a matter to be seriously considered and one that presumably will only disappear in time with a politically informed and educated electorate.

The more modest, intellectual and professorial leaders of Russia's Choice, or candidates like Yavlinsky, lacked the kind of charisma necessary to engage a disenchanted society. The campaign run by Russia's Choice veered between serious discussions for the highbrow and an inordinate number of pop political commercials in which pro-democratic singers and comedians were wheeled on irrelevantly to support the bloc, giving more the impression of a music video than a commercial with a political message. To see Gaidar in one political video solemnly walking as the saviour to the sounds of 'Bolero', with archival footage in the background of coups and disturbances from the past – a montage of billowing black clouds, tanks, blood – or the intrusion of Yeltsin saying 'I am committed to Gaidar', seemed both mindless and in bad taste. Nor did it make good sense to have a Russian singing in English, as if to demonstrate pro-Western sentiments and a commitment to the IMF. Serious discussions like the round table with Gaidar, former privatization minister Anatolii Chubais and former finance minister

Boris Fedorov, in which they attempted to explain Russia's difficult economic plight, were impressive, if for a minority audience, but the constant refrain about inflation, privatization and the market had a numbing effect on viewers generally. There was hardly any appeal to moral values or uniting the country in common endeavour other than the promise of market changes, which was almost Soviet in its certainty that economic determinism was the answer to all problems. The damage the bloc inflicted on its own image was supplemented by the harm caused by its political rivals. The snide comment by former Moscow mayor and leader of the Russian Movement for Democratic Reforms (although he did not stand for election), Gavriil Popov, that the bloc's good-quality political posters were bought with American money, or Govorukhin's various insinuating allegations, including the claim that on the night of 3–4 October Gaidar had paid one billion roubles to get supporters out on the streets (this figure being increased a few days later to 11 billion), left seeds of doubt which, foolishly, Russia's Choice did not consider it necessary to refute.

For all his intelligence and wit, Gaidar's public image has never held broad public appeal. Television has not been kind to him, although he has improved considerably since his first performance on television in January 1992 when he appeared flushed, licking his lips and moving jerkily. Even the well-made party broadcast which placed him in his family surroundings could not dispel the image of an inaccessible, closeted economist uncomfortable with the public. A student street survey of 452 Muscovites who were asked what animals they identified with particular political leaders inevitably associated Gaidar with a piglet; Zhirinovsky was a wolf, after his patronymic, and also a hyena; Shakhrai a polecat; (Prime Minister Viktor) Chernomyrdin a boar and Yeltsin a bear, mostly a polar bear, which is the stronger animal in folklore.[13] Despite the frivolous nature of the survey, it is significant that all the leaders except Gaidar were associated with either strength or cunning. An animal analogy could not be found for Yavlinsky, which confirms his somewhat anonymous profile in the public eye and coincides with his relatively low results in the elections, despite being the intellectual alternative to Gaidar. His Yabloko bloc ranked number two in virtually all public opinion polls published ten days before the elections, the crucial point at which public opinion began to switch. His decision to play down television advertising on principle, saying that victory should be achieved not on television performance but on party platforms, may well have been to blame. In fact the elections were run more on personalities than on party platforms, as Zhirinovsky's victory demonstrates.

The concept of paying for television advertising has, curiously, not been seen as an issue, although its potential for debasing and corrupting the electoral process is obvious. In the regions, access to money played a particularly important role, enabling the *nomenklatura* to consolidate its position and debarring independent candidates from the race. Paid advertising in Orenburg, for example, cost 250,000 roubles for 1.5 minutes on the screen. Out of 150 candidates in Orenburg only thirty could afford to buy air time during the 2–3 hours that regional TV broadcasts on the national state channel. Moreover, the place of murky money in the Russian economy is so widespread that one would have thought a more critical attitude would have been taken of the Central Electoral Commission's decision to introduce this practice into election campaigning. It is not after all a common procedure. Only four democracies in the world allow paid advertising on television during elections: Israel, Canada, Australia and the United States; and only in the United States is there no free time and no limit to the amount of time that can be bought. In the United States, however, the source of income must be declared to enable the electorate to judge what interests lie behind a candidate. Such a mechanism has no way of being realistically applied in Russia, with its resourceful ways of concealing dirty money (so-called *chernyi nal'*).

Although the Central Electoral Commission has issued figures on expenditure from the election fund, in which most of the parties' budgets should have been held, there were other ways that sponsors' money could be transferred to the parties' and blocs' accounts without the Commission's knowledge. If we take these official and manifestly unreliable figures, we learn that Russia's Choice spent 1.3 billion roubles on television advertising, Civic Union paid one million and the LDPR paid 86 million. When the Central Electoral Commission applied to various organizations and commercial firms to explore the sources of financing more deeply, the only response they got was from the state TV companies. From them we know that the advertising company Premier paid 33 million roubles to

Russia's Choice for radio programming, that the enterprise Mars paid 62 million roubles for DPR's TV commercials, and that the leisure centre Sokol' paid 75 million roubles for Zhirinovsky's TV air time.[14] Little detail is known about financial sources, other than fairly general information that major banks and trade corporations sponsored both Russia's Choice and Yavlinsky and that the centrist blocs received money from former state enterprises. Only the Communist Party received funding from its party members. With its stable, voting-conscious membership, the party's decision not to buy TV advertising must have rested on the calculation that it could not widen its electoral base. Zhirinovsky's sponsors remain a mystery, the only officially registered ones being fairly minor firms which could not have covered his costs. The fact that political advertising had such an effect on voting demonstrates that money necessarily dominated the elections and paid time on television exceeded free time. If it was not those with the most money (or credit) that won, it is also the case that without substantial sums of money it would not have been possible to win.

Newspaper and radio coverage

Unlike television, the press was less restricted and compensated for some of the gaps in television coverage. The quality pro-government newspaper *Izvestiya* in particular distinguished itself, running investigative pieces (such as the article on shady dealings in the campaign in Sochi),[15] challenging questionable facts and not permitting candidates to get off the hook as easily as they had done on television. Thus, with rare precision for the Russian media, inaccurate, off-the-cuff statements were examined: for example, Civic Union's I. Yurgens's comment that the standard of living had dropped six-fold while prices had risen a thousand times was referred to the relevant ministry, whose expert put the subject in its context and through argument concluded that the real income of the population had dropped 2.5 times. In the same way Zhirinovsky's statement that former republics such as Azerbaijan were bleeding Russia dry was refuted and it was shown that, on the contrary, Russia owed the former Soviet republic 65 billion roubles.[16] Although ministry figures may also be unreliable, the attempt to use argument and seek reputable sources stands as a lesson to those papers that regularly disseminate undocumented and unresearched information. A series of page-long interviews with most of the leading candidates and penetrating articles from *Izvestiya*'s political commentator, Otto Latsis, consistently took candidates, including pro-democrats, to task for false pronouncements, but the paper did not disguise where its heart lay and hardly uttered a word of criticism about Russia's Choice.

Of other well-known newspapers, the liberal-centrist *Segodnya* gave the broadest and most thorough coverage of the campaign, but lacked clarity and astuteness. The defence ministry's paper, *Krasnaya zvezda* (Red Star) according to one source was the most detached and objective of all because, as the paper claimed, 'we can't bring a split along party lines in the army'. The liberal daily *Nezavisimaya gazeta*, whose leading articles have steadily become more irascible and bitter, the more so since the newspaper turned against Yeltsin after October 1993, supported Shakhrai's party; while *Moskovskie novosti* provided reports on all election blocs but slanted its coverage in favour of Yavlinsky and Shakhrai. The conservative *Pravda* suspended publication for much of the official campaign due to financial difficulties and came out only two days before the elections after a donation from DPR's Travkin.[17] Such nationalist papers as *Zavtra* and *Slovo Zhirinovskogo* (Zhirinovsky's Word) continued to be sold by supporters in the metro's underpasses and in certain institutions like the police force and the army.

The subject of the electoral process itself, both the regulations and the irregularities, comprised the larger part of electoral coverage during the first two weeks of the campaign, at the expense of the longer-term social, political, economic and legal problems which the elections would decide. *Izvestiya* published twenty articles criticizing poor media performance. During the course of the campaign the number of election-related items increased dramatically (see Table 5.3).

Different standards distinguished the central from the regional newspapers. Moscow's national papers tended to be more objective and analytical, even when indicating a political preference, and made greater use of public opinion polls and sociological surveys. The issue of the constitution was covered at greater length than in the regions and the document itself was finally published in a

118 *Daphne Skillen*

Table 5.3 Number of items relating to the elections published in selected newspapers during the 1993 electoral campaign

	Weeks 1–2	Weeks 3–5	Total
Moskovskie novosti	56	154	210
Rossiiskie vesti	43	132	175
Segodnya	27	116	143
Krasnaya zvezda	31	93	124
Izvestiya	24	97	121
Moskovskii komsomolets	15	41	56

Source: Russian-American Press and Information booklet.

number of national papers. More attention was given to parties and blocs than to individual candidates, particularly candidates in the far-flung constituencies of the country. This meant that very few new names emerged and, without them, there was a sense of limited scope for the future. Inevitably the journalist's ego intervened – a self-importance common to Moscow's journalistic corps, which often sees the reporter competing with his interviewee for attention and indulging in long-winded and tedious verbosity. Some journalists with whom I spoke conveyed the same weariness reflected in the population at large at having yet another election and even petulantly remarked that they would not take part in 'all this dirty business' – as if a reporter had a choice.

For all the many words addressing these elections as 'new' and 'different', the coverage showed that journalists had not adapted to the conditions of a pluralistic society. The Soviet mentality of disregarding detail and nuance and perceiving society as one monolith, without special class or group interests (the army, farmers, miners, etc.), impoverished the level of discussion. Little differentiation was made between candidates and opposing views. Nor was it made clear who stood behind candidates, what their background or past history was, or what it meant when a candidate asserted that he or she was 'independent'. There was little discussion of political programmes and the stance taken by parties on education, health, housing or the many other problems directly affecting people's lives. A whole range of issues was simply ignored: campaign financing, the role of lobbies or the initial registering of signatures to get candidates on the ballot, which had apparently taken place with serious violations. Apart from a generalized cynicism that malpractice was possible anywhere, little attempt was made to forewarn of suspect constituencies, so that some months later evidence of falsifications in the counting of votes, seriously changing the Central Electoral Commission's official voting results, came as a surprise.[18]

The growing importance of regional papers in affecting votes was a new development. One of the recent consequences of decentralization is that for the first time more people are reading regional than national papers: 58 per cent read papers based in their own cities.[19] The politics of the Kremlin no longer count for as much in the lives of ordinary people as local economic and political news or local advertising. As a result it was local candidates and not national parties and blocs that became the focus of attention in the regional press. Inevitably, the element of partisanship was greater in the provinces and more attention was given to those candidates tied to the local government apparatus. Interviews often took the form of either obviously agitational pieces or the reverse, bland interviews without comment or investigation. A large number of articles were written by local professionals, lawyers or academics, which showed both a high level of local public activity and a lower level of journalistic specialization than in the capital. The trend towards greater localization was not accompanied by a corresponding interest in area sociological surveys, which practically do not exist, and little coordination was shown between regions and the centre in achieving a balanced perspective.

The new status of the regional press, however, has promoted the first signs of serious and independent journalism coming from the provinces. During the electoral campaign I co-directed a competition called 'School of Parliamentary Journalism', which was held by the Cultural Initiative Foundation (Soros Foundation) to evaluate the best electoral coverage in the media, with prizes totalling $250,000. Out of some 730 materials we received, 380 came from the regional press. The general rise of creative and critical writing from all parts of the country, despite limited resources and the greater difficulties of working in the regions, was impressive. The standard of, for example, Tat'yana Shchipanova's article on the constitution in *Novgorodskie vedomosti* (Novgorod Herald) or

Svetlana Mironova's balanced interview of an independent candidate in *Chelyabinskii rabochii* (Chelyabinsk Worker) was on a par with anything coming from the capital.[20] Moreover, the greater power wielded by the local political apparatus and local interests have always made 'objective' journalism a more difficult and dangerous affair in the regions. One writer from the Vladimir region had taken on the pseudonym M. Mikhailov because of constant threats from communist opponents due to his pro-democratic sentiments. His article in the Vladimir paper *Prizyv* (The Call) was a model of investigative, critical writing. On the one hand he described the devious manner in which two papers joined up to promote the interests of an influential communist businessman; on the other hand he lamented the political ambitions of the democrats, of the likes of Sobchak, Yavlinsky and Popov, who opposed Russia's Choice although, he argued, neither they nor the man in the street could tell the difference between their policies. The end result, he claimed with a clever piece of prognosis, was that Zhirinovsky stood a greater chance of winning than Zyuganov.[21] Quality articles of this sort, if they continue to appear, will change the attitude of readers to regional papers. At the moment, although more people are reading their local papers, 33 per cent still perceive the national media and national institutions of power as more accurate sources of information.[22]

The potential of radio for giving fuller information than television and the advantage of being switched on as a background noise were not made full use of. Throughout the country radio has become more a vehicle for popular music than for news. However, state-run Radio Russia, with its obligation to give free time to parties and blocs, aired almost 23 hours of election information. More partisan in its coverage than television, it made no bones about promoting the draft constitution and tended to favour Russia's Choice, Yabloko and the Russian Movement for Democratic Reforms, giving Gaidar 1 hour and 40 minutes of total air time, Zyuganov 50 minutes and Zhirinovsky 19 minutes. The only other influential Moscow-based radio station, Echo Moscow, which is privately owned and consequently was not required to give free air time, covered the elections with great detail and gave more time to them (33 hours) than Radio Russia. With a firmly pro-democratic corps of journalists, it invited representatives of most parties to be interviewed, but since it felt free to criticize and even to ridicule conservatives and democrats alike, not all candidates accepted the invitation. Obviously, remarks such as 'the only good communist is a dead communist', or a warning to Shakhrai that 'Lefortovo jail is waiting for you', frightened off candidates not used to tough political debate with the irreverent but intelligent journalists on the station.[23]

Conclusion

The media, therefore, played a central role in the electoral campaign and television was the primary medium of voters' information on election-related events and on the contestants. Electoral associations utilized a variety of techniques to bring their messages to the voters, including party political broadcasts and interviews. Television news also covered the blocs' activities. Despite the serious attention and large amount of time that the media, and television in particular, devoted to the campaign, election coverage was, by and large, deficient in comparison to Western standards of political reporting. There was bias in the amount of time devoted to Russia's Choice, information on campaign financing was in short supply and candidates displayed their inexperience in competitive politics by avoiding televised debates with each other and engaging in exchanges of insults instead of discussions of issues. Most important, however, the absence of Russian television journalists' and presenters' critical comments and summaries did not assist the electorate in making reasoned choices from the alternatives presented to them in their living rooms. Given this fact, it is not so surprising that nearly a quarter of Russian voters, in an atmosphere of economic hardship, rising crime rates and political instability, voted for Zhirinovsky's LDPR with its easy answers to complex problems.

It would have been unreasonable to expect the media's role in the 1993 multiparty elections to go entirely smoothly; some mistakes were inevitable, even some which would have serious consequences. It is more worrying, however, when the same mistakes are repeated. One month after the elections the programme *Itogi* ('Sum-up') on NTV ran a five-minute footage, without text or commentary, inviting us to laugh once again at Zhirinovsky's latest antics on the day the new parliament opened – this dubious piece of reporting coming from the top current affairs programme in the country. A few days after the elections Ostankino TV's chief, Bragin, was sacked for his mishandling of the television campaign and Zhirinovsky's success, and since then substantial changes have taken place in the reorganization of the main television channels. Perhaps there will be enough time to digest the experiences of the 1993 media campaign before the next elections are held.

Notes

1. These figures reflect the percentages of votes that the Liberal Democratic Party of Russia won through party list seats. See 'The Final Tally', *The Economist*, 8 January 1994, p. 30.
2. *Moscow Times*, 19 November 1993.
3. VTsIOM (Vserossiiskii tsentr izucheniya obshchestvennogo mneniya), *Monitoring obshchestvennogo mneniya*, no. 1, 1994 (January), p. 21, and ibid., no. 2, 1994 (March–April), p. 31; also from the centre's database.
4. Post-Factum report, 5 November 1993.
5. ITAR-TASS report, 6 November 1993.
6. Post-Factum report, 25 November 1993.
7. *Moscow Times*, 26 November 1993.
8. *Izvestiya*, 1 December 1993.
9. *Byulleten' Tsentrizbirkoma*, no. 4, 1993 (November), p. 13.
10. VTsIOM, *Monitoring*, no. 2, 1994 (March–April), p. 31; A. Olson and E. Petrenko, 'Parlamentskie vybory 12 dekabrya 1993 goda: sotsiologiya elektoral'nogo povedeniya' (Moscow: Fond Obshchestvennoe mnenie, 1994), p. 72.
11. *Russian Media Coverage of the Campaign*: booklet of a study conducted by the Russian-American Press and Information Center, 2–3 Khlebnyi pereulok, Moscow.
12. *Izvestiya*, 2 December 1993.
13. T. Furman, 'Televidenie i vybory: neosoznannye fantazii i utrachennye illyuzii' (unpublished degree thesis, Moscow State University, 1994), p. 33.
14. *Moskovskie novosti*, no. 18, 1994 (1–8 May).
15. *Izvestiya*, 1 December 1993.
16. *Izvestiya*, 25 November 1993 and 27 November 1993.
17. See Russian-American Press and Information booklet.
18. *Izvestiya*, 4 May 1994.
19. VTsIOM, *Monitoring*, no. 1, 1994 (January), p. 20.
20. *Novgorodskie vedomosti*, 30 November 1993; *Chelyabinskii rabochii*, 2 November 1993.
21. *Prizyv* (Vladimir), 4 December 1993.
22. VTsIOM, *Monitoring*, no. 1, 1994 (January), p. 21.
23. Russian-American Press and Information booklet.

6 Parties and Voters in the Elections

MATTHEW WYMAN, BILL MILLER, STEPHEN WHITE and PAUL HEYWOOD

The elections of December 1993 were a dramatic affair. They represented the first free multiparty vote in Russia for three-quarters of a century, and their results came as a considerable surprise. The majority of commentators before the election had assumed an easy victory for the pro-government bloc Russia's Choice (VR), led by former acting prime minister and architect of Russia's economic reforms Yegor Gaidar, in the wake of President Boris Yeltsin's dissolution of the Russian parliament that October. Opinion polls carried out by reputable organizations had consistently shown substantial VR leads.[1] Yet when the votes were counted, VR, with 15 per cent of the votes in the party list section of elections to the new Federal Assembly, trailed well behind the 23 per cent won by the Liberal Democratic Party of right-wing populist Vladimir Zhirinovsky. Collectively, parties of self-styled democrats, that is those favourably disposed to the Yeltsin administration, gained the support of just one-third of those who voted, representing just over one in six of the total electorate.

This chapter seeks to analyse this party vote and to uncover its social and political origins. It is based primarily on a study of the 1993 election designed by the authors and carried out by Russian Public Opinion and Market Research (ROMIR) in two waves, before and after the voting.[2] As a representative survey of the whole of Russia, rural as well as urban, this research gives us unique information about trends during the campaign, electoral participation, and the emerging social base for political parties of various ideological positions.

Turnout

As with all recall polls, the Glasgow study overestimates turnout — putting it at 67 per cent, compared with the official figure of 55 per cent, with the latter itself probably inflated by electoral malpractices of various kinds.[3] Respondents throughout the world are reluctant to admit to interviewers that they have not voted. This is clearly a source of some error, but analysis can in any event be justified by the observation that even if a respondent did not in fact vote, the party they claim to have voted for does reflect their political identification at the time of interview. Furthermore, analysis of turnout suggests some clear and plausible conclusions.

What characteristics are commonly associated with political participation? Studies identify several factors.[4] A major predictor is clearly level of interest in politics. Interest tends to be increased by lengthy exposure to the educational system, and therefore education is normally strongly related to turnout. Income is also a good predictor, in part because the better-educated tend to earn more, but also because greater wealth tends to lead to increased satisfaction with the existing system. Young people are less likely than older generations to participate, because they tend to be more mobile both psychologically and physically. However, in some, although not all, countries, institutions such as political parties or trade unions are influential enough to mobilize the poorer and less well-educated, that is the less politically interested, to go out and vote through the effectiveness of their ideological appeal or on-the-ground organization. The seminal seven-nation study by Verba, Nie and Kim found that such parties existed in Sweden, Austria and Japan, counterbalancing the normal education and income effects, but in the United States and Yugoslavia existing parties represented the interests of the socially advantaged, and therefore the more marginalized sections of society participated in substantially lower numbers. In the recent period, however, some analysts have suggested that the increasing impact of the media, in particular television, on the electoral process has tended to counteract such

Table 6.1 Political interest and electoral participation

		% very or quite interested in politics	% voted on party list	Difference
All		32	70	+38
Gender	Male	41	74	+33
	Female	24	66	+42
Age	18–29	21	56	+35
	30–54	33	71	+38
	55+	39	79	+40
Education	Elementary	25	73	+48
	Secondary/Vocational	29	68	+39
	Higher	52	73	+21
Class ID*	Manager	60	71	+11
	Businessperson	37	65	+28
	Intelligentsia	45	74	+29
	Worker	27	68	+41
	Farmer	28	77	+49
Rurality	Rural	28	78	+50
	City under 100,000	32	69	+37
	City 100,000–1 m.	31	71	+40
	City 1 m. and over	37	57	+20
Income	Not enough	26	66	+40
	Just enough	40	75	+35
	Enough for fair/good standard of living	38	71	+33

* Class ID indicates response to question: 'Would you describe yourself as . . .?'
Source: Glasgow project. Table based on post-election wave, $N = 1043$.

effects in democratic political systems. Party organizations are no longer able to mobilize voters.[5]

Table 6.1 relates political interest and electoral participation in Russia. In some respects the data are as expected. Older people were more likely to vote than the young, and managers and the self-defined intelligentsia more than industrial workers. The unemployed (57 per cent) and housewives (51 per cent) voted in the smallest numbers.

However, these data show, surprisingly, that there is virtually no relationship between education, income and turnout. Those with less than secondary education and those who assessed their family income as not enough to live on voted in virtually the same numbers as the wealthier and more highly educated, despite being substantially less interested in politics. High percentages of farmers and other inhabitants of rural Russia voted, despite their low levels of political interest, whereas voters in the big cities, where there is much more interest in politics, voted at much lower levels. Of those not interested in politics, many more women than men took part. This reflects the considerable success in the December elections of parties that sought to mobilize the more excluded sections of the Russian electorate: the Agrarian Party of Russia (APR), the bloc Women of Russia (ZhR), the Communist Party of the Russian Federation (KPRF), and Zhirinovsky's LDPR. The APR and KPRF of course benefited in this from having inherited former CPSU organizational structures. Those who argue that there is only a weak connection between existing Russian parties and the electorate would do well to take note of these findings.

Trends during the campaign

How did voting preferences change during the last three weeks of the campaign? The Glasgow project concurs with research by other organizations showing a clear late surge of support for the LDPR. The pre-election wave, conducted in the three weeks before the vote, put the Liberal Democrats in joint second place at 12 per cent, whereas support more than doubled to 27 per cent in the post-election wave. (The slight [4 per cent] overestimation of LDPR support in the post-election sample in all probability represents a 'halo effect' common to recall election polls. People like to identify themselves with the way in which those around them turn out to have behaved.)[6] On these data, and others, the main loser appears to have been Nikolai Travkin's Democratic Party of Russia (DPR), whose support halved over the same time period.[7]

From where did the more successful parties gain support, and how did the social base of the party vote change in the course of the campaign? Table 6.2 illustrates the trends.[8]

Table 6.2 Trends in party support during the campaign

		KPRF −	KPRF +	APR −	APR +	DPR −	DPR +	ZhR −	ZhR +	Yabl. −	Yabl. +	VR −	VR +	LDPR −	LDPR +	Against all −	Against all +
All		7	9	7	8	12	6	11	8	9	10	19	17	12	27	8	5
Gender	Male	8	9	8	8	14	9	3	3	10	10	20	18	15	30	7	4
	Female	6	8	5	9	10	3	18	14	7	9	18	17	9	24	8	6
Age	18–29	2	1	4	8	15	3	13	5	7	15	14	16	14	31	9	6
	30–54	6	7	7	9	10	8	12	9	9	8	20	17	15	29	8	4
	55+	11	16	8	7	12	5	10	10	9	7	20	18	7	21	7	6
Education	Elementary	7	12	10	8	10	4	11	12	6	7	16	15	17	29	7	6
	Secondary	5	7	6	8	13	7	13	7	8	10	18	16	12	28	9	5
	Higher	10	10	5	8	8	4	5	9	14	12	25	27	6	16	6	3
Class ID	Manager	9	8	9	14	4	10	8	4	15	19	22	26	18	8	8	4
	Professional	4	6	12	7	8	5	16	17	12	14	17	27	4	13	8	3
	Engineer	5	2	0	7	16	7	19	10	13	14	12	32	16	19	9	0
	Clerical	3	10	0	14	11	3	22	8	5	0	17	11	3	25	5	8
	Skilled worker	7	7	6	5	18	10	8	6	8	9	14	11	21	39	6	5
	in cities under 100,000	8	6	0	0	23	7	3	7	7	10	8	5	29	63	8	0
	in defence sector	8	3	23	6	19	13	8	8	5	0	5	5	13	50	5	3
	Unskilled worker	4	7	0	3	11	6	21	12	7	3	13	21	21	36	9	6
	Farmer	4	7	19	27	11	7	14	3	8	6	17	12	14	23	10	6
	Housewife	6	6	0	10	5	5	17	17	9	10	24	4	12	33	7	3
	Student	0	0	5	12	22	8	8	0	15	21	22	16	7	26	4	4
	Unemployed	0	0	3	5	4	0	6	2	8	15	20	22	10	44	19	9
	Pensioner	13	18	9	6	10	4	8	11	6	8	22	17	7	17	8	6
Rurality	Rural	8	9	17	22	10	4	17	9	6	6	11	11	13	25	7	8
	Cities under 100,000	9	9	2	3	15	5	12	7	9	11	14	12	12	40	8	4
	Cities 100,000–1 m.	5	9	3	3	14	6	9	8	9	10	21	19	14	26	8	5
	Cities 1 m. and over	5	7	1	6	6	10	5	10	13	13	29	32	8	13	9	3
N =		43	61	43	56	79	42	75	59	58	66	126	122	81	186	54	36

Source: Glasgow project. The table is based on intending and actual voters, that is 'don't know' and 'won't/didn't vote' responses excluded.
− indicated pre-election sample   + indicates post-election sample

Let us first consider the LDPR. Before 12 December, support for the Liberal Democratic Party of Russia was heavily concentrated among particular social groups, especially the manual working class. During the campaign, Zhirinovsky appears to have extended his coalition to appeal to a much broader section of Russian society. His core support remained among workers, in particular workers in the defence industries. In retrospect this does not seem surprising. Workers in state enterprises were the group which analysts identify as having benefited the most from the 'social contract' policies of the Brezhnev era, and by contrast a group which has suffered disproportionately badly as a result of economic restructuring.[9] While mass unemployment had not come about as of December 1993, workers in the 'rust belt' of loss-making factories were fearful for their future, and angry about a present where they were often not paid on time or at all, where the fringe benefits such as housing and recreational and child-care facilities previously provided by enterprises had been cut back, and where they often saw their managers continuing to pay themselves, as well as benefiting from various types of insider privatization.

Where a loss-making enterprise is the sole employer, as is the case in many of Russia's smaller towns and cities, insecurity about the future is particularly acute. Because of Russia's low population density, these places are often very remote, and in any case the virtual absence of a housing market creates huge obstacles to labour mobility.[10] In this context, it should come as no surprise that the LDPR was able to more than treble its support in smaller towns, to four in ten of the population. The party also scored heavily among the unemployed, many of whom no doubt preferred Zhirinovsky's promise not to allow unemployment to the Gaidar line that it was an economic necessity that they should be left without any useful social purpose.

During the campaign, the Liberal Democrats appear also to have been able to increase their share of the vote most among the young (including students) and the middle-aged, those with less formal education, and housewives. Certain sections of society remained reluctant to vote for Zhirinovsky, in particular managers and professionals of various kinds, and inhabitants of Russia's biggest cities. Overall, then, the LDPR represents the political expression of various groups of the more marginal and excluded in Russian society.

The same can be said of two more parties clearly in opposition to the Yeltsin administration, the Communists and the Agrarian Party. These proved to be based on clearly identifiable social groups. The KPRF gained the most support among older people, in particular pensioners. It evidently had no appeal to young people, gaining the support of just 1 per cent of voters aged under thirty. The traditional base for communist parties in the manual working class scarcely existed here: the KPRF polled less strongly among these groups than in the population as a whole.

The Agrarians, by contrast, were able, through their stress on protecting the welfare of all rural inhabitants, to appeal to a section of the working population – farmers – among whom they outpolled the LDPR. They were also much more successful in projecting an appeal to younger people than was the KPRF.

During the campaign, much of the support for Nikolai Travkin's Democratic Party of Russia appears to have drained away, and it is noteworthy that the groups among whom the DPR lost the most votes – students and young people generally, the working class and inhabitants of small and medium-sized cities – are groups among whom the LDPR gained heavily. While it is not possible to prove with those data that these groups switched directly, it is certainly plausible that many anti-government voters who had initially been impressed with the strength of Travkin's criticisms of the Yeltsin administration decided ultimately to vote for an even harsher critic of the current situation.

Women of Russia voters are a coalition of two distinct groups. The bloc evidently appealed more to older than to younger women, and more to the less well-educated and the poor, to unskilled workers (women of course do many of the most boring and routine jobs in Russia, as elsewhere) and housewives. They did less well in rural areas, where people may be more concerned with place than gender. However, there was also strong support among professional groups such as teachers and doctors, the vast majority of whom are female.

What then of support for the more pro-government parties, Russia's Choice and the Yavlinsky-Boldyrev-Lukin bloc (Yabloko)? The two present a contrast. Both appealed to the less excluded sections of society – inhabitants of the big cities, managers and professionals, the highly educated – and both increased their support among these groups during the campaign. However, Russia's Choice voters were much wealthier than the voters for Yabloko; the former comprising those actually benefiting from the transition, the latter being made up of the potential beneficiaries of change, such as students and young people more generally. Russia's Choice also gained votes from some older people, from sections of the unemployed and from unskilled workers, reflecting perhaps the operation of a deference factor in favour of the government party.

Overall then, comparing the situation before and after 12 December, one sees each of the most popular parties strengthening its support among distinct sections of the electorate. The data give a sense of the dynamic process whereby the conduct of democratic elections forces parties to begin to focus their appeal on particular interests within society, which is a major element in a country's democratization.

Attitude changes during the campaign

The election campaign was reported as a victory for extreme nationalist views. Zhirinovsky's comments about, for example, restoring the former tsarist empire, dumping nuclear waste in the Baltic states, unleashing nuclear war on Germany and Japan, and harassing non-Russians within Russia were widely commented on.[11] But did the electorate become more nationalistic as the campaign progressed?[12] Table 6.3 provides some clues.

It is evident from these data that the election made very little difference to people's views on nationalistic issues. Marginally more Russians opposed the right of Jews (and indeed of the other ethnic minorities we asked about, Gypsies and Muslims) to hold public meetings, but a similar one in two thought that Russia should own parts of other countries, and one in four thought that military action should be threatened if necessary to defend Russians living in the former Soviet republics. These positions reflected the attitudes of a wide section of Russian society both before and after the elections.

Furthermore, as support for the LDPR grew, its voters actually became less nationalistic, although they still remained the most likely to adopt hostile attitudes towards minorities and foreign

Table 6.3 Attitude changes during the campaign

	All Russians Pre-	All Russians Post-	Communist Party Pre-	Communist Party Post-	Russia's Choice Pre-	Russia's Choice Post-	Liberal Democrats Pre-	Liberal Democrats Post-	Non-voters Pre-	Non-voters Post-
(a) Views about parties and elections										
Election will be/was free and fair	44	64	16	58	73	84	42	68	26	43
No party represents the interests and views of people like me (% disagreeing)	28	33	59	56	44	52	44	44	8	16
(b) Economic attitudes										
Market economy right for Russia	55	51	31	28	82	70	43	44	47	51
Unemployment is unacceptable	47	53	63	77	25	40	52	63	43	49
(c) Political values										
Oppose right of Jews to hold public meetings	53	56	63	48	45	60	55	63	54	50
A strong leader whom the people trust should not be restricted by law (% agreeing)	23	21	7	26	22	32	21	31	25	15
In the event of disputes, the government should be able to override parliament	28	28	12	16	51	56	20	13	22	22
(d) Nationalist values										
There are parts of other countries that should belong to Russia	51	49	64	54	47	43	67	60	40	43
Military action should be threatened to defend the rights of Russians living outside Russia	25	25	17	31	17	25	41	31	29	24

Source: Glasgow project.

countries. It was in fact voters for other parties who became more likely to adopt a nationalistic stance.

Over the course of the campaign there did, however, appear to be some shift in the electorate's attitudes towards economic change, with a fall in support for a market economy, and a rise in the number of people who thought that unemployment was unacceptable, and that the state should control prices for basic goods. These trends were most strongly observed among supporters of parties hostile to rapid economic change, the KPRF and Agrarians. The election campaign exposed voters to anti-government arguments in greater intensity, which helped to legitimize such views.

Possibly the most significant attitudinal change which occurred in the course of the election campaign, however, related to the views of Russian voters about the elections themselves. In the wake of the 'October crisis' and the suspension by the government of various opposition parties there had been some doubt as to whether there could in fact be free elections. However, the Glasgow data show a dramatic 20 per cent rise during the campaign in the number of people who thought that the elections were 'free and fair'. This rise was most marked among opposition voters. Clearly, acceptance by all sections of society of the legitimacy of a particular set of 'rules of the game' for choosing leaders is an important element in democratic consolidation, and in this respect the elections represent an encouraging development. Also important is the development of attachments to particular parties among voters. After the campaign, some one in three Russians were willing to say that there was a party which represented the interests and views of people like them. While not high by Western standards, this level of party identification represents significant progress from the situation before the elections. Previous work with which we have been involved suggested that at the end of 1992, just one in five Russians said that they felt close to some or other party.[13] While, therefore, the elections might not have been good for the 'democrats', in many respects they can be seen as having been good for democracy.

The attitudes of party voters and non-voters

As well as party identification, which forms the basis of the voting decision in most well-established democracies, development of the party system in Russia would benefit from there being some relation between the views of political elites and the views of their supporters. Without this, parties would be operating at a level remote from the concerns of the ordinary Russian, which would tend to increase disillusionment and lack of interest in politics in general.

Let us first consider democratic values. The opposition parties, in particular the LDPR and the KPRF, were labelled 'enemies of democracy' by many commentators during the campaign, whereas the government forces were portrayed as its friends. To what extent is this reflected by the nature of party voters? Table 6.4 provides some answers.

Clearly when one considers lip service to the idea of democracy, more pro-government VR and Yabloko voters were likelier to say that the concept was broadly acceptable. However, just one in five even among LDPR and Communist voters felt that there was a better alternative, and only slightly more than this favoured a one-party system or the abolition of all parties.

To what extent is lip service to democracy transferred into democratic instincts in response to various scenarios we asked about? The Glasgow data are intriguing in suggesting that many voters for VR were, to say the least, permissive in their attitude towards the rights of government against its political opponents and against ordinary citizens. Fifty-six per cent of Russia's Choice voters thought that the government should be able to overrule parliament, and nearly one in three that it should be able to overrule the constitutional court. A third thought that a strong leader should be unrestricted by the law, and a sixth that the government should ignore public opinion if it disagreed with it. A staggering 49 per cent thought that it was acceptable for citizens' rights to be suspended in order to combat a campaign of slander against the government. A third thought that the KPRF should be banned and half that the Liberal Democrats should be illegal. Instincts among many VR voters, then, were to allow the government to operate unrestrained by other political or social institutions, or by ordinary citizens. Voters for the KPRF, APR and LDPR were on each of these measures more likely to want the power of government to be restricted. Clearly, being in opposition increases voter awareness of the potential for governments to abuse their power.[14]

Table 6.4 Political attitudes of party voters and non-voters

	All Russians	LDPR	KPRF	APR	DPR	ZhR	Yabloko	VR7	Non-voters
Idea of democracy is:									
broadly acceptable	48	44	42	45	47	38	67	69	45
there is no alternative	15	13	11	17	35	17	25	12	12
there is a better alternative	16	20	22	16	8	20	3	7	17
There should be a one-party system/no parties at all	25	28	26	14	14	41	14	16	28
If the government wanted to take action but was opposed by the *new* parliament, elected in December, who should have the final say? (% saying government)	28	13	16	26	22	38	46	56	22
If the government wanted to take action but the constitutional court said it violated the constitution, who should have the final say? (% saying government)	18	15	12	14	24	23	19	28	14
A strong leader who has the trust of the people should not be restricted by the law	21	31	26	18	19	19	10	32	15
Governments should ignore public opinion if they think it is wrong for the country	11	10	3	9	12	14	14	15	11
Acceptable for government to suspend citizens' rights:									
to combat corruption and mafia crime	76	77	74	88	88	78	83	82	70
where there is a campaign of slander against the government	36	33	21	41	37	33	30	49	47
Ban KPRF	16	14	0	5	5	18	17	32	15
Ban LDPR	26	2	21	29	15	30	32	54	27
Ban Russia's Choice (VR)	12	19	20	15	14	5	4	0	11

Source: Glasgow project.

During the campaign, each party except Russia's Choice was to some extent critical of the government's handling of the economy, but none were openly opposed to the creation of a market economy. In this respect, KPRF and APR leaders were not as hostile to the government as their voters, among whom opponents of the market outnumbered supporters. Voters for these groups, and also for the LDPR and ZhR, were also the most likely to believe that the economic role of the state should remain fairly similar to that in the past; that it should forbid unemployment, run heavy industry, control prices, and intervene to ensure egalitarian income distribution. These data are shown in Table 6.5. Many of them expressed highly unfavourable attitudes towards the 'new rich' who have appeared in recent times.

Voters for the Democratic Party of Russia, by contrast to those for other parties critical of the government, were much more favourable towards the market and willing to tolerate its undesirable consequences. However, the most pro-market of all were Yabloko voters, some three-quarters of whom, for example, were willing to accept the inevitability of unemployment. Nevertheless, among both VR and Yabloko voters, statist economic instincts remain, with majorities favouring price controls and state provision of health care. There is very little mass support for libertarian economic policies among any groups at all.

Zhirinovsky had created widespread concern during the campaign by his openly expansionist and racist comments, leading many to label him a fascist. As established above, the exposure these comments received in the media did not increase support for discrimination against minorities, territorial claims against other countries or the threat of military force to defend Russians living outside the Russian Federation. But to what extent were these right-wing views typical of LDPR voters? Table 6.6 sets out the findings of the Glasgow project on this matter.

These data suggest that LDPR voters were indeed the least likely to support the right of Jews to hold public meetings, and equally least likely to support an equivalent right for Gypsies. Communist voters were substantially the most tolerant in this respect. Further breakdown of the figures begins to suggest an explanation for these findings. Big cities, which are more cosmopolitan, are more permissive about minority rights. However, the LDPR support is

Table 6.5 Economic attitudes of party voters and non-voters

	All Russians	LDPR	KPRF	APR	DPR	ZhR	Yabloko	VR	Non-voters
Creation of a market economy right for Russia	51	44	28	31	77	50	81	70	51
Creation of a market economy wrong for Russia	28	34	54	45	16	25	13	13	23
Which one of these statements comes nearest to your view about unemployment? Unemployment is:									
unacceptable	53	63	77	63	42	67	26	40	49
unavoidable because loss-making factories must be closed	30	18	15	17	31	24	52	48	33
necessary to make people work hard	13	14	7	17	23	8	19	9	13
Which one of these comes closest to your attitude towards the 'new rich'? Do you:									
admire them	9	9	4	7	5	8	12	11	9
feel indifferent towards them	43	40	16	34	40	41	62	54	47
dislike them	30	31	54	36	29	30	21	24	28
feel they should be jailed	13	17	21	16	14	13	1	3	11
The state not private business should run car factories	58	61	73	69	43	59	47	54	59
The government not private business should set prices for basic goods and services	80	85	87	83	69	88	63	76	79
The government not private business should provide health care	75	75	88	85	72	76	72	78	69
More important to give people freedom to make as much money as they can	42	44	27	36	45	26	60	60	41
More important to ensure gap between rich and poor does not become too wide	51	48	65	45	52	67	35	36	53

Source: Glasgow project.

Table 6.6 Nationalist values among party voters and non-voters

	All Russians	LDPR	KPRF	APR	DPR	ZhR	Yabloko	VR	Non-voters
Recent changes are turning us into a colony of the West (agree)	49	63	72	73	46	44	40	24	44
Parts of neighbouring countries should belong to Russia (agree)	49	60	54	57	35	51	43	43	43
18–29 years	48	72	n/a	72	81	33	35	40	38
30–54	48	58	52	58	31	47	40	40	47
55+	51	53	57	46	25	60	59	49	40
Threaten military action to defend rights of Russians outside Russia	25	31	31	19	31	15	24	25	24
18–29 years	31	49	n/a	35	47	0	18	37	26
30–54	22	28	18	17	22	14	27	21	21
55+	24	20	35	13	42	21	25	22	23
Would you support or oppose the right of each of the following to hold public meetings and rallies? (% supporting):									
Jews									
Rural areas	29	20	40	24	31	27	34	29	32
Cities under 100,000	22	22	40	27	20	15	18	20	20
Cities 100,000–1 m.	24	10	15	n/a	7	29	28	16	20
Cities 1 m. and over	27	21	53	n/a	32	21	35	21	27
Elementary or incomplete secondary education	47	48	46	n/a	50	53	50	48	54
Secondary or vocational education	22	23	26	28	32	19	36	31	18
Higher/incomplete higher education	29	22	37	18	21	35	32	30	32
Gypsies	44	43	42	10	43	36	49	48	45
Rural areas	24	19	38	18	18	17	30	26	25
Cities under 100,000	18	22	35	19	12	10	9	20	8
Cities 100,000–1 m.	22	10	30	n/a	0	18	22	16	23
Cities 1 m. and over	20	20	46	n/a	16	10	29	19	17
	38	45	35	n/a	34	38	52	43	39

Source: Glasgow project. Table based on post-election wave; $N = 1043$.

concentrated outside these places, in small towns and rural areas, where suspicion of outsiders is much stronger. The rural-urban effect appears in this context rather stronger than the traditional relationship between education and political tolerance, also shown in Table 6.6.

What then of externally oriented nationalist values? It would appear that Communist and Agrarian voters are substantially more suspicious of the intentions of the West and Western business than LDPR voters, reflecting their greater hostility to a market economy. However, territorial claims on other countries were expressed by six out of ten Liberal Democrat voters, the largest proportion, and one in three were prepared for Russia to threaten force to defend kinfolk outside the Russian Federation. Communist and DPR voters were just as willing to threaten force. However, in both these respects LDPR voters were not substantially more aggressive towards the outside world than supporters of the 'democratic' parties. Many (43 per cent) of VR and Yabloko voters also thought that some parts of their neighbouring countries should belong to Russia, and around a quarter agreed that force should be threatened where necessary to defend ethnic Russians. These views are widespread in Russian society.

Among LDPR voters, however, there was a significant difference between the young and the old. Liberal Democrats aged over 55 were no more likely than elderly VR or Yabloko voters to claim parts of neighbouring lands or believe in the use of force, but younger Zhirinovsky supporters proved significantly the most nationalistic. This suggests that the motivations of different generations for casting an LDPR vote were significantly different. The origin of aggressive nationalism among young Russians remains something which is not fully understood by analysts.[15]

Conclusions: Parties and voters in post-communist Russia

Evidence from the Glasgow project leads us to some important conclusions about the December 1993 elections. We find that as the campaign progressed parties increasingly came to represent distinct sections of Russian society. We find a clear link between party platforms and the attitudes of party voters. We find support for the idea of having elections and belief that they are free and fair boosted as a result of the vote. Party identification, although still weak, was boosted as a result of the campaign. All of these are good news for the democratization process, helping to move Russia on from what was a nascent party system to one which, while still diffuse and weak, has at least become more visible.

However, to end on a less sanguine note, if parties fail to deliver substantial benefits, there is clearly a danger of this process being reversed and of disillusionment with the democratic process rapidly setting in, as happened in southern Europe during the late 1970s and early 1980s.

Notes

Part of the discussion presented in this chapter was previously published in Matthew Wyman, Bill Miller, Stephen White and Paul Heywood, 'Public Opinion, Parties and Voters in the December 1993 Russian Elections', *Europe-Asia Studies*, vol. 47, no. 4 (June 1995), pp. 591–614. The authors are grateful to the publishers for their kind permission to reproduce it in this volume.

1. Polls by the All-Russian Centre for Public Opinion Research (VTsIOM) can be found in *Segodnya*, 25 November 1993; *Segodnya*, 11 December 1993; and for their post-election study, *Ekonomicheskie i sotsial'nye peremeny: monitoring obshchestvennogo mneniya*, 2 (1994), p. 70.
2. The Glasgow poll consisted of two representative samples of the Russian adult population (18 plus), covering the whole country, urban and rural. There were 2,136 interviews carried out, with respondents selected according to a five-stage probability sample. Results were post-weighted by age, sex, education and rurality. Interviews were conducted at 128 sampling points in two waves:
   - the pre-election wave of 1,091 interviews between 25 November and 9 December 1993
   - the post-election wave of 1,045 interviews between 12 December (after the polls closed) and 13 January, concentrated on the weekend after the elections, that is 18–19 December.

   The same sampling points were used for both waves to enhance comparability, though the persons interviewed were different. Interviews took place in the respondent's home, covered a wide range of questions, and averaged 60 minutes each. The response rate was 79 per cent, which is typical for Russian surveys at this time. Sampling, translation and interviews were carried out by ROMIR (Russian Opinion and Market Research) in association with GALLUP UK, where Allan Hyde and

Gordon Heald provided invaluable assistance. The survey forms part of a five-nation study of *Public Opinion and Democratic Consolidation in Russia and Eastern Europe*, carried out by the authors and funded by the ESRC under grant number R000 23 3538.
3 For evidence of manipulation of turnout figures in the December elections see, for example, Kronid Lyubarsky, 'Fal'sifikatsiya', *Novoe vremya*, 7 (1994), pp. 8–12; Aleksandr Minkin, 'Opyat' "dvoika"?', *Moskovskii komsomolets*, 11 January 1994, p. 1; Valerii Vyzhutovich, 'Tsentrizbirkom prevrashchaetsya v politicheskoe vedomstvo', *Izvestiya*, 4 May 1994, p. 4; Larisa Aidinova, 'Fal'shivnye vybory, mertvye dushi?', *Vek*, 18 (13–19 May 1994), p. 3; Mikhail Malyutin, 'Fal'sifikatsiya zakonchena: zabud'te', *Novaya ezhednevnaya gazeta*, 11 May 1994, p. 6.
4 Two classical studies of participation are Sidney Verba and Norman H. Nie, *Participation in America: Political Democracy and Social Equality* (New York: Harper and Row, 1972), and Sidney Verba, Norman H. Nie and Jae-On Kim, *Participation and Political Equality: A Seven-Nation Comparison* (Cambridge: Cambridge University Press, 1978).
5 For example, Kay Lawson and Peter Merkl (eds), *When Parties Fail: Emerging Alternative Organizations* (Princeton, NJ: Princeton University Press, 1988).
6 For a technical discussion see, for example, Richard G. Niemi, Richard S. Katz and David Newman, 'Reconstructing Past Partisanship: The Failure of Party Identification Recall Questions', *American Journal of Political Science*, vol. 24, no. 4 (November 1980), pp. 633–51; on the psychological basis for a halo effect, see Elisabeth Noelle-Neumann, *The Spiral of Silence: Public Opinion – Our Social Skin* (Chicago and London: Chicago University Press, 1984).
7 Other data which suggest a similar pattern are cited in Inga Mikhailovskaya and Yevgenii Kuzminsky, 'Making Sense of the Russian Elections', *East European Constitutional Review*, vol. 3, no. 2 (Spring 1994), p. 62.
8 Previous versions of this section can be found in Matthew Wyman, Bill Miller, Stephen White and Paul Heywood, 'The Russian Elections of December 1993', *Electoral Studies*, vol. 13, no. 3 (September 1994), pp. 254–71, and Matthew Wyman, Stephen White, Bill Miller and Paul Heywood, 'Public Opinion, Parties and Voters in the December 1993 Russian Elections' (typescript, 1994).
9 Linda J. Cook, *The Soviet Social Contract and Why it Failed* (Cambridge, MA, and London: Harvard University Press, 1994).
10 Philip Hanson, 'The Future of Russian Economic Reform', paper presented to the Regional Security Conference of the International Institute for Strategic Studies, St Petersburg, 24–27 April 1994; also Susan Richards, 'Steppes to the Right', *Times Higher Educational Supplement*, 21 January 1994, pp. 14–15.
11 Richard Sakwa, 'The Russian Elections of December 1993', *Europe-Asia Studies*, vol. 47, no. 2 (March 1995), pp. 195–227.

12 We deal with this issue also in Bill Miller, Stephen White, Paul Heywood and Matthew Wyman, 'Zhirinovsky's Voters', Glasgow University Press Release, issued 16 February 1994.
13 For evidence about party identification in Russia in late 1992, see Stephen White, Matthew Wyman and Olga Kryshtanovskaya, 'Parties and Politics in Post-communist Russia', *Communist and Post-communist Studies*, vol. 28, no. 2 (1995), pp. 1–20.
14 This, in a cross-national context, is the theme of our previous paper: Bill Miller, Stephen White, Paul Heywood and Matthew Wyman, 'Democratic, Market and Nationalist Values in Russia and East Europe', presented to the 1994 Annual Conference of the Political Studies Association, Swansea, March 1994 (see, for example, p. 14).
15 On this, though, see Hilary Pilkington, *Russia's Youth and its Culture* (London: Routledge, 1994).

7 Stabilization or Stagnation? A Regional Perspective

ELENA OMEL'CHENKO and
HILARY PILKINGTON

Given the dramatic circumstances in which they were launched, the December 1993 elections in the Russian Federation were remarkably uneventful. Despite minor accusations and counter-accusations of irregularities – concerning, in particular, the falsification of votes in the plebiscite to ensure the requisite voter turnout to validate the constitution[1] – on their own these have not sufficed to invalidate the elections or the electoral process. Moreover, the early part of 1994 was marked by greater political tolerance at the highest level and the emergence and/or consolidation of political anchors in the form of Prime Minister Viktor Chernomyrdin (whose retention of his post marks a significant and important compromise by the radicals), and the speakers of the new upper and lower houses (Vladimir Shumeiko and Ivan Rybkin). If these individuals continue to use their political weight as effectively as they do now the pro-presidential imbalance created by the new constitution might be, at least partially, rectified. Moreover, the impact of the 'media event' of the elections, the apparent success of Vladimir Zhirinovsky (leader of the Liberal Democratic Party of Russia) in the party lists vote, has been minimized. While his ability to shift tacitly the political spectrum cannot be denied, he and the Liberal Democratic Party as a whole have been successfully frozen out of key committee posts and have failed to forge any parliamentary alliance with life-threatening consequences for the president.[2]

The apparent uneventfulness of the electoral process might lead the optimistic political scientist to begin talk of a 'democratic consolidation' achieved via the success of particular political procedures (multiparty elections and a national referendum) and leading to the further legitimation of key political institutions (parliament, presidency, political parties and constitution). To explain such an outcome one might turn to modernization theory, or one of its variants, to suggest that the basis for a democratic polity – in the form of urbanization, education, professionalization, and the media and communications revolution – had been forged in the pre-Gorbachev period.[3] Alternatively, one might tread the path of 'transition theories', which hold the additional advantage for political scientists of firmly positing the motor of change to be political, as opposed to social, forces.[4] The present authors also seek to balance the social and the political in explaining current processes of change and, as sociologists rather than political scientists, they hope to add to the debate by locating the December 1993 elections in their micro-sociocultural context. This contextualization leads them to raise a number of questions about the extent to which the December 1993 elections have facilitated the 'normalization' or 'stabilization' of the political process in Russia, at least in the form one might expect from a modernization or transition theory perspective. This does not necessarily entail a rejection of the empirical tenets of the modernization thesis as applied to Russia (even though deterministic variants of modernization theory must clearly be questioned, and with regard not only to Russia). Nor does it imply the adoption of an unreconstructed 'legacies of totalitarianism' conceptual model of contemporary Russia, resting on a mechanistic employment of variables such as the notoriously amorphous concept of 'political culture'.[5] The aim of the current chapter is, rather, to consider concrete political *behaviour* – as opposed to *attitude* – in its full social, economic and cultural context and to suggest how this kind of study might inform our understanding of current political processes.

The focus of this exploration is the election process in the Ul'yanovsk region (*oblast'*).[6] Such are the regional specifics of the current political process in Russia that it would be impossible to make any broad generalizations from the empirical material presented. However, the case study itself has useful typicalities and peculiarities. In its typicalness a study of Ul'yanovsk should illustrate the contours of political behaviour in those regions where there is a very strong local administration. Local (as opposed to national) political culture, it will be argued here, is a significant, although frequently missing, factor in explaining political behaviour and should be considered alongside the more widely discussed phenomena of the '55th parallel factor' and city versus rural mentalities as a key dimension of the post-Soviet political picture. In its very peculiarity, on the other hand, the Ul'yanovsk phenomenon plays an important role in the unfolding of Russian politics. Not only does the region have a notoriously 'conservative' reputation among outsiders, but it perceives itself as an island of stability in the midst of growing disorder and seeks, via its conservative positioning, to spread this stability to the rest of the country.

The authors thus seek to consider a two-way process: the influence of socio-cultural and local political factors on political behaviour in the elections of December 1993; and the likely impact of the experience of those elections on political behaviour in the future. The local political culture of Ul'yanovsk presents some interesting challenges to top-down and centre-out approaches to understanding the process of political change in post-Soviet Russia, particularly with regard to the unreflective employment of the notion of 'political stabilization'. This chapter seeks to raise questions and challenge assumptions about the process and direction of change in Russia by exploring the components which account for the peculiar political stability in Ul'yanovsk today. Is Ul'yanovsk an early vision of the future of Russia as its democratic structure 'stabilizes' and solidifies? Is it, alternatively, an island of the Russian past, a 'Brezhnevian paradise' as Hanson calls it,[7] which has only a limited lifespan in a rapidly (re)modernizing society? Or is Ul'yanovsk simply part of Russia's richly diverse *present* about which we know far too little?

Democratic consolidation or political stagnation? The election process in Ul'yanovsk

There is nothing immediately striking about voting patterns in the Ul'yanovsk region (see Table 7.1). The only significant features are

Table 7.1 Voting patterns in Ul'yanovsk (party-list vote as % of total vote)

	Turnout	LDPR	KPRF	APR	VR	ZhR	PRES	DPR	YBL	RDDR	GS	BRNI	KEDR	DiM
Ul'yanovsk	55.1	23.4	16.6	13.3	11.6	7.6	5.8	5.2	4.5	2.8	1.5	1.0	0.6	0.6
Russia (average)	52.9	22.8	12.2	8.0	15.7	8.0	6.6	5.5	7.9	4.1	2.0	1.3	0.8	0.7

Key:
LDPR = Liberal Democratic Party of Russia
KPRF = Communist Party of the Russian Federation
APR = Agrarian Party of Russia
VR = Russia's Choice
ZhR = Women of Russia
PRES = Party of Russian Unity and Accord
DPR = Democratic Party of Russia
YBL = Yavlinsky-Boldyrev-Lukin Bloc
RDDR = Russian Movement for Democratic Reforms
GS = Civic Union
BRNI = Future of Russia – New Names
KEDR = Constructive Ecological Movement of Russia
DiM = Dignity and Charity

Source: Figures taken from official government information release of provisional results by region, 'Vybory v gosudarstvennuyu dumu RF po obshchefederal'nomu okrugu'.

a slightly higher than average turnout and an exaggerated squeezing of the centre vote in the party list section of the voting. Single-mandate votes in the two electoral districts of the Ul'yanovsk region returned to the State Duma V.A. Sychev (deputy head of the regional administration with responsibility for youth affairs) and L.A. Zhadanova (a senior doctor at the children's hospital and affiliated to the Communist Party). The pattern of voting in elections to the Federation Council was also not dissimilar from elsewhere in the country. The two representatives were well-known figures of the local administration: Yu.F. Goryachev (head of the regional administration) and S.N. Yermakov (mayor of Ul'yanovsk city and formerly the chair of the city council executive committee). Public opinion surveys conducted by the Sociological Laboratory of Moscow State University's Ul'yanovsk branch from 21 November to 5 December 1993 showed these two candidates to be persistently the most popular, followed by the directors of the two main enterprises in Ul'yanovsk: P.P. Lezhankin, director of the UAZ automobile factory, and V.V. Mikhailov, director of the Aviastar aircraft factory (see Figure 7.1).

Interpreting this pattern of voting as a whole is problematic. One reading might be that the relatively high level of participation, together with the squeezing of the vote for the indeterminate centre, suggests a knowledgeable and decisive electorate born of an emergent civic culture accompanying the consolidation of democracy. An alternative reading would be that, in the Russian context, high voting levels may be correlated on the contrary to low 'democratic' civic culture,[8] since voting is above all associated with the expression not of individual political choice but of collective duty and the manifestation of loyalty to local bosses. Given the favouring of conservative political blocs (note especially the high showing of the Communist Party of the Russian Federation and the Agrarian Party of Russia) and the poor showing of Russia's Choice (see Table 7.1), the second hypothesis appears immediately the more tenable.

In order to be able to confirm or refute these possible interpretations an additional variable must be interposed; that of 'political knowledge'. The electoral process in Ul'yanovsk must be examined in detail to ascertain to what extent people were voting for particular parties with known programmes, or, alternatively, for individuals regardless of party affiliation and out of a sense of duty

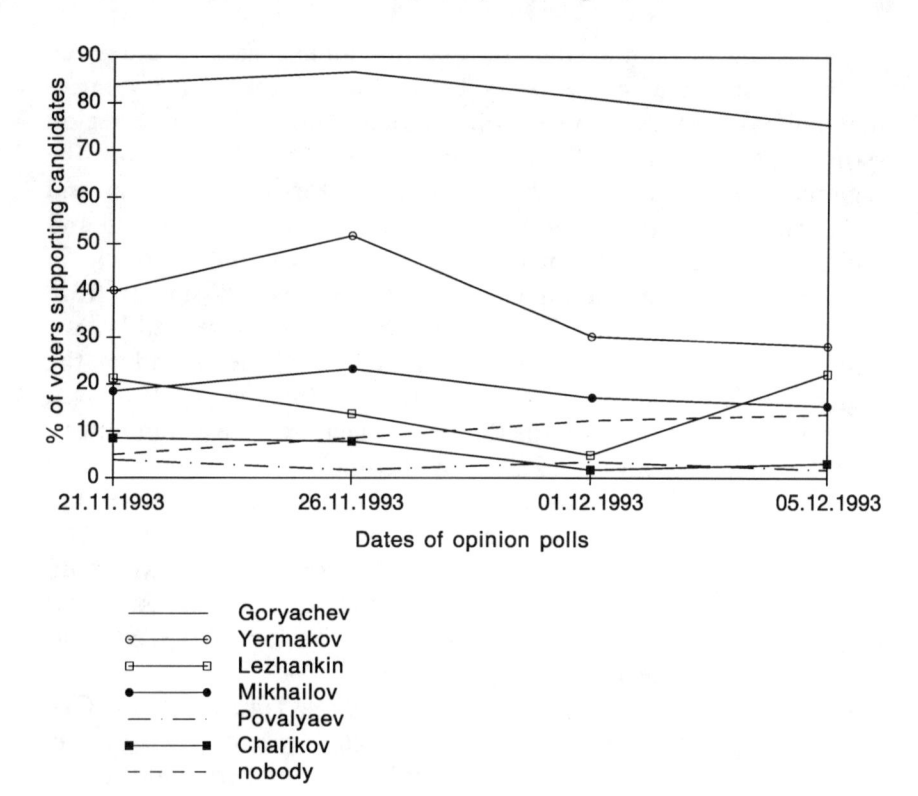

[Figure: line chart showing % of voters supporting candidates across four poll dates: 21.11.1993, 26.11.1993, 01.12.1993, 05.12.1993. Candidates: Goryachev, Yermakov, Lezhankin, Mikhailov, Povalyaev, Charikov, nobody.]

Figure 7.1 Popularity of candidates

Source: Data from SocLab, MGU; published in E. Omel'chenko (ed.), *Byulleten' sotsiologicheskoi informatsii: Analiticheskii obzor issledovanii* (Ul'yanovsk: Sotsart, MGU, 1994), pp. 7–8.

and habit rather than civic conscience. Such an examination is undertaken below, via a study of key socio-cultural factors and institutions shaping voting patterns in Ul'yanovsk in December 1993.

Programmes, parties or personalities? The role of the media in informing the electorate

The media played a central role in the electoral process in December 1993. They largely determined both the breadth and the depth of the electorate's knowledge of the individual candidates' and electoral associations' programmes and, given the complexity and novelty of the electoral system in Russia, were crucial in explaining the voting process itself. They were potentially also central to ensuring a free and fair contest between candidates. An analysis of how the media performed this multifaceted role, therefore, may significantly aid our interpretation of the results of the elections.

Firstly, the media were central to the focusing of political issues, and Ul'yanovsk was no exception to the general pattern whereby attention centred on single-mandate district candidates to the State Duma and representatives being elected to the Federation Council, rather than on the federal-level vote for party lists. Thus, just as in other provincial areas, the elections in Ul'yanovsk were not about which electoral association would be most prominent in the State Duma, but about who would be going to Moscow from (and for) Ul'yanovsk. Thus, although the elections were clearly multiparty in form, they were only partially so in content.

This focusing of the issues did not facilitate the role the media might have played in clarifying the confusing voting process. The mechanism of voting and the choices which had to be made remained unclear even as people went to the polls. The inadequate fulfilment of this informational role also had significant implications for the electoral process. The absence of detailed information about differences between candidates, electoral blocs, programmes and different mandates in the new system further encouraged the process of voting for well-known individuals rather than for particular political policies or philosophies. Advertising or simple exposure thus became the most important weapon in winning votes, making the electorate volatile and easily manipulable. The personalization of the campaign gave a natural advantage to candidates of, or supported by, the local administration, and in particular the powerful head of administration, Goryachev. Those who were able to distribute their leaflets to outlying areas in the region could easily win over public opinion. The local administration was clearly advantaged in this respect by its extensive networking system in the region. The media were also prey to more open abuse by those in power. All organs of the press to a greater or lesser extent were (and are) subject to pressure from the local authorities in Ul'yanovsk and any candidate protected by the head of administration had an immediate advantage. Of all the local newspapers *Gubernskie vedomosti* was the most openly supportive of regional administration candidates during the election campaign. It was forthright in its support of Goryachev and Sychev and, to a lesser extent, Yermakov (the city mayor) whilst conducting both overt and covert negative coverage of other candidates. It also published regular 'sociological surveys' on the front page which showed 100 per cent support for Goryachev.[9] The paper *Narodnaya gazeta* – established by the regional administration and supportive of its policies – also persistently favoured Goryachev. However, it did not sink to publishing rumours or smear campaigns against other candidates. *Ul'yanovskaya pravda* – the most conservative of the local papers, with a readership among mainly middle-aged and older generations – supported the leaders of the communist bloc (the Communist Party of the Russian Federation and the Agrarian Party of Russia) and published virtually no material about any other candidates. The only opposition newspaper was *Simbirskii kur'er*, which published articles highly critical of decisions taken by the regional administration as well as material in support of candidates of the democratic blocs and the local enterprise directors Lezhankin and Mikhailov.[10]

Local television and radio stations gave one hour of air time per day to covering the election campaign and candidates were given the opportunity to speak in turn. However, Goryachev, Yermakov and Sychev received constant, indirect publicity and help. The presenter of the television election programme was openly biased and broadcast daily the results of the aforementioned sociological surveys published by *Gubernskie vedomosti*. The form of television coverage also strengthened the hand of the administration. The favouring of debates between individual candidates showed local administrators, steeled in the presentation of policy, in a good light while revealing the weaknesses of other individuals. Thus, candidates supported by the regional administration in general received significant additional support from local television and radio coverage, although sometimes other candidates themselves were to blame for not seeking more air time.[11]

Having administrative control of the city allowed Goryachev to ensure that posters put up by opposition candidates could 'disappear' overnight. Smear campaigns were also not unheard of:

one candidate, on the list of the Democratic Party of Russia, suddenly found himself subjected to rumours that he was gay.[12] By far the greatest single advantage for those already in positions of authority in terms both of receiving and of influencing election coverage, however, was financial. Although each candidate received 1.5 million roubles from the state to run his/her campaign, this did not cover the costs of efficient campaigning and thus access to extrabudgetary funds was crucial.[13] This was particularly important in the final week of the campaign when media time granted without charge to candidates had generally dried up; the nationwide late surge of the Liberal Democratic Party illustrates well the importance of this factor.

There is no conclusive evidence that serious electoral misconduct, to ensure the election of the local head of administration or those he supported, occurred in Ul'yanovsk, as appears to have been the case, for example, in Krasnodar territory (*krai*) or Lipetsk region.[14] However, it is clear that while the content of the law on elections might have been followed, its spirit was not. The local media did not significantly raise the level of political knowledge of the electorate during the election campaign.[15] Many voters remained extremely confused about the election rules and procedures, about the programmes and policies of individual candidates and about their party affiliation. After the first presentation of local candidates published in *Simbirskii kur'er* which included party or electoral association affiliation and programmes, no subsequent presentations of candidates made reference to such affiliations. Moreover, in many newspaper articles it was unclear whether what was written was a candidate's own advertising or an editorial viewpoint. This is not to say that the media in Ul'yanovsk were monolithic or even consistently biased but rather, as Hansson notes of the role of the media in Novosibirsk during the election campaign, that they 'acted as megaphones for the politicians, and not as free and critical media'.[16]

Who votes for whom, and why? Social stratification, social stereotyping and voting patterns

Given little hard information about the differences between electoral associations or candidates, it would appear that people in the

Ul'yanovsk region voted for candidates according to two general criteria: what they had done for the region; and their professional profile (see Figure 7.2).

The most popuar candidates were those from respectable, caring professions (doctors, lawyers and teachers) and the most unpopular were business people. The two representatives elected via the single-mandate elections to the State Duma were Sychev – who as deputy head of the regional administration would score highly on the 'what he/she has done for the region' factor – and Zhadanova, who was a paediatric doctor. When the electorate in Ul'yanovsk was asked in a survey what the greatest motivation for their voting behaviour in the December elections had been, the single most often mentioned factor was, 'Goryachev is a person trying to improve (*oblegchit'*) the life of the region's residents.'

The pattern of voting in Ul'yanovsk thus reveals an inward-looking and protectionist political mentality. Figure 7.2 shows that policies, campaigning and image (reputation and appearance) were secondary in the minds of the electorate to their general social respectability (as representatives of the region) and, above all, the ability of the candidate to 'get a good deal' for the region once elected.

It would be wrong, of course, to talk of a political *mentalité* manifest uniformly across the population. Indeed the use here of electoral voting patterns to elicit political behaviour and attitudes overemphasizes certain sections of the community, and specifically those most likely to hold conservative positions. Figure 7.3 shows how key socio-demographic and socio-professional groups (pensioners and military personnel) were significantly more likely to use their right to vote than other groups (business people and students).[17]

The consideration of voting patterns and motivations for voting in Ul'yanovsk region invokes a startling vision of Homo Soveticus alive and well. Homo Soveticus (or Sovok as he/she is more affectionately known these days) is a complex social being manifesting a peculiar mixture of *Gesellschaft* and *Gemeinschaft* mentalities, and legal, rational and blood/patronage allegiances. His/her leaders are required to be both 'good at their jobs' but also, and equally, 'to concern themselves with the welfare of those under their leadership'.[18] In Ul'yanovsk those whose welfare must be protected are, first and foremost, the inhabitants of the region, and being 'good at

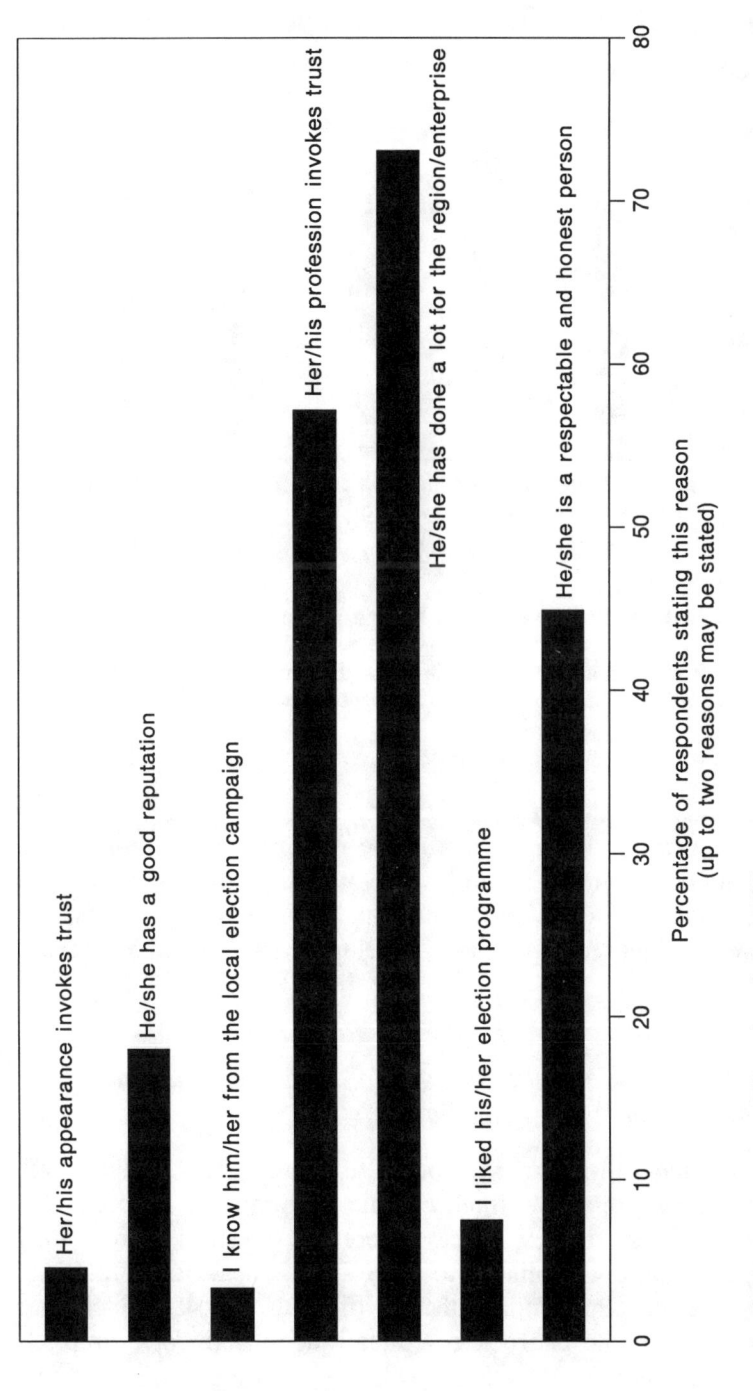

Figure 7.2 Reasons for voting for candidates

Source: Data from SocLab, MGU; published in E. Omel'chenko (ed.), *Byulleten' sotsiologicheskoi informatsii: Analiticheskii obzor issledovanii* (Ul'yanovsk: Sotsart, MGU, 1994), pp. 7–8.

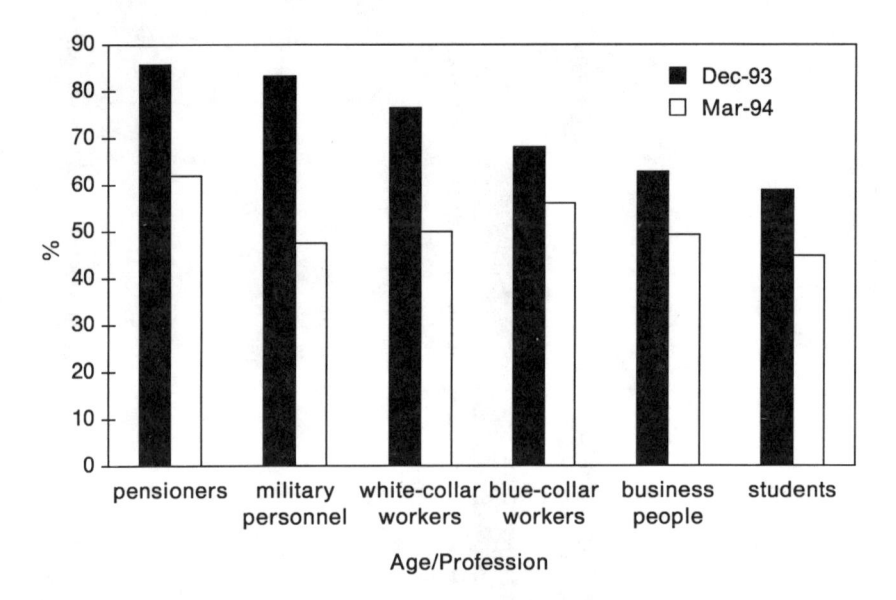

Figure 7.3 Participation in elections by age and profession

Source: Data from SocLab, MGU; published in E. Omel'chenko (ed.), *Byulleten' sotsiologicheskoi informatsii: Analiticheskii obzor issledovanii* (Ul'yanovsk: Sotsart, MGU, 1994), pp. 7–8.

one's job' means standing up for the region against Moscow and in this way securing a 'good deal' for the region's population. Social stereotyping and regional identification, it is argued here, are crucial factors in understanding and conceptualizing voting patterns and their implications for political developments in contemporary Russia.

Shaping the regional political agenda: The socio-cultural context of Ul'yanovsk voting patterns

Despite frequent, ill-informed reports to the contrary, Ul'yanovsk has not had its pre-revolutionary name of Simbirsk restored but, rather, it is one of the few places where the question of renaming has not arisen and is unlikely to arise in the near future. This is partially due to the 'monoculture' of Ul'yanovsk, which has traditionally been the bedrock of education by Leninist example.[19]

However, as is argued here, the region is more than just a leftover from a dictatorial regime for which there is no place in the future.[20]

There is a conservative political culture and natural sense of stability in Ul'yanovsk quite independent from the attachment to Vladimir Il'ich. Ul'yanovsk is indeed *Soviet*, but in the most positive sense of the term. It is a multi-ethnic region (Russians constitute about 70 per cent of the population of the region (*oblast'*) although there are over eighty nationalities altogether, including significant minorities of Tatars, Chuvash and Mordvins), but one in which ethnic tensions do not figure high on the political agenda. Research on ethnic relations conducted in the region in 1992 showed that almost half (49 per cent) of the people thought that all ethnic groups had equal rights and opportunities while about 32 per cent thought those of Russian ethnic origin had some advantages. Of the Russians surveyed 69 per cent thought that ethnic relations would carry on unchanged and 10 per cent thought they would actually improve. Respondents of non-Russian nationalities were even more optimistic; 22 per cent thought relations would improve. The regional culture is also collectivist; there is a strong sense, not of bullish nationalism, but of 'local patriotism' which encourages people to see themselves not as individuals but as acting as representatives of the region and bearing the full responsibility which that entails. Finally, it is a region which retains a now rare sense of a 'bright future'. Levels of social optimism are significantly higher in Ul'yanovsk than elsewhere in the Russian Federation.

Given the connections all too readily made between the ongoing socio-economic crisis in Russia and the potential for the rise of the extreme right (symbolized by the Zhirinovsky vote) the counter-example of Ul'yanovsk is important and requires further explanation. The social optimism of Ul'yanovsk is, of course, a result of more than the spirit of Lenin which certainly always has lived, still lives and will live in the region. It is also a product of current social circumstances which may perhaps best be described as significant cushioning from economic crisis. This cushioning is a result of two factors: the Ul'yanovsk economic heritage, and the current economic policy of the regional administration.

On the first count, the Ul'yanovsk regional economy is dominated by two industrial giants: Aviastar (producing primarily large cargo aircraft) and the UAZ automobile factory (famous for its jeeps).[21] The national importance of these two enterprises has allowed Ul'yanovsk to retain its level of industrial output,[22] and to continue receiving subsidies from the government (at least in the case of Aviastar).[23] The presence of these enterprises thus has a direct impact on the social situation in the region.

At the same time, however, the regional administration of Ul'yanovsk has been conducting a unique economic experiment with some very interesting results. The policy focuses on the maintenance of living standards, a minimization of social tension and continued economic growth. Thus, rationing of some basic food products has been retained, prices of staple goods regulated, and a committed policy of social partnership followed.[24] Those who view the process more negatively might suggest that this has been achieved via a policy of half-hearted privatization plus the use of extrabudgetary funds to keep prices artificially low and production high. The money for the non-budgetary fund is generated from thirty different sources but especially from penalties and fines of various kinds, taxes on advertising, on market trade and on excess profit of monopolist enterprises. The result has been to give Ul'yanovsk the lowest cost of living in Russia, as well as to ensure that it remains free from the continued foodstuffs shortages suffered in other regions.[25]

However, as Ivanov also notes, it is within the Ul'yanovsk tradition to seek a unique path. In the late 1970s the local authorities adopted a self-sufficiency policy as far as consumer goods and foodstuffs were concerned which successfully provided a more stable and higher standard of living than in other regions.[26] Today, therefore, the aim of regional policy need not necessarily be motivated ideologically – to slow down privatization and resist price liberalization policy being implemented from Moscow. It might rather be seen as a continuation of that policy of self-sufficiency and local improvement (e.g. of vegetable storage) which directly improves local living conditions without impacting negatively on the development of other regions, as would have been the case, for example, if the region had used money which should have gone to Moscow in taxes to cushion the local population.[27]

The regional political agenda in Ul'yanovsk has some peculiar contours. The region is not simply another provincial backwater breeding resentments and jealousies towards the privileges of the centre. It is rather consciously conservative and inward-looking and reveals a, perhaps foolhardy, self-confidence in the correctness of its chosen path. On the other hand, it enjoys an enviable standard of living, low levels of social tension and a positive self-image among its inhabitants.

Coming to terms with hermeneutics: The impact of the elections on the future political process

Thus far it has been argued that the micro-sociocultural context (in this case the regional dimension) shapes current political activity in Russia. In the final section of this article, the impact of the political on the social will be considered as an attempt is made to assess the likely impact of participation in the elections of December 1993 on the future political process.

Election overload and voter weariness

The first noticeable impact of the December elections was a general reluctance to repeat the electoral exercise. Local elections in the spring of 1994 suffered from extremely low turnouts and a number of local elections which took place in March 1994 were rendered invalid because fewer than 25 per cent of the electorate went to the polls.[28]

In Ul'yanovsk public opinion surveys of voting intentions showed that interest in elections had declined considerably (see Figure 7.3 above). This was due not only to general overload but also to disappointment felt immediately after the elections as things continued as before with little real change to people's lives. Awareness of this disillusionment led Goryachev to attempt to alter the electoral rules to ensure that greater weight was given to the rural electorate (traditionally solidly pro-Goryachev). However, the voting arrangements issued by the head of administration – which would have led to twice as many deputies being elected from the region as from the city – seriously contravened the presidential decree on electoral procedures. After the intervention of the editor of the only opposition newspaper in the region, a presidential order was issued cancelling the elections, just three days before they were due to take place. In the scandal that followed, falsified (already completed) voting papers were also discovered. As a result, the elections were rescheduled to take place in November 1994.

Strengthening of the regions

Of course, a significant proportion of people had never held much hope that things would improve dramatically after the elections. Despite the atypically high level of social optimism noted above, a public opinion survey in the region conducted on 1 December found that the majority of respondents thought the situation in Russia would not be significantly changed after the elections (54 per cent), while 12 per cent thought it would actually get worse (see Figure 7.4).

This reflects the fact that although the question of president versus parliament may have been resolved via the dubiously democratic adoption of a new constitution, many of the key problems plaguing Russian politics will not be solved by the 1993 elections. The relationship between the regions and the centre occupies the first place on the reformulated agenda.

Existing tensions were significantly heightened by the events of September–October 1993 and the associated sacking of a number of heads of administration. Arguably, the widespread election of regional governors to the Federation Council may act to coopt them into working with rather than against Moscow. Wishnevsky, for example, reports accusations that the heads of administration and others from the presidential administration are beginning to play a similar role to that formerly played by the Central Committee of the CPSU.[29] Equally, however, elections to the Federation Council could give many heads of administration, such as Goryachev, the popular mandate and independent power base which, as presidential appointees, they previously did not have. Certainly, the first indications from Ul'yanovsk suggest no weakening of regional power.

This is not surprising, given that the campaign run by Goryachev overtly employed regionalist sentiments as a central element. His campaign leaflet was headed by a quote from Solzhenitsyn stating: 'Vote for those you know, who live alongside you.' Underneath was

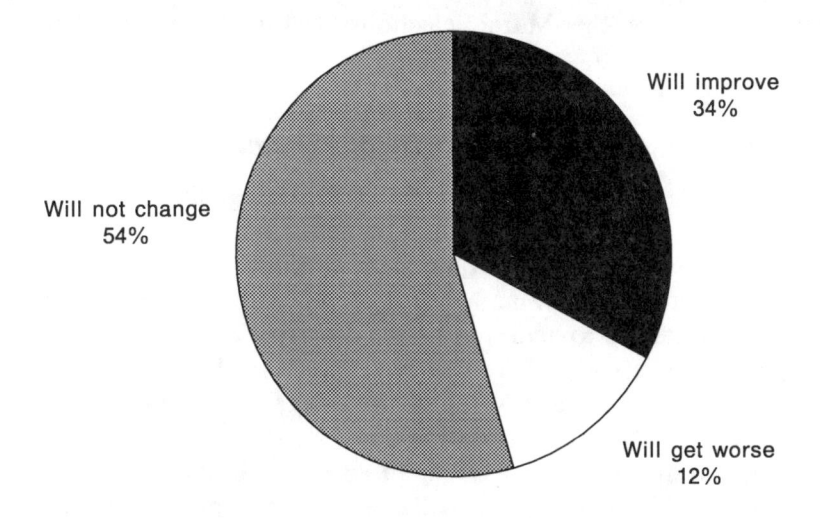

Figure 7.4 'How will the situation change in Russia after the elections?'

Source: Data from SocLab, MGU; published in E. Omel'chenko (ed.), *Byulleten' sotsiologicheskoi informatsii: Analiticheskii obzor issledovanii* (Ul'yanovsk: Sotsart, MGU, 1994), pp. 7–8.

a photograph of Goryachev with the caption 'A person everyone knows.' This was followed by a list of things he was standing 'for' and 'against'. On the 'for' side was 'a strong region', 'low prices' and 'stability' (i.e. Ul'yanovsk regional policy), while on the 'against' side was 'politicking', 'empty words' and 'corruption' – all metaphors for Moscow politics.

This regionalist ticket was appropriated by the other candidate eventually elected to the Federation Council – Yermakov, the city mayor. His slogan was 'Vote for Goryachev and Yermakov' in a historically familiar attempt to associate himself with the popularity of the head of administration. In this way the two poles of power – region and city – were seen to be pulling together in the interests of Ul'yanovsk.

If anything then, the electoral process reinforced the power of the regions and their heads of administration. They were shown to have the clearest programmes of action, the clearest means of articulating their message and to meet little real opposition. Other candidates stood against them with the resignation of a loyal opposition, and by the March elections it was difficult to find anyone to stand at all.

Consolidation of civic culture or rise of extremist politics?

If the resolution of the power struggle in Russian politics was one hope from the elections, the second (at least among liberal academics) was surely that they would help consolidate a multiparty system and electoral choice as a norm of political behaviour. The reasons for the failure to achieve this are discussed elsewhere in this volume, and the discussion here will be confined to the implications of the unexpectedly strong showing of the Liberal Democratic Party of Russia.

It was not so much the relatively high vote for Zhirinovsky which was shocking, as the complete collapse of the centrist electoral associations, proving there was no politically attractive centre in the political spectrum except in the form of the Women of Russia bloc.[30] The late surge towards the Liberal Democratic Party meant that its growing support was not captured in public opinion surveys (which were not allowed to be published in the last few days before the elections) and so Zhirinovsky's success came as just as great a shock in Russia as it did in the West. The more sober reaction which prevailed in Russia, however, is explained not only by Zhirinovsky's maverick reputation but also by the knowledge that his success was at least partially attributable to the comparatively feeble campaigns mounted by other electoral associations and parties.

Nevertheless, the 'normalization' of extremist positions remains a disturbing sign for the future, even if the centre gained a tacit victory via the large number of 'independents' elected in the single-mandate constituencies. It means that any acute worsening of economic or ethnic relations could rapidly change the political agenda. Even in the 'Brezhnevian paradise' of Ul'yanovsk, public opinion surveys on voters' concerns reflected above all the negative effects of the market. At the beginning of December the electorate's five greatest concerns were: price rises, the growth of crime, the growth of unemployment, the threat of civil war, and corruption in organs of power. Thus, although the level of social tension in Ul'yanovsk currently remains relatively low, the kind of protectionist culture which prevails has the potential to breed an exclusivist mentality which might be turned against sections of the community, especially foreigners, newcomers to the region or ethnic minorities.[31]

Russia remains a highly politicized and inward-looking society. A survey in July 1993 eliciting the names of those people mentioned most often in central Russian newspapers showed that politicians had a virtual monopoly on public life; it was not until fiftieth place that anyone other than politicians (i.e. business people, academics, sports stars, actors, etc.) was mentioned.[32] The December 1993 elections – themselves a product of high political drama – did not solder an ideal-type liberal-democratic political culture based on political knowledge, a sense of efficacy and a belief in procedural, representative democracy. The political behaviour of the electorate suggests rather the use of extremist candidates to punish a central government which had ceased to protect properly the welfare of its subjects, as well as revealing a growing disillusionment with the more removed institutions of the political system. This behaviour suggests much in common with other East European societies as they become increasingly disillusioned with their 'new democracies' as well as with the actually existing (as opposed to their ideal-types often found in academic literature) liberal-democratic societies of Western Europe and North America.

Conclusion

The task originally set the authors was to consider the social and cultural obstacles to political stabilization in the Russian Federation. In exploring the electoral process in Ul'yanovsk, however, they came to the conclusion that, in this region at least, the interaction between the social and the political was in fact reversed; it was political stability which was acting as a brake on social, economic and cultural change. Of course Ul'yanovsk region is in no way 'typical' of Russia, but it nevertheless is part of the rich diversity which constitutes contemporary Russia, and the fact that it causes problems for our frameworks of understanding current political processes is extremely useful in the process of refining and improving those frameworks.

The reason, it has been argued above, that the example of

Ul'yanovsk disrupts our thinking about the Russian political process is that political behaviour cannot be explained by reference to a single set of national political markers. In fact, as the authors have tried to show, the political behaviour of both electorate and elected during the December 1993 elections in Ul'yanovsk region reveals a political stability and continuity which contrasts with the high tension and brinkmanship of the Moscow political scene. This raises important questions about the viability of a central project of 'democratic transition' aimed at dragging up the level of 'civic culture' of a 'backward hinterland' and in this way 'stabilizing' and 'normalizing' the political spectrum of Russia.

Questions are also raised about the self-legitimating principles of procedural democracy which suggest that, given more practice at the procedures of democracy (such as multiparty elections), Russia will improve its performance of these procedures and thereby become a more stable political democracy. In fact, in December 1993, the procedures of democracy were more or less adhered to (bar of course Yeltsin's calling of the elections in the first place). In Ul'yanovsk, at least, however, the practice of democratic procedure revealed a correlation between participation and 'civic culture' which was the inverse of that which might have been expected. It also suggested not a legitimating but a delegitimating effect of democratic procedure, evident in the manifest desire of the ruled not to participate and of the rulers not to play the procedural game during the run-up to the aborted elections in spring 1994.

No conclusions can be offered as yet as to the long-term implications of the trends suggested here. The authors seek no more than to raise awareness of some regional specifics of the Russian political scene and to suggest that Ul'yanovsk region is not a conservative blip on the path to 'democratic transition' but a useful and indicative example of the way in which politics is conducted in regions with strong identities and regional administrations. It is perhaps also indicative of the still far from secure formulation of the relationship between power, authority and democracy in contemporary Russia. While democratic and electoral procedure is important (witness the struggle over the adoption of the new constitution), in practice political power still overrides and determines democratic procedure, while that procedure (including elections) is perceived to be about the allocation and division of such power.

Notes

1. V. Tolz and J. Wishnevsky, 'Election Queries Make Russians Doubt Democratic Process', *RFE/RL Research Report*, vol. 3, no. 13 (1994), pp. 1–6.
2. The party does hold chairs of five committees but they are not ones which, as yet, have allowed them significant impact on the political process.
3. For classic, but nevertheless culturally sensitive, applications of the principles of modernization theory to Russian development, see M. Lewin, *The Gorbachev Phenomenon* (Berkeley: University of California Press, 1988); G. Lapidus, 'State and Society: Toward the Emergence of Civil Society in the Soviet Union', in S. Bialer (ed.), *Politics, Society and Nationality Inside Gorbachev's Russia* (Boulder, CO: Westview Press, 1989); and A. Inkeles, 'The Modernization of Man in Socialist and Non-Socialist Countries', in M. Field (ed.), *Social Consequences of Modernization in Communist Societies* (Baltimore: Johns Hopkins University Press, 1976). Alternative, 'revisionist' modernization theses are put forward by Richard Sakwa through his notion of 'mismodernization': see R. Sakwa, *Russian Politics and Society* (London: Routledge, 1993), or R. Sakwa, 'Democratic Change in Russia and Ukraine', *Democratization*, vol. 1, no. 1 (Spring 1994), pp. 41–72. Also Thomas F. Remington, who focuses on the political pressures resulting from the *negative* rather than positive consequences of the modernizing process: see T. Remington, 'Regime Transition in Communist Systems: The Soviet Case', in F. Fleron and E. Hoffmann (eds), *Post-Communist Studies and Political Science* (Boulder, CO: Westview Press, 1993), pp. 265–98.
4. Perhaps the boldest examples of transition theories as applied to Russia are those which advocate 'authoritarian transition'; see, for example, articles by Migranyan and Klyamkin in the collection introduced by E. Berard-Zarzicka, 'The Authoritarian Perestroika Debate', *Telos*, no. 85 (Summer 1990), pp. 115–41. Commentators more removed from the political debate itself, however, tend to focus on discerning and describing key factors influencing the process of 'transition': see, for example, J. Linz and A. Stepan, 'Political Identities and Electoral Sequences: Spain, the Soviet Union and Yugoslavia', *Daedalus*, vol. 121, no. 2 (Spring 1992), pp. 123–40; and R. Bova, 'Political Dynamics of the Post-Communist Transition: A Comparative Perspective', in Fleron and Hoffmann (eds), *Post-Communist Studies and Political Science*, pp. 239–64.
5. See, for example, Z. Brzezinski, 'Soviet Politics: From the Future to the Past?', in P. Cocks, R. Daniels and N. Whittier Heer (eds), *The Dynamics of Soviet Politics* (Cambridge, MA: Harvard University Press, 1976), pp. 337–54; Z. Brzezinski, *The Grand Failure: The Birth and Death of Communism in the Twentieth Century* (New York: Charles Scribner's and Sons, 1989); and M. Malia, 'A Fatal Logic', *The National Interest*, no. 31 (Spring 1993), pp. 80–90, or, writing under the pseudonym 'Z', 'To the Stalin Mausoleum', *Daedalus* (Winter 1990), pp. 295–342. For a useful

critical overview see A. Dallin, 'The Uses and Abuses of Russian History', in Fleron and Hoffmann (eds), *Post-Communist Studies and Political Science*, pp. 131–43.

6 The bulk of the empirical material is based on three surveys conducted by the Sociological Laboratory of Moscow State University (Ul'yanovsk branch) at three key moments in time: September 1993 (just after Yeltsin's dissolution of parliament), immediately before the December 1993 elections, and immediately before the local elections due to be held in March 1994 but subsequently postponed. Each survey was conducted on the basis of a representative sample (across the city and region) used regularly by the Sociological Laboratory for public opinion surveys. For each of the surveys referred to here between 500 and 700 responses were recorded.

7 P. Hanson, 'The Center Versus the Periphery in Russian Economic Policy', *RFE/RL Research Report*, vol. 3, no. 17 (29 April 1994), pp. 23–8, at p. 27.

8 Certainly voter *abstention* was positively correlated to high political (dissident) activity under the former one-party system of the Soviet Union. See R. Karklins, 'Soviet Elections Revisited: Voter Abstention in Non-Competitive Voting', *American Political Science Review*, vol. 80, no. 2 (June 1986), pp. 449–66.

9 See *Gubernskie vedomosti* from 18 November to 6 December 1993.

10 The university's weekly paper *Vestnik* also retained a critical stance.

11 The reasons for the relatively poor performance of candidates opposing the regional administration are explored below.

12 This was not published in the local newspapers, but as soon as it became clear that the candidate was gaining popularity, rumours began to circulate to this effect.

13 As a rule organs of the media gave free advertising space to those candidates being supported openly or covertly by the publication or television or radio station, while other candidates were charged advertising rates for exposure.

14 In Krasnodar the head of administration, Yegorov, appears to have interfered in the selection of members of both the constituency election committee and its 'working group', while in Lipetsk illegal practices in the election of the head of administration, Narolin, to the Federation Council were discovered. See K. Lyubarsky, 'Fal'sifikatsiya', *Novoe vremya*, no. 7 (1994), pp. 4–11.

15 For a more detailed discussion of the election campaign and the media's importance to it in Ul'yanovsk see E. Omel'chenko, 'K vyboram 12 dekabrya', *Vestnik* (3 December 1993); E. Omel'chenko, 'K vyboram 12 dekabrya', *Vestnik* (10 December 1993); E. Omel'chenko, 'Zhena Tsezarya vne podozreniya', *Vestnik* (17 December 1993).

16 O. Hansson, 'Novosibirsk', in 'The Russian Parliamentary Elections. Monitoring of the Election Coverage in the Russian Mass Media. Final Report, The European Institute for the Media', *International Affairs*, no. 5 (1994), pp. 3–78, at p. 54.

17 Voting behaviour recorded for December 1993 refers to respondents' reports of whether or not they voted. Figures for March are based on reported intentions to vote by respondents.
18 A survey conducted by the All-Union Centre for the Study of Public Opinion (VTsIOM) in November 1989 as part of the research programme 'Sovetskii Chelovek' found that the key qualities for leaders were held to be 'knowing one's job well' (stated by 51 per cent of respondents) and 'caring about one's subordinates' (49 per cent). See Yu. Levada (ed.), *Sovetskii prostoi chelovek: Opyt sotsial'nogo portreta na rubezhe 90-kh* (Moscow, 1993), p. 63.
19 The city's name derives from Lenin's original surname, Ul'yanov, since the city was his birthplace.
20 Here the authors are taking issue with Hanson's description of the region's prospects as comparable to an 'Enver Hoxha theme park' (Hanson, 'The Center Versus the Periphery', p. 28).
21 Ul'yanovsk region is dominated by the *oblast'* centre; of its 1,462,200 population 661,100 live in Ul'yanovsk city itself: see *Narodnoe khozyaistvo oblasti za 1992* (Goskomstat RSFSR Ul'yanovskoe Oblastnoe Upravlenie Statistiki, Ul'yanovsk, June 1993), p. 72. In general, however, the region's urban population (72.3 per cent) is slightly below the average for Russia as a whole (74 per cent): see *Narodnoe khozyaistvo oblasti za 1992*, p. 70; *Chislennost'. Sostav i dvizhenie naseleniya v Rossiiskoi Federatsii* (Goskomstat Rossii – RITs, Moscow, 1992), p. 3.
22 The decline in industrial production in 1992 in Ul'yanovsk was less than a third of the Russian national average while the first half of 1993 saw a stabilization of consumer goods production.
23 Hanson, 'The Center Versus the Periphery', p. 24.
24 N. Burkin, 'Ul'yanovskaya oblast': sotsial'noe partnerstvo radi cheloveka', *Chelovek i trud*, no. 8 (1993), pp. 35–7.
25 N. Ivanov, 'The Ulyanovsk Region: Own Way in Reform?', *Russian Business Monitor*, no. 6 (1993), pp. 42–9, at p. 45.
26 ibid., p. 44.
27 ibid., pp. 45–6.
28 In twenty-five regions where regional and local elections were held on 20 March, the turnout was very low, dropping to 13 per cent in places. See Tolz and Wishnevsky, 'Election Queries Make Russians Doubt Democratic Process', p. 6.
29 J. Wishnevsky, 'Problems of Russian Regional Leadership', *RFE/RL Research Report*, vol. 3, no. 19 (1994), p. 6.
30 For a more detailed discussion of the success of the Women of Russia electoral association see H. Pilkington, 'Can "Russia's Women" Save the Nation? Survival Politics and Gender Discourses in Post-Soviet Russia', in S. Bridger (ed.), *Women in Post-Communist Russia*, Interface: Bradford Studies in Language, Culture and Society, no. 1 (University of Bradford, Spring 1995), pp. 160–81.

31 Although attitudes towards refugees and forced migrants, for example, are not negative as yet, growing competition for housing, employment and state benefits may change the situation in the future.
32 'Indeksy upominanii v iyule 1993-go', *Reputatsiya*, no. 1 (August 1993), p. 13.

PART IV
The Framework of a New Political Order

8 The Development of the Russian Party System: Did the Elections Change Anything?

RICHARD SAKWA

Political parties have a fundamental role to play in the development of modern representative democracy.[1] They connect civil and political society, advance the perceived interests of individuals, groups and social strata while aiming consciously to develop these constituencies, and provide a link between civil society and the state, espousing the claims of the one and enforcing the rules of the other.[2] In post-communist Russia the emerging parties and party system only marginally fulfilled these functions. The relative independence of government from both parliamentary supervision and party control and its interweaving but not fusion with the presidential system gave rise to what can be called 'regime politics', occupying the space between an ill-formed state system and a rudimentary civil society. The unstructured party system was unable to assert its role against other potential political actors like the military, industrial interest groups and the government itself, giving rise to a distinctive form of inclusive corporatism.[3]

The development of an effective party system in Russia has been inhibited by four groups of factors: the provenance of parties as part of the insurgency against the decaying communist regime; regime system patterns of politics and governance; the post-totalitarian legacy of a fractured and amorphous society; and the general crisis of parties in modern societies. Given this context, it is surprising just how much was achieved by the nascent party-political system in Russia.

Periodization

Before discussing the factors giving rise to regime politics we will briefly outline the three stages in the evolution of the multiparty system in Russia. The first was the insurgency stage of movements and *neformaly* (informal organizations) accompanying the dissolution of the power of the Communist Party of the Soviet Union (CPSU) during perestroika. The second stage accompanied the triumph of what can be called the August regime, the period between August 1991 and October 1993 of relatively liberal economic policies and, in the absence of elections, of a peculiar sort of 'phoney democracy' as the regime born of the August coup consolidated itself. The third stage was inaugurated by the dissolution of the old Russian Congress of People's Deputies and its Supreme Soviet led by Ruslan Khasbulatov, on 21 September 1993, and the events of 3–4 October, when the White House was stormed and President Boris Yeltsin's opponents crushed. This adaptation stage was marked by the adoption of a new constitution and the first genuine national multiparty elections, on 12 December 1993. The elections began to clarify the pattern of party affiliation but failed to consolidate the party system.

The insurgency stage

The democratic insurgency against the communist regime was characterized by the proliferation of movements covering social, environmental, gender and other issues, as well as the formation of the first political popular fronts and proto-parties.[4] The tumultuous proliferation of informal organizations and an independent press revealed the strong currents of civic endeavour flowing beneath the stagnant surface of Soviet life, demonstrating the vitality of the Russian social organism.[5] While the politics spawned by the insurgency phase might have been untidy and anarchic, they were nevertheless stamped by a profound commitment not only to democratic goals but also to the democratic method, and demonstrably repudiated political cultural theories that stressed Russian passivity and innate authoritarianism.[6] The integration of this upsurge of civic activism into a new polity, however, remained problematical.

Despite the Stalinist terror and decades of stifling one-party rule, the elements of continuity with the pre-revolutionary experience of party formation should be stressed. One analysis noted that pre-revolutionary Russia was characterized by hundreds of societies and clubs, and that this rich associational life continued into the early Soviet years but thereafter dried up to the degree that only three social organizations were created in the Brezhnev years.[7] Early studies of the *neformaly* blurred the distinction between political and social activities, but this was understandable since the key point at this stage was precisely independence from administrative structures, and interest orientation was a secondary consideration. This autonomy, however, was at first conceived of as part of the shift from 'administrative command' to hegemonic strategies of rule within the framework of perestroika.[8]

By contrast with Poland, the insurgency phase in Russia was both shorter in time and more anarchic, with no single umbrella movement spearheading the opposition, although Democratic Russia came closest to fulfilling this role. (Solidarity later split to spawn a number of post-communist parties in Poland. In Hungary, to take another example, the opposition played a lesser role in the transformation of the system, and here a more traditional form of party politics was the first to emerge.) The establishment of the Democratic Union on 9 May 1988 can be taken as the beginning of the renewed era of multiparty politics in Russia. Rejecting Gorbachev's attempts to expand the base of the party regime by incorporating new social forces in an expanding consensus, the new party declared its outright opposition to Soviet power and allegiance to a 'peaceful democratic revolution'.[9] The memoirs of one of the leaders of the party, Valeriya Novodvorskaya, provide a vivid illustration of the intellectual and personal factors shaping the path to insurgency by the new generation.[10] By late 1990 there were at least 457 political or politicized organizations in Russia, confronting analysts with major problems of classification.[11] Broadly speaking, this period can be characterized as a bipolar struggle between communist and liberal movements, with the embryonic national-patriotic movements torn between the two.

The end of the CPSU's constitutionally guaranteed monopoly on power in March 1990 allowed informal movements to take on more structured forms and gave way to a rudimentary multiparty system.

The elections held in the first stage, notably in March 1990 to the Russian Congress of People's Deputies, were dominated by the antipolitics of opposition to the communist regime. The social movements associated with the insurgency phase were largely unable to make the transition from mobilizational to representational politics, whereas Solidarity in Poland gradually differentiated between its trade union and party functions.[12] Unity in the insurgency phase of party formation was forged by the negative programme of opposition to the communist regime, in favour of greater civic freedom and a looser form of federation. Practically all respondents in a survey of middle-level Democratic Russia activists stressed that the movement prospered because of its commitment to the removal of the CPSU from power and the transition to a new social order.[13]

The informal movement origins of most parties left its stamp on the nascent party system. Civil society-type 'antipolitics' was typical of the insurgency phase, marginalizing political parties as instruments of mobilization and political communication.[14] Experience of earlier revolutions, however, demonstrates that it is difficult to institutionalize the aspirations of the politics of insurgency, and more effective (often authoritarian) forms are established that 'betray' the revolution while at the same time maintaining its core principles. Both the French and Bolshevik revolutions reflect this pattern, and now, in a different way, the anti-communist democratic revolution had to be 'saved' at the expense of sacrificing some of its participatory and spontaneous forms. This was the function of the regime system. As Michels long ago demonstrated, political parties, whatever their programmatic aspirations, tend to succumb to the oligarchical tendencies inherent in modern social organizations,[15] but Russia appears to have fallen victim to this iron law even before party life had become routinized and bureaucratized.

Consolidation: the August regime, August 1991–October 1993

Duverger stresses the electoral and parliamentary origins of modern political parties,[16] and in the absence of either in the consolidation phase party formation inevitably stagnated. If the *leitmotiv* of the alternative society in the insurgency phase had been unity, across the political spectrum and between republics, the *zeitgeist* of the

The Development of the Russian Party System 173

August period was disintegration. Unity was shattered by differing responses to the disintegration of the USSR and the onset of radical economic reform. In this period the development of the party system was inhibited by the emergence of a distinctive type of dual power in which a presidential apparatus was superimposed on the nascent parliamentary system with little coordination between the two. While the government gained a degree of institutional autonomy, parties were left hanging in the air with little constructive purpose.

The second stage was marked by the decline of the movements associated with the politics of insurgency. Environmental movements were marginalized under the impact of severe economic recession, and housing and other movements failed to respond to the new challenges. The official trade union movement was reformed and de-étatised, while the new trade unions were subject to the factionalism and splits typical of the pseudo-parties.[17] The democratic anti-communist revolution ceded ground to numerous patriotic and nationalist movements. The ideological homogeneity of the insurgency phase now gave way to programmatic divergence over such issues as the powers of the presidency, relations with the 'near abroad' and, above all, economic reform. Programmes now reflected the realities of contemporary Russian politics rather than idealized versions of abstract transitional processes to 'the market'.[18]

The coup was followed by the decline not only of movements but also of many of the parties spawned by the struggle against communism. Most were not proto-parties, destined with time to become fully fledged parties, but pseudo-parties sustained by a variety of extraneous circumstances that did not reflect either their popular appeal or their organizational resources. According to Gavriil Popov the democratic movement could not have been expected to achieve much since its social base was so heterogeneous, from intellectuals to security officials to pensioners, united only by their 'hatred for the bankrupt CPSU regime'.[19] The failure of social movements to 'particize' themselves, notably in the case of Democratic Russia and also the Civic Union later, is one of the distinctive features of the transition in Russia.[20] The dominance of Democratic Russia on the reformist flank inhibited the development of more sectional party politics.

After December 1991 'national' politics was defined on a smaller scale, but numerous parties were unable to adapt to the new conditions and continued to support some larger political entity to cover the former Soviet Union. The disappearance of the CPSU removed the incentive for the 'opposition' to unite, while much of the old CPSU elite made a smooth transition and became part of the new establishment, disorienting groups like Democratic Russia, which responded by calling for lustration laws and a continued mobilizational effort against manifestations of the old regime, something that now threatened Yeltsin's own position. A gulf remained between the parties emerging from below and official representation in the legislature, with parliamentary and popular organizations operating on separate levels, inhibiting the development of distinct party identities and organizations.

Four major tendencies can be identified in this period in party formation: liberal democrats and entrepreneurs; representatives of state industry; communist statist organizations; and national patriotic movements.[21] The communist statist tide became less and less distinguishable from the national patriotic movement. The Communist Party of the Russian Federation (KPRF), revived at a congress in February 1993 and claiming to be the successor to the old Communist Party, was one of the few political forces that transcended the politics of insurgency and could draw on reserves of organizational and political experience matched by few other parties.

Thus the proto-parties of the first stage of party formation gave way to a period marked not by their evolution into fully fledged parties but by a system marked by numerous pseudo-parties, all seeking a niche in the ideological spectrum and organizational life of the post-communist polity. Parties neither nominated the president nor formed the government, and parliament and the parties in it were marginalized. The absence of disciplined party blocs endowed parliamentary politics with a fractious fluidity, and the parties were often divided internally and unable to play an effective role. The failure to integrate parties into the operation of the political system undermined the stability of the new democratic institutions and forced ever greater reliance on a technocratic ideology of democratic and marketizing reforms from above (the regime system).

The absence of a multiparty system impeded the development of serious parties, but at the same time the absence of serious parties inhibited the development of a multiparty system. Parties emerged but not a party system, and the new parties only fitfully fulfilled the communicative and link functions between the political elite and the people. Party formation in this period was marked by groups, and above all their leaders, trying to sustain autonomous organizations while at the same time forming blocs with kindred parties, contradictory impulses that imbued the whole period with a hall of mirrors quality.[22] Every party produced programmes in abundance, but it was the government, standing as it were above politics in a form of technocratic rule, that formulated its own policies largely independent of any party, movement or bloc. The kaleidoscopic shifts between numerous pseudo-parties suggested that while a multiparty system might in time emerge, the instability of the social structure and the mimetic pluralism that was such a strong feature of post-communist Russian society inhibited the development of any party system, let alone a functioning two-party system.

The adaptation stage

In this stage the pseudo-parties of the August regime were faced with the hard school of an election, in which their inflated claims of support could finally be put to the test. Few withstood the challenge, and most faded into the obscurity whence they had come. The elections contributed to the development of parties by forcing the development of organizations and alliances, but it was the adoption of the constitution in a plebiscite also on 12 December 1993 that provided an institutional framework in which parties could operate. The establishment of a bicameral Federal Assembly, and in particular the lower house, the State Duma, finally created a forum in which multiparty politics could flourish in Russia's third attempt at parliamentarianism. A new generation of parties emerged, most of which drew their provenance from earlier stages but had been able to respond to the dramatically changed political climate following the October events.

Yeltsin's decree of 21 September 1993 dissolving the old Russian legislature was followed by the imposition of an electoral system designed above all to encourage the development of a multiparty system. Following world practice, the electoral system was manipulated by democratic reformers to advance specified goals.[23] The electoral law provided for a mixed system in which half the seats to a new 450-member State Duma would be elected by the traditional first-past-the-post single-member constituencies, but the other half would be elected from party lists according to a weighted system of proportional representation. In order to be eligible to stand a party or bloc required at least 100,000 nominations with no more than 15,000 signatures drawn from any one of Russia's 89 regions and republics, so that the bloc or party had to have demonstrable support in at least seven regions or republics.[24] This provision was designed to stimulate the creation of a national party system and to avoid the dominance of Moscow, and at the same time to force the creation of larger blocs to overcome the fragmentation of Russian political life. The adoption of a mixed proportional and constituency system according to Viktor Sheinis, one of its main advocates, was not only to accelerate the creation of a party system but also to avoid 'an atomized parliament with fractions like those we have today, representing no more than interest clubs'.[25]

A 5 per cent hurdle was incorporated into the 'list' system to prevent the proliferation of small parties. To enter parliament a party had to take at least 5 per cent of the national vote, with the whole country considered one giant constituency. It was assumed that this would give reformist candidates an advantage since their natural strength in the big cities, above all Moscow and St Petersburg, would counteract the conservatism of rural areas, where in any case a low turnout was more likely. In contrast to earlier practice the elections were to be held in one round, and the old minimum turnout requirement of 50 per cent was reduced to 25 per cent. The elections to the upper house of the Federal Assembly, the Federation Council, were conducted almost entirely on an individual rather than a party basis.

According to Nikolai Ryabov, the head of the Central Electoral Commission, the proportional elections played a positive role 'in the development of the parties and movements themselves, assisting the development of multipartyism in Russia'.[26] The electoral process was indeed a major stimulus for the development of parties and a party system, but the adoption of this hybrid system only revealed more starkly the fault lines in Russian society. Thirteen parties and electoral blocs negotiated the hurdles to stand in the election, and of these only eight cleared the 5 per cent threshold. Thus the aim set earlier by Gavriil Popov to 'parliamentarianize' the opposition by offering them a forum away from their accustomed street politics was only partially fulfilled.[27]

The elections, moreover, once again gave rise to a fragmented party system in parliament, with nearly a dozen relatively small factions preventing the establishment of a stable majority, inhibiting the development of parliamentary government and helping to perpetuate the supraparty system of regime politics. The major centres of power were based on personalities, many of whom were outside the parliamentary and party system altogether (such as the prime minister, Viktor Chernomyrdin and the mayor of Moscow, Yurii Luzhkov), and within the parties links between the leadership and membership were tenuous. The overpartification of Russian politics gave rise to the tendency to shift from party to bloc politics, illustrated by the shift in the Movement for Democratic Reforms' policies at its congress on 29 January 1994. The movement's chairman, Popov, claimed that the 'Westernizing' model of Russian reforms had failed and called for the creation of a 'Democratic Alternative for Russia' bloc as a 'constructive opposition' not only to the policy of 'shock therapy' but also to 'the reform model based on Western prescriptions'.[28]

The elections were followed by a new wave of party creation, in which some of the electoral blocs sought to turn themselves into fully fledged parties. Yegor Gaidar tried to convert Russia's Choice into a party uniting all the radical democrats, but with only limited success. The other democratic parties were busy converting their blocs and electoral alliances into more stable party organizations to prepare themselves for the presidential elections, due in 1996, and were unwilling to compromise either their organizational or their ideological independence by allying with what appeared to be a discredited figure. Gaidar's main hopes rested with Democratic Russia as the largest and most experienced of the democratic organizations.

Here too, however, he was rebuffed. A plenary meeting of its Council of Representatives on 19–20 February 1994 revealed the bitterness of the movement's regional organizations, condemning the dominance of the 'communo-democratic *nomenklatura*' in the regions, and criticizing the leaders of Russia's Choice for their incompetence in the elections. They insisted that in the local and regional elections Russia's Choice candidates stood little chance of winning unless they proclaimed their sympathies for a more successful bloc, like the Agrarian Party of Russia (APR). One of Democratic Russia's leaders, Lev Ponomarev, noted that support for the democrats continued to decline throughout Russia. The movement was torn between support for a hypothetical presidential party or for Gaidar's group, and in the event, not surprisingly, voted to retain their political independence and not to join Gaidar's party.[29] As with the transformation of Solidarity into a governing bloc, so too activists condemned Democratic Russia's 'degeneration' from a movement expressing the aspirations of the people into the 'bourgeois' Russia's Choice.[30] Democratic Russia was a classic case of the failure to move from the mobilizational politics of insurgency to representational politics typical of a revolution's consolidation phase, and only at moments of crisis against a clearly defined enemy was it able to find a role for itself.[31]

On 12–13 June 1994 the founding congress of the new 'liberal conservative' party, Democratic Choice of Russia, elected Gaidar its leader, although the Democratic Choice movement continued to exist in parallel alongside the new party, causing considerable confusion. The new party sought to accelerate market-oriented reform by representing the beneficiaries of the reforms: bankers, businesses, the directors of newly privatized enterprises and those regional leaders who had been able to take advantage of the new opportunities.[32] Russia's Choice was the single largest party in the Duma, with 75 deputies in its faction, and had branches in 68 of Russia's federal components. Many of Democratic Russia's activists joined the new party, and in the regions in particular the choice between remaining in Democratic Russia or joining Gaidar's party was a difficult one.[33]

According to Sergei Shakhrai's not unbiased view 'the Beer Lovers' Party has better prospects' than Gaidar's Russia's Choice. According to Shakhrai, only three tendencies had any realistic prospect: the social democrats, as represented by the reformed communists; the conservatives, with groups like his own Party of Russian Unity and Accord (PRES); and the 'liberals in the European sense', Gaidar and his ilk.[34] Yeltsin made it clear that he did not consider Russia's Choice the presidential party, and indeed he now disclaimed any need for such a party, but noted that he would 'rely' on Russia's Choice since it was the one closest to his own views.[35] Thus once again the idea of a presidential party was buried. In the meantime plans to turn Grigorii Yavlinsky's Yabloko into a fully fledged party appeared stalled, the group seeming incapable even of thinking up a proper name for themselves. Attempts to unite the democratic forces behind a single presidential candidate came to nothing, and the attempt was postponed to 1995.[36]

In the centre Arkadii Vol'sky talked of turning his Russian Union of Industrialists and Entrepreneurs into a fully fledged Industrial Party, but hesitated out of fear of creating 'yet another flash-in-the-pan party formed "from the top"'.[37] Nikolai Travkin's Democratic Party of Russia (DPR) faced considerable difficulties in maintaining its earlier momentum, and his attempts to build a genuine organization by establishing a strictly hierarchical structure contrasted with Civic Union's more flexible response.[38] Neither approach appeared to be effective, and by late 1994 the DPR was severely weakened by the desertion of its regional membership, while the Civic Union withered away.

Following the elections the right also began to regroup. The Third Congress of the Russian All-People's Union (ROS) met on 19–20 February 1994 and decided to reconstitute itself as a party. It clearly sought to take advantage of the demise of the National Salvation Front and act as the pre-eminent national-patriotic organization. ROS was indeed the strongest of all the national-patriotic movements, with 139 delegates representing some 40 Russian regions attending the congress, in which such prominent oppositionists as Viktor Alksnis and Yurii Golik (former deputies to the USSR Congress of People's Deputies), Nikolai Pavlov and Iona Andronov (former deputies to the Russian Congress) and the writer Vasilii Belov participated. The putative party, however, was torn by ideological conflicts. Pavlov insisted that the new party should be strongly patriotic, whereas other delegates feared that this might lead to its degeneration into a sectarian nationalist organization. State Duma deputy Vladimir Tikhonov stressed that the party should aim for a broad appeal, and warned that: 'It is important that national self-identity should not develop into nationalism.' Another contentious issue was whether the party should nominate a presidential candidate immediately, a view supported by Pavlov, who argued that Sergei Baburin should be nominated, but the congress left the question open.[39]

At its second congress on 21 May 1994 former vice-president Aleksandr Rutskoi's People's Party of Free Russia changed its name to the Russian Social Democratic People's Party and elected Rutskoi as chairman. The revamped party sought to attract those disaffected by the KPRF's turn towards social democracy, and at the same time Rutskoi urged all patriotic forces to form a united front in opposition to the existing regime, and called for early presidential elections. Rutskoi's primitive view of politics was reflected in his statement: 'If we are talking about an opposition, then it has to be uncompromising. Why not uncompromising? What's the point of an opposition otherwise?'[40] In the absence of a ruling party opposition was bound to take on some unusual features, and in post-communist Russia the opposition was marked by its extremism, ideological incoherence and factionalism.[41] Rutskoi went on to create the Derzhava (Great Power) organization in an attempt to unite the national-patriotic movements.

The KPRF itself had gained in political weight in the elections, ending up with 45 deputies in its faction in the State Duma, but had not done as well as it might have if Vladimir Zhirinovsky's Liberal Democratic Party of Russia (LDPR) had not diverted votes away from it. In the months following the election the KPRF became thoroughly 'parliamentarianized', but certain identity problems remained. While it pledged to support 'workers' collectives', these were divided by industry and profession, and the Communist Party's relationship with enterprise managers was ambivalent. Over 80 per cent of directors implemented with a greater or lesser degree of enthusiasm Gaidar-type policies.[42] The KPRF had some 550,000 members and 20,000 primary organizations, making it by far the largest party, but the absence of a clear-cut ideology and the aged profile of its membership inhibited the mobilization of these resources. The party placed itself firmly in the camp of the constitutional opposition, but its economic programme was populistic, its calls for the reunion of the former Soviet republics smacked of imperialism, while its Eurocommunist-style political programme was as contradictory as that of the original Eurocommunists in the 1970s.[43] While it questions the viability of the smaller Russia to survive, doubts remain over the degree that the party has embraced pluralistic politics. Its nationalist aspirations and its democratic commitments are not yet convincingly integrated.

In an attempt to heal the wounds inflicted by the October events, and to stabilize the political situation, Yeltsin sponsored a Charter for Civic Accord, signed on 28 April 1994 by 148 political, trade union, religious and public figures.[44] The president promised not to launch early parliamentary elections, while the signatories in return promised not to demand them, and a ban on strikes was to be observed. Zhirinovsky signed up, but the opposition was notable by its absence, with the KPRF and the APR refusing to sign, while Yavlinsky did not even attend the ceremony, regarding the whole exercise as pointless, imposing no obligations on anyone.[45] The opposition, meanwhile, had organized its own Accord for Russia, including the KPRF, the APR, Rutskoi, and the former head of the Constitutional Court, Valerii Zor'kin. Both the oppositional Accord for Russia and Civic Accord reflected the traditional pattern of bloc politics and harked back to the inclusive 'popular front' politics of the insurgency phase.

The frantic regrouping of parties in the adaptation phase could not disguise the weakness of the party system. According to one commentator:

Russian politics is increasingly becoming restricted to private, top-level intrigues. One can talk of retrogression: Before, a proto- (or quasi-) multiparty system ensured a semblance of feedback between the authorities and society and guaranteed a certain transparency of political life, but today the rudimentary multiparty structure is drying up.[46]

With their roots in the insurgency phase when success had fallen like a ripe fruit into their hands, reformist parties failed to broaden their appeal from the capital's intelligentsia to the needs of the provinces and ordinary wage earners.

No overall legislation had been adopted in Russia by late 1994 to regulate the sphere of social organizations. The absence of direct instructions in the new constitution concerning the adoption of a law on political parties was seen by the opposition as part of the broader chaos in political relations, inhibiting effective work in the Duma, and as one of the reasons for the disorganization of local elections. The lack of rules concerning the financing of political organizations meant that commercial organizations were given a free hand, and sought to ensure the maximum benefit from their 'investment'. In the absence of structured party politics lobbies formed their own parties, as with the Agrarian Party. At the same time, the executive branch created all sorts of organizations – e.g. the Public Chamber under the Presidency, the Department for Relations with Parties and Social Organizations of the Presidential Administration – ensnaring parties in an administrative nether world. The aim allegedly was clear: to make political parties dependent on the executive authorities and to bring the opposition to heel.[47]

The retrogression can partly be explained by the type of resources available for party formation. In the insurgency phase mobilization took place largely on ideological grounds, whereas during the consolidation of the August regime this shifted to a variety of forms but was marked by the weakness of organized social groups in civil society coming together to seek political representation. For example, Shakhrai's PRES was created largely by drawing on the organizational facilities and resources of his Ministry of Nationality Affairs and Regional Policy. In party formation as elsewhere a process of territorialization of Russian politics was marked, with insiders carving out areas of concern and resources to further their own political ends. The role of prominent personalities, often with access to sources of financial support, is striking in Yanitsky's interviews with leaders of informal movements.[48] The career of Konstantin Borovoi, the founder of Russia's first post-Soviet commodity exchange and of the Party of Economic Freedom, is a case in point.[49]

Regime politics

Party development in Russia reflected in an exaggerated form processes common to most post-communist countries. How can we explain the amorphousness of Russian party development? Is there something specifically post-totalitarian inhibiting the development of an effective party system, or is the problem broader, reflecting a general crisis of party systems in mature industrial democracies? It might be noted that postwar Japan has also been characterized by an extreme form of regime politics, institutionalized until recently in the dominance of the Liberal Democratic Party in the Diet and by innumerable informal links with business and other constituencies. The dissolution of Soviet-style governance, where the party's leading role was institutionalized in the form of party control over the state, has been replaced in Russia by a system where it is unclear who controls the government, let alone who dominates the state, giving rise to much speculation about the dominance of dark forces and the mafia. Regime politics lacked a mechanism for the interaction of parties and the authorities.[50] In the absence of a law on political parties the relationship lacked juridical foundation and encouraged the development of subaltern organizations, like Civic Accord and the Public Chamber, lacking autonomous political weight yet acting as mechanisms for the incorporation of parties into the regime system.

Classical analyses, notably that of Stein Rokkan, attribute the features of emerging party systems to the cleavage lines generated by the great processes of nation and state building: workers and capitalists, church and state, centre and periphery, giving rise to certain categories of parties (socialist, Christian, conservative, liberal and so on), although the correspondence between the cleavage and a particular party may be based on any number of independent variables.[51] In addition, according to Rokkan, there is an extraordinary continuity in the political alignments and party systems in Europe between those of the 1920s and those of the 1960s, suggesting that parties first in the game capture most of the resources available to support a party (voter loyalty, programmes and so on) leaving the system 'frozen' and making it very difficult for new parties to break in, irrespective of the changes that may have transformed society.[52] Rokkan suggested differing processes of political mobilization between the establishment phase of party alignment and the continuity phase, with changes later tending to be channelled through existing parties rather than through the establishment of new ones.

The formative phase of a social formation is crucial, and in Russian party formation, as in so many other spheres, insurgency, consolidation and adaptation politics each left their mark on the shape of the party system. The manner in which the old regime dissolved gave rise to a distinctive establishment phase, while continuity with pre-revolutionary parties is marked but at the same time problematical. The consolidation phase marked the transition from an expanding political community to the restriction of political activism to a relatively small elite in which regional and other forms of cleavage in effect failed to gain autonomous party representation.

The politics of insurgency

The fluid politics associated with the insurgency phase continued into later years. The negative connotations of the concept of 'party' led many groups to call themselves 'unions', 'movements' or 'associations'. As part of this general revulsion against Bolshevik organizational practices, most parties avoided rigorous membership criteria, and allowed both group and individual membership. This led to many peculiar situations in which, for example, individuals in the regions could maintain simultaneously their membership of Democratic Russia and of the DPR, even though the latter at the national level had left the movement in November 1991. Another feature of insurgency politics was the weakness of the link between parties and political representation in legislative bodies. A great mass of deputies had been swept into the soviets as part of the democratic tide of 1990, yet once elected they lacked a structured political identity and as a mass reflected the amorphousness of the party system in its entirety. Above all, the politics of insurgency were marked by the ability of groups and leaders to achieve victories and fame with relatively small organizational, membership and, indeed, financial, resources. Parties were stamped by the formative stage and largely remained elitist organizations with a fairly small mass base and fluid organizational structures.

The dissolution of the CPSU itself had left a great mass of public officials and activists without a home. Some of them joined a new party with which they maintained only tenuous relations. In the great majority of cases, however, they emerged as perhaps the single largest group in Russian politics, formally independent but tied by tradition and sentiment to what is usually called the *nomenklatura* elite. The major legacy of the politics of insurgency, indeed, is the gulf between the elite and the mass membership. While Democratic Russia had established itself as an effective grassroots organization, it failed to become a party, while parties lacked the sort of lower-level activism typical of Democratic Russia.

Patterns of politics

It is not always possible to distinguish between short-term factors arising out of the actual processes of historical change and the more profound elements of a society's political culture and traditions, although the attempt must be made. It is often asserted that Russian political culture is hostile to the emergence of political parties because of a popular commitment to collective values and a predilection for a single authoritative source of political authority.[53] As Stephen Welch has pointed out, however, the traditional counterposing of interests and culture in the debate over political culture is far from adequate. In its place, Welch suggests a more dynamic model stressing the evolutionary dynamics of political culture.[54] In the United States, for example, as Richard Hofstadter demonstrated in his *The Idea of a Party System*, the atmosphere was originally hostile but gradually a party system became accepted.[55]

The state did little to assist the development of parties or a party system, and little came of Yeltsin's promise to provide assistance at a meeting with the leaders of fifteen of the largest parties on 12 December 1991.[56] The government was chosen on a non-party basis, and the emergence of presidential government inhibited the emergence of a party system. Yeltsin declared himself to be above party politics, and on resigning from the CPSU in July 1990 declared that he would join no party. He missed perhaps the best moment to establish a presidential party in the autumn of 1991 when, following the coup, his prestige and support were at their height. At his press conference on 21 August 1992 Yeltsin observed that he was often asked to create a presidential party, but he refused because 'my support is the Russian people'.[57] Yeltsin once again took up the idea of creating a presidential party following the elections of December 1993, but gave no firm indication of how this was to be achieved,[58] and instead Gaidar, as we have seen, sought to fill the vacuum by creating a party that could be called presidential. Yeltsin's understandable desire to be president of all Russians only strengthened the tendency towards charismatic above-party leadership implicit in the regime system in post-communist Russia. Yeltsin clearly felt more at ease working through his own 'command', free of political or social control.

If the presidency did little to encourage the development of a party system, the old Supreme Soviet did even less. While the 'speaker' of the Russian parliament, Ruslan Khasbulatov, stressed the importance of the development of multiparty politics,[59] in practice representation of parliament as a single entity, as a 'party' in and of itself acting as the 'opposition' to presidential government, undermined the development of party politics in parliament. The establishment of electoral blocs for the December 1993 elections allowed numerous small parties, which independently would not have been able to cross the 5 per cent threshold, to gain seats in the new Duma. Travkin noted that electoral pacts undermined the development of a normal parliamentary system.[60] His warnings were only partially justified, and deputies elected on the party list system began to feel, if not the whip, then the pull of party discipline in their activities in the State Duma. Even Zhirinovsky's LDPR, where 40 per cent of the deputies elected under its banner were not even members of the party, remained together as a faction.

The elections played a significant role in parliamentarianizing the nascent party system. Elections make parties, but party affiliation made little difference to the vote in the constituencies. Nearly half the State Duma deputies were elected as independent deputies rather than on the party principle, and this was then reflected in the fluidity of factions in the Duma, although the factional system predominant in the old Supreme Soviet remained strong. The formation of parliamentary committees on the party principle was yet another attempt to kick-start the party system into operation. According to Mikhail Mityukov, the chair of the Presidential Commission on Legislative Proposals and the main author of the regulations governing the work of the new assembly, the rules prevented the emergence of a new Khasbulatov and by focusing on party factions promoted the development of a party system. The chair of the Duma and the two vice-chairs were to belong to different factions, and instead of a Presidium there was a Conference made up of the three chairs and delegates from factions and groups with voting power in proportion to the size of the faction. The Conference's role was to be purely organizational. The rules, moreover, allowed a faction or bloc to recall a deputy and replace him or her with one further down the party list.[61]

The distinction between parties in government and those in

opposition was unclear, and instead a syncretic political process predominated. In establishing Russia's Choice as a party, it was not clear whether it would be of the government or in opposition, including as it did both the foreign minister Andrei Kozyrev and Sergei Filatov, the president's chief of staff. Voters understandably were confused by the 'choice' offered to them, and even more so since the relationship with Democratic Russia was not clear. Yeltsin's advocacy of Civic Accord in early 1994 reaffirmed his commitment to a vision of social harmony in which contestatory parties were to be subordinated to the national interest. The Accord reflected Yeltsin's traditional incomprehension of the operation of a multiparty system and his attempts to incorporate active political forces into a dynamic and mobile form of consensus politics run firmly from the top. Yeltsin's apparent attempt to bring in the KPRF by offering them places in a coalition government was in keeping with the inclusionary tendencies of the regime system.[62]

The totalitarian society

The legacy of the unprecedented concentration of political power and claims to ideological predominance by the CPSU provided an inauspicious terrain for parties to claim a share in power. Postcommunist Russian politics does not operate on a *tabula rasa* but in a context where traditional social institutions and groups try to preserve their position while being challenged by new social actors. The deceptive ease with which the old regime finally fell masked the resilience of the former structures, both formal (e.g. the *nomenklatura* elite) and informal (mafia-type structures). Kulik noted the emergence of a vicious circle in which parties developed but were weak because of the 'post-totalitarian condition of Russia', while society could not be democratically integrated into the state without powerful parties.[63]

Bureaucratic state socialism had undermined the autonomy and scope for reciprocal interaction of groups in society and instead pluralistic politics was limited to interest groups like the military, industry and agriculture competing for scarce resources allocated by the central administrative system. Links were primarily vertical, between a group and the government, rather than horizontal, between groups themselves. In post-communist conditions, however, the weakness of the state encouraged a form of horizontal bargaining, particularly in the economic sphere, that gave rise to a form of mimetic pluralism that stimulated parties and political movements to develop but incorporated them not into full-blown corporatism (the polity was too fluid for that) but into the soft authoritarianism of the regime system.

The current fever of party formation has much in common with Russia's first attempt to establish a multiparty system between 1905 and 1917. The dominance of individuals, the relative lack of influence on government, shifting leadership alliances, poor ties with the mass membership, wild sloganeering and the tendency for abstract ideological demands to take the place of immediate political programmes were all reminiscent of the earlier period.[64] In addition, the upsurge of party formation and hopes for a fundamental constitutionalization of Russian politics between 1904 and 1907 was ultimately constrained by the reconstitution of imperial power;[65] and likewise the insurgency phase of party formation up to 1991 was eventually channelled by the emergence of the regime system. The question of why the Bolsheviks, being only one among many political parties, were able to come to power and establish a one-party system is an ever-present warning of what might come of Russia's contemporary bacchanalia of party formation and mutation.[66] According to a survey ranging from 1917 to 1990, the central feature of Russian party formation has been the absence of a broad social basis and the presence of archaic monolithicity in both tsarist and Bolshevik forms combined with statist forms of industrial development.[67]

Following the elections of December 1993, boycotted by none of the significant parties, a parliament has come into being, called by some the Fifth Duma to stress, for good or ill, its lineage with its four pre-revolutionary counterparts that despite their restricted powers had the potential to become the forum for political dialogue and a genuine legislative body. The majority of parties, moreover, were less doctrinaire than their pre-revolutionary counterparts, and took to parliamentary life with gusto. Even the Communist Party under Zyuganov rapidly became parliamentarized, while LDPR deputies worked effectively in committees. The rump extra-parliamentary opposition was rapidly marginalized.

As in the earlier period, the relationship between party formation and social structure remains obscure. If indeed the formation and development of political parties is 'organically linked with the division of society into classes and with the heterogeneity of these classes ... the way in which classes and separate layers fight for their interests',[68] then what classes can we talk about today? Party formation in contemporary Russia suffers from a two-fold dependence, from the past and from the West, in which the expression of socio-economic and other social interests takes the form of 'pressure politics' within the context of regime politics. Both the interests themselves and their expression are too fluid to be harnessed by relatively inflexible party structures.

While parties in democratic societies are an essential element of civil society, they can in certain circumstances act as the substitute for civil society. According to Vaclav Havel, this was the case in the First Republic (1918–38) in Czechoslovakia.[69] At the same time, the Russian post-socialist experience would suggest that the general debilitation of all social forces was compensated for by the emergence of regime governance. The latter could have been institutionalized in the form of one-party predominance if, instead of taking the presidential path, Yeltsin's insurgency had transformed itself into a single governing party. This outcome was improbable since, unlike Poland and Czechoslovakia, where the powerful insurgency movements, Solidarity and Civic Forum respectively, later splintered to give birth to a 'normal' spectrum of political parties, Russia's insurgency was inchoate and only loosely structured and lacked the civic movement cum political party of the other countries.

One can talk in terms of 'concept parties', those formed in the minds of their leaders or designed to fill a perceived niche in the political spectrum. Lacking stable sources of funding, offices, administrative resources, quite apart from often offering no original socio-political programme, most parties can be seen as little more than electoral clubs or narrow interest organizations unable to generalize and appeal both to universal values and generalized interests. In certain respects, the Civic Union could be described as a concept party, receiving only minimal support in the December 1993 elections and thus called a 'fictitious political force'.[70] The veteran human rights activist Kronid Lyubarsky goes so far as to argue that 'the attempt to conduct "party" elections in an atomized and essentially "non-party" country failed'. Instead of allowing parties to represent the interests of specific social groups, the elections only contributed to the political chaos and allowed full rein to the ambitions of individual leaders, and the resulting parliament in his view did not reflect the real balance of forces in society.[71]

The general crisis of parties

The problem of party formation in Russia reflects the general crisis, or at least the 'unfreezing', of parties in European politics.[72] The shift from materialist to post-materialist preferences in the value system of voters and the apparent decline in the role of parties as such, eclipsed by new forms of participation (such as social movements) and alternative forms of political communication (such as television), have given rise to a new volatility in established party systems. The fluidity, and possibly indeed exhaustion, of existing party political systems has been exacerbated by the demise of the bloc politics associated with the Cold War that provided an artificial environment sustaining continuities that might otherwise have given way to new forms of voter alignment and political participation. In particular, the old cleavage between left and right had long become an unclear compass in the confused modern political terrain, and the idea of the left as a party has certainly come to an end.[73] The age of mass parties appears over, and parties in general appear obsolete as vehicles of popular mobilization, regional and national identity, individual development, and, in the Russian context, even as instruments of power.

The Christian Democratic Party in Italy, having dominated the political scene since 1948, in effect disintegrated, while the Liberal Democratic Party in Japan split and thus lost its accustomed predominance. In America, too, parties are seen as being in a state of possibly terminal decline.[74] The counterview, that parties continue to function as an effective element in democratic systems, translating the preferences of citizens into votes, legislative seats, policies and ultimately laws, is still made, but for only a relatively small number of states.[75]

Party formation in the post-communist democracies is thus taking place at a time of profound changes. In Eastern Europe party formation has followed only slightly less of a tortuous path than in Russia.[76] While the notion of 'redemocratization' is often applied to some of the more westerly parts of the region, in Russia the notion has little resonance. By the same token, the question of continuity in Central Europe in the birth (or rebirth) of new parties has to be treated differently further east. The degree of discontinuity in Russia has been the subject of considerable controversy, and while very few parties (e.g. the Constitutional Democrats) seek to draw their genealogy back to before the revolution, broader continuities (as we have seen) in processes and challenges remain. The range and diversity of Russia's parties, which lasted into the 1920s, should not be underestimated.[77] The Soviet regime itself, however, is another question, and the 74 years of Bolshevik power make this a far more potent source of continuity. The KPRF in its programmatic declaration adopted on 14 February 1993 explicitly claimed to be the continuer party of the old CPSU.[78] In addition the parties and movements associated with the insurgency against the communist regime drew some of their roots from the various so-called 'dissenter' communities, often based on moral imperatives such as truth-telling and non-violence. All these provide the matrix in which new political alignments and parties are developing.

These traditions condition certain sets of choices, but overall there is an open political market in Russia, not monopolized by any single party or category of parties, and bearing little relation to the past. However, the potential market finds very strong 'consumer' resistance to joining parties and political activism. Two sets of reasons can be postulated to explain this resistance. The first looks to the emerging parties, which have been fractious and incompetent in achieving mass appeal; while the second suggests that however effective parties might be, in existing post-communist conditions in Russia there are few takers, explained by such factors as alienation because of the Bolshevik experience, the struggle to survive today, and the charismatic type of politics that has emerged, focused on presidential politics. Only the new generation remains untainted by participation, if only through passive acquiescence, in the politics of the old regime. The very absence of youth in political processes suggests some more universal process leading to the decay in political participation. The communist regime had destroyed not only opposition parties but the very basis on which political affiliation could take place. From a Rokkanian perspective, those cleavages characteristic of the early part of the century, notably those based on class politics, had been superseded. The traditional class structure had been overturned, organizations and associations destroyed, and quasi-political forms of mobilization instituted that tended later to delegitimize political participation in its entirety.

The Rokkanian problematic, however, remains, in that Russia is undergoing a state- and nation-building endeavour that matches any in history, yet the language and processes defining this transition remain indistinct. New cleavages have indeed emerged, based above all on those able and willing to take advantage of the new, more risk-oriented, society and those committed to or dependent on security-oriented policies. The social basis of the August regime is strong where people can take advantage of the new opportunities, such as the industrial north, Moscow and St Petersburg. In this context social democracy has little to offer in the transition, but might well be able to take advantage of the aspirations for security and a degree of social justice of those classes who have survived and benefited from the transition, the new middle and upper working class of capitalist Russia.

In addition, the centre-periphery cleavage in Russia has lost none of its force, but the language of 'national self-determination', for example, has become somewhat compromised. The astonishing fact of post-communist Russian party formation is the weakness of regionally based parties. (By contrast, Catalan aspirations after Franco found a strong and self-sufficient party ready to express them.) Parties based on ethnic politics are wholly delegitimated, while those in favour of new state identities are as yet weak. In Tatarstan, for example, in the forefront of the struggle for autonomy if not yet independence, the leading role is taken not by a party but by a social movement, the Tatarstan Social Centre (TOTs), based, like most nineteenth-century national movements, overwhelmingly on the intelligentsia. The case of Chechnya is a maverick one in all respects and can hardly be fitted into our perspective of party-building. The case does, however, illustrate the importance of understanding the processes underlying the decay of the old regime, above all the clannification of *nomenklatura* politics.

The secular-religious divide also appears in a new light in post-communist conditions, although it should be stressed that in the

West, too, the party alignments derived from this cleavage are waning. In Russia the Orthodox Church had acquiesced in its own subservience to the regime, and this ambiguity tended to undermine its political and moral authority in the post-communist period. Even in Poland where the Catholic Church had been unambiguous in its call for political openness, the advanced secularization of society prevented the emergence of a serious religious-based party in the aftermath of Solidarity.

It might well appear that Christian democracy (and perhaps social democracy, too) has had its day and was a phenomenon of the late nineteenth to the mid twentieth century, inappropriate to the challenges facing the world on the eve of the twenty-first century. A response to modernization, industrialization and the onset of mass society, and a reflection of resistance to the market economy and the secularization and individualization of social life, the apparent triumph of liberalism has left the distinctive features of alternative politics without an anchor. Both Christian and social democracy, for example, were responses to the traumas accompanying the rise of market capitalism, but have found it difficult to sustain alternative policies in mature industrial societies.

In Russia, of course, the capitalist social formation is only now emerging and their critiques are acutely relevant. Their weakness, therefore, is all the more mystifying. Part of the answer lies in the perceived problem of choicelessness of which regime politics was both a cause and a consequence. In the early stages of party formation the monolithicity of the CPSU was reproduced in an inverted form by the emerging oppositional movements, united only in their desire to destroy the communist monopoly. This negative unity was perpetuated after the fall of the regime by a commitment to the broad principle of creating a market system in Russia. Even those movements which evinced a growing suspicion of capitalism were unable to sustain an effective alternative programme. In this limited sense we can argue that post-communist party formation was inhibited by the post-historical period in which it was born, using history in the sense argued by Fukuyama, namely the absence of a universal alternative to liberal capitalist modernity.[79]

In this context no party was able to sustain a genuine and viable democratic alternative to the neo-liberal policies pursued by Gaidar, or to generate indeed a convincing counter-hegemony to 'joining

Western civilization' or 'becoming normal'. As the economic crisis worsened in 1993 and people were alienated by the apparent equation between democracy and poverty, the absence of a genuine constitutional oppositional policy in the form of social Christian or social democratic policies untainted by association with 'imperialists' or 'statists' inflated support for more extremist groups.

The general crisis of parties, however, also has deeper causes. While post-modernism might well be an overused and abused term, it does nevertheless signal problems characteristic of our times. In particular, the fusion of microprocessing technology and communications has accelerated the creation of an information society in which politics has become even more spectral, reduced to the level of images and attractions that bear little relation to the irreducible realities of public life. As Jacques Derrida has noted, the media have rendered the professional politician 'structurally incompetent' by generating a set of demands associated with performance on air and image projection, and at the same time a political space has been formed that displaces parties and parliaments.[80]

Parties are an expression of the attempt to institutionalize the diverse interests of civil society but, given the fracturing of social activism today, there might be reasons to suspect that parties are no longer the predominant political vehicle for this process. The consolidation of democracy appears to be a far broader process than the formation of a multiparty system; parties are only one aspect of the representative structure of complex democratic societies.[81] Thus the formation of a structured party system is inhibited both by the intrinsic weakness of civil society, and by the rise of new forms of representing social interests. The 'American exception' – the absence of clearly, ideologically defined mass parties of the socialist sort – has now become the norm.

Conclusion

The Russian party system is still in its infancy and, despite the tendency to force social processes that is a defining feature of post-communist transitions, there is no reason to believe that what took decades in the West can be accomplished in a matter of years in Russia. The Russian party system is atomized, with every category contended by numerous groups in a constant process of formation and separation. The concept of proto-parties suggested a natural evolution into full-blown parties, whereas most organizations established in the insurgency phase and, to a lesser degree, in the adaptation stage, were pseudo-parties, marginalized by the December 1993 elections and destined to wither away. Contrary to the Rokkanian perspective, the multiparty system in Russia today reflects not profound social cleavage (although there is no shortage of these) but the struggle of a relatively small elite. Zhirinovsky's party, coming from outside the existing political elite, in effect confirmed the resilience of the existing elite system.

The formation of a multiparty system was inhibited by three sets of factors: the political and institutional context, above all the emergence of a presidentialist regime system; the post-totalitarian social structure prone to a lobbying type of politics marked by the weakly structured representation of interests, such as trade unions; and cultural habits, with popular attitudes resistant to the partization of politics and fearing the Weimar syndrome of a new authoritarianism marching through the gates of multiparty democracy.

The amorphousness of political parties in Russia reflects not only the weakness of social interests and the instability of political structures, but also the structural gulf between the state and society. The death of the Soviet system put an end to some of the cruder forms of the antagonism between the state and society, regulated by the ubiquitous security apparatus, but in new forms the divisions continued. The gulf between power and the individual remained, and the failure of Russian political parties to fulfil the traditional role of channelling political communication between the elite and the people was the subjective aspect of a structural problem. This gave rise to a regime politics that undermined the classical approach to the separation of powers. The inability of the new parties to act as intermediaries between state and society created a political vacuum that stimulated the rise of a regime system of government that can be characterized as 'soft authoritarianism', having the potential to evolve either into fully fledged democracy or into full-blown authoritarianism.

The pseudo-party system was both cause and consequence of the regime system, in which political parties were marginal to the operation of governance. While in Japan the regime system focused on one party, the Liberal Democratic Party, in Russia, after domination by the one-party system for so long, another path evolved focusing on supraparty technocratic government. A coalition of political forces emerged, encompassing the presidency, regional and republican leaderships, the 'power' ministries (including the military), privatized enterprises and the governing elite, whose interests were best served by this hybrid system. In the State Duma parties played an important role, but the relative marginalization of parliament meant that the links with government were weak, while the upper house was based not on party but on regional representation. Just as there was no governing party, so too there could be no official opposition. Instead, the government was faced with a vigorous but inchoate opposition both within the legislature and beyond, elements of which it sought to incorporate through pacts and coalitions.

The regime-based coalition, however, probably only represented a phase in Russian politics, and sources of weakness became increasingly apparent. The radical democrats, for example, had earlier supported the 'firm hand' as a way of implementing radical reform, but their own political marginalization following the December 1993 elections led them to favour a more party-based system of government. The threat of presidential elections, moreover, could challenge the whole basis of regime politics. Above all, regime politics was predicated on limited popular political mobilization, undermining the common notion of 'democratization' as extending mass democracy through active citizenship. The formation of political parties appeared to be a way of communicating within the elite and of mobilizing ideological and political resources in an intra-elite struggle, undermining the functionalist approach that suggested that certain tasks have to be performed in any society and that parties are responsible for political communication between leadership groups and the people. In post-communist (and, indeed, 'postmodernist') societies, this communicative function is apparently performed (in so far as it is performed at all) by a range of alternative structures, above all social movements and the media. Thus the functions and the very definition of a political party are brought into question.

However, while the functionalist approach might have come

under attack in Western scholarship and the strains of post-communist transition have tested the very notion of a political party, the case still remains that a structured party system is an essential element in pluralist democracy. It is not inconceivable, however, that it simply might not emerge in Russia, having missed the golden age of party politics in the late nineteenth and early twentieth centuries. The crystallization of a party system inevitably takes a number of years, but there is nothing inevitable about this taking place. There is no guarantee that two or three parties will emerge triumphant to allow the classic alternance between governing and oppositional party. The distinctive conditions of the Cold War perpetuated the age of political parties by a generation or two, but now with the end of the glacial overlay that had frozen political development for so long new forms of political and social interaction have begun to emerge. The question of whether these new patterns are more or less democratic lies beyond the scope of this paper.

Notes

1 This chapter takes further the analysis in Chapter 4 of my *Russian Politics and Society* (London and New York: Routledge, 1993) and a subsequent article 'Parties and the Multiparty System in Russia', *RFE/RL Research Report*, vol. 2, no. 31 (30 July 1993), pp. 7–15.
2 Giovanni Sartori, *Parties and Party Systems: A Framework for Analysis* (Cambridge: Cambridge University Press, 1976) and his *The Theory of Democracy Revisited* (Chatham: Chatham House Publishers, 1987); see also Jean Blondel, *Comparative Government: An Introduction* (Hemel Hempstead: Simon & Schuster, 1990), part II.
3 According to Philippe C. Schmitter:

> Corporatism can be defined as a system of interest representation in which the constituent units are organized into a limited number of singular compulsory, non-competitive, hierarchically ordered and functionally differentiated categories, recognized or licensed (if not created) by the state and granted a deliberate representational monopoly within their respective categories in exchange for observing certain controls on their selection of leaders and articulation of demands and supports.

See Philippe C. Schmitter, 'Still the Century of Corporatism?', in Frederick Pike and Thomas Stritch (eds), *The New Corporatism* (Notre Dame, IN: Notre Dame University Press, 1974), pp. 93–4.

4 See Judith B. Sedaitis and Jim Butterfield (eds), *Perestroika from Below: Social Movements in the Soviet Union* (Boulder, CO: Westview Press, 1991).
5 See Gail Lapidus, 'State and Society: Toward the Emergence of Civil Society in the Soviet Union', in Alexander Dallin and Gail Lapidus (eds), *The Soviet System in Crisis* (Boulder, CO: Westview Press, 1991), pp. 130–47; Victoria Bonnell, 'Voluntary Associations in Gorbachev's Reform Program', also in *The Soviet System in Crisis*, pp. 151–60.
6 Cf. Steven Fish, 'The Emergence of Independent Associations and the Transformation of Russian Political Society', *Journal of Communist Studies*, vol. 7, no. 3 (September 1991), pp. 299–334.
7 A.V. Gromov and O.S. Kuzin, *Neformaly: kto est' kto?* (Moscow: Mysl', 1990), pp. 11–15.
8 For example V.A. Pecheneva (ed.), *Neformaly: kto oni? Kuda zovut?* (Moscow: Izdatel'stvo politicheskoi literatury, 1990).
9 Vladimir Pribylovsky, *Dictionary of Political Parties and Organizations* (Moscow: PostFactum; Washington, DC: Center for Strategic and International Studies, 1992), pp. 28–32.
10 V. Novodvorskaya, *Po tu storonu otchayaniya* (Moscow: Novosti, 1993).
11 The figure comes from V.N. Berezovsky et al., *Rossiya: partii, assotsiatsii, soyuzy, kluby: spravochnik* (Moscow: RAU Press, 1991), vol. 1 (1), p. 3, with a discussion of classification on pp. 5–9.
12 See Michael Waller, 'Political Actors and Political Roles in East-Central Europe', *Journal of Communist Studies*, vol. 9, no. 4 (December 1993), pp. 21–36.
13 L. Gordon and E. Klopov (eds), *Novye sotsial'nye dvizheniya v Rossii* (Moscow: Progress-Kompleks, 1993), p. 25.
14 Cf. Paul Lewis, 'Civil Society and the Development of Political Parties in East-Central Europe', *Journal of Communist Studies*, vol. 9, no. 4 (December 1993), pp. 5–20.
15 Robert Michels, *Political Parties: A Sociological Study of the Oligarchical Tendencies of Modern Democracies* (New York: The Free Press, 1962).
16 Maurice Duverger, *Political Parties: Their Organization and Activity in the Modern State* (London: Methuen, 1954).
17 The best analysis of the post-communist trade union movement is in *Kto est' chto: politicheskaya Moskva, 1993* (Moscow: Catallaxy, 1993), part 5.
18 See V.G. Golovin, 'Ekonomicheskie vzglyady politicheskikh partii i blokov Rossii', in *Partii i partiinye sistemy sovremennoi Evropy* (Moscow: INION, 1994), pp. 142–71.
19 *Izvestiya*, 24 August 1992.
20 On the Civic Union, see Michael McFaul, 'Russian Centrism and Revolutionary Transitions', *Post-Soviet Affairs*, vol. 9, no. 3 (1993), pp. 196–222.
21 B.I. Koval' and V.B. Pavlenko, *Partii i politicheskie bloki v Rossii*, 1st edition (Moscow: NIPEK, 1993), pp. 11–17.
22 ibid., p. 9.

23 Arend Lijphart, *Electoral Systems and Party Systems: A Study of Twenty-Seven Democracies, 1945–1990* (Oxford: Oxford University Press, 1994).
24 'Polozhenie o vyborakh deputatov Gosudarstvennoi Dumy', *Izvestiya*, 24 September 1993, pp. 3–5.
25 *Moskovskie novosti*, no. 25 (20 June 1993), p. A9.
26 *Byulleten' Tsentral'noi izbiratel'noi kommissii*, no. 1 (12), 1994, p. 28.
27 *Konstitutsionnoe soveshchanie*, no. 1 (August 1993), p. 33.
28 *Segodnya*, 1 February 1994, p. 2; *CDSP*, XLVI/5 (1994): 15.
29 *Nezavisimaya gazeta*, 22 February 1994, p. 1.
30 *Nezavisimaya gazeta*, 27 May 1994, p. 2.
31 See Yitzhak M. Brudny, 'The Dynamics of "Democratic Russia", 1990–1993', *Post-Soviet Affairs*, vol. 9, no. 2 (1993), pp. 141–70.
32 Vera Tolz, 'Significance of the New Party Russia's Democratic Choice', *RFE/RL Research Report*, vol. 3, no. 26 (1 July 1994), pp. 25–30.
33 Interview with Lev Ponomarev, '"Demokraticheskaya Rossiya" nikogda ne stanet sotsial-demokraticheskoi partiei', *Russkaya mysl'*, 4046 (5 October 1994), p. 9.
34 *Segodnya*, 31 March 1994, p. 1.
35 *Segodnya*, 5 April 1994, p. 1; 15 June 1994, p. 2.
36 *Kommersant" daily*, 19 August 1994, p. 3.
37 *Segodnya*, 31 March 1994, p. 2.
38 Wendy Slater, 'The Diminishing Center of Russian Parliamentary Politics', *RFE/RL Research Report*, vol. 3, no. 17 (29 April 1994), pp. 13–18.
39 *Nezavisimaya gazeta*, 22 February 1994, pp. 1, 3.
40 BBC *Summary of World Broadcasts* SU/2004 B/1, 25 May 1994.
41 Cf. Nikolai Troitsky, 'Groznaya sila, kotoroi net', *Stolitsa*, no. 22 (132), 1993, pp. 11–13.
42 *Pravda*, 28 December 1993, p. 2.
43 Cf. Wendy Slater, 'The Russian Communist Party Today', *RFE/RL Research Report*, vol. 3, no. 31 (12 August 1994), pp. 1–6.
44 Vera Tolz, 'The Civic Accord: Contributing to Russia's Stability?', *RFE/RL Research Report*, vol. 3, no. 19 (13 May 1994), pp. 1–5.
45 *Izvestiya*, 29 April 1994, p. 1.
46 Maksim Sokolov, *Kommersant"*, 1 April 1994, p. 1.
47 Yurii Dmitriev, 'Politicheskie prava i svobody grazhdan v novoi Konstitutsii Rossii – shag vpered ili nazad?', *Konstitutsionnyi vestnik*, no. 1 (17), 1994, pp. 66–7.
48 O.N. Yanitsky, *Sotsial'nye dvizheniya: 100 interv'yu s liderami* (Moscow: Moskovskii rabochii, 1991), e.g. p. 27.
49 For his own views, see K. Borovoi, *Tsena svobody* (Moscow: Novosti, 1993), in which the very title of his autobiography reinforces the financial aspect.
50 Cf. Z.M. Zotova, *Partii Rossii: ispytanie vyborami* (Moscow, 1994).
51 S.M. Lipset and S. Rokkan, 'Cleavage Structures, Party Systems and Voter Alignments: An Introduction', in S.M. Lipset and S. Rokkan (eds), *Party Systems and Voter Alignments: Cross National Perspectives* (New

York: The Free Press, 1967); see also S. Rokkan, *Citizens, Elections, Parties* (Oslo: Universitetsforlaget, 1970). For an attempt to apply Rokkanian analysis, see Maurizio Cotta, 'Building Party Systems after the Dictatorship: The East European Cases in a Comparative Perspective', in Geoffrey Pridham and Tatu Vanhanen (eds), *Democratization in Eastern Europe* (London and New York: Routledge, 1994).
52 Lipset and Rokkan, *Party Systems and Voter Alignments*, pp. 50–51.
53 For example Nikolai Biryukov and V.M. Sergeev, *Russia's Road to Democracy: Parliament, Communism and Traditional Culture* (Aldershot: Edward Elgar, 1993).
54 Stephen Welch, *The Concept of Political Culture* (Basingstoke: Macmillan, 1993), p. 149.
55 Richard Hofstadter, *The Idea of a Party System: The Rise of Legitimate Opposition in the United States, 1780–1840* (Berkeley: University of California Press, 1970).
56 *Kommersant"*, no. 48 (98), 16 December 1991, p. 23. A few favoured groups supported by Gennadii Burbulis did get premises, but Yeltsin's reneging on this promise for the others was yet another reason for the bitter hostility against him among growing sections of the new political elite.
57 *Nezavisimaya gazeta*, 22 August 1992, p. 1.
58 *Nezavisimaya gazeta*, 23 December 1993, p. 1.
59 Ruslan Khasbulatov, *The Struggle for Russia: Power and Change in the Democratic Revolution*, edited and introduced by Richard Sakwa (London and New York: Routledge, 1993), p. 230 and *passim*.
60 *Izvestiya*, 24 November 1993, p. 4.
61 *Izvestiya*, 24 December 1993, pp. 1–2.
62 *Independent*, 5 October 1994.
63 A. Kulik, 'Posttotalitarnye partii v politicheskom protsesse', *MEMO*, no. 2 (1994), pp. 27–38, at p. 29.
64 Erwin Oberlander, 'The Role of the Political Parties', in K. Katkov et al. (eds), *Russia Enters the Twentieth Century* (London: Temple, Smith, 1971), pp. 60–84.
65 Cf. Terence Emmons, *The Formation of Political Parties and the First National Elections in Russia* (Cambridge, MA: Harvard University Press, 1983).
66 A.I. Zevelev (ed.), *Istoriya politicheskikh partii Rossii* (Moscow: Vysshaya shkola, 1994); N.V. Orlova, *Politicheskie partii Rossii: stranitsy istorii* (Moscow: Yurist, 1994).
67 Igor' Malov and Maksim Khrustalev, 'Mnogopartiinost' v Rossii, 1917–1990', *Problemy vostochnoi Evropy*, no. 31–32 (Washington, DC, 1991), pp. 79–163.
68 Orlova, *Politicheskie partii Rossii*, p. 3.
69 Cited by Jiri Pehe, 'Civil Society at Issue in the Czech Republic', *RFE/RL Research Report*, vol. 3, no. 32 (19 August 1994), p. 16.

70 Vladislav Sukhopol'sky, cited by Kronid Lyubarsky, *Novoe vremya*, no. 7 (1994), p. 8.
71 Kronid Lyubarsky, *Novoe vremya*, no. 7 (1994), p. 12.
72 For example R. Inglehart, 'The Changing Structure of Political Cleavages in Western Societies', in R.J. Dalton et al. (eds), *Electoral Change in Advanced Industrial Democracies: Realignment or Dealignment?* (Princeton, NJ: Princeton University Press, 1984).
73 Cf. Richard Flacks, 'The Party's Over – So What is to Be Done?', *Social Research*, vol. 60, no. 3 (Fall 1993), pp. 445–70.
74 Cf. Martin P. Wattenberg, *The Decline of American Political Parties, 1952–1988* (Cambridge, MA: Harvard University Press, 1990).
75 For example Ian Budge and Hans Keman, *Parties and Democracy: Coalition Formation and Government Functioning in Twenty States* (Oxford: Oxford University Press, 1993).
76 Cf. Gordon Wightman (ed.), *Party Formation in East-Central Europe: Post-Communist Politics in Czechoslovakia, Hungary, Poland and Bulgaria* (Aldershot: Edward Elgar, 1994).
77 One of the best analyses of Russia's first parties is V.V. Shelokhaev (ed.) et al., *Politicheskaya istoriya Rossii v partiyakh i litsakh* (Moscow: Terra, 1993).
78 *Rossiya: politicheskie partii i obshchestvennye ob"edineniya (1991–1993gg.)*, 1st edition (Moscow, 1993), pp. 56–62.
79 Francis Fukuyama, *The End of History and the Last Man* (Harmondsworth: Penguin, 1992).
80 Jacques Derrida, *Spectres of Marx* (London and New York: Routledge, 1994); see also his 'Spectres of Marx', *New Left Review*, no. 205 (May–June 1994), pp. 31–58.
81 Cf. Philippe C. Schmitter, 'Interest Systems and the Consolidation of Democracies', in G. Marks and L. Diamond (eds), *Reexamining Democracy* (London: Sage, 1992), pp. 156–81.

9 The Presidency and Political Leadership in Post-Communist Russia

STEPHEN WHITE

Presidential government in Russia is of recent origin. Mikhail Gorbachev was elected the first (and as it turned out, last) executive head of state of the USSR in March 1990; Boris Yeltsin became the first president of Russia in June 1991. Some of the other republics and even lower levels of government had begun to adopt presidential forms of administration even earlier. At the end of 1991, as Soviet rule came to an end, cartoonists asked: 'In what does the USSR lead the United States?' The answer was 'In the number of its presidents.' The presidency, it was established by this time, was normally an elective office, and was a position of executive authority (neither Gorbachev nor Yeltsin, as the former prime minister Nikolai Ryzhkov remarked, liked the idea of 'reigning like the Queen of England').[1] Indeed in Russia, after December 1993, it was the presidency that defined the character of the political system, as Yeltsin used his ascendancy after the dissolution of parliament to secure the adoption of a constitution that extended his already considerable powers.

A strongly personalist political leadership was of course a long-standing Russian tradition, extended into the Soviet period by the dominance of the general secretary of the Communist Party. Gorbachev, when he became party leader in 1985, was (as he put it) more powerful than any of the other leaders that he confronted on the world stage: the virtually unchallengeable leader of a party that could not itself be challenged through the ballot box, the media or the courts of law.[2] And yet, even in the Soviet period, there were countervailing forces. Leadership, after Stalin, was increasingly collective. The general secretaryship was separated from the position of prime minister after 1964 to avoid an excessive concentration of power in the hands of a single person. The state system itself was strengthened, through the reform of local government and an expanded committee system within the USSR Supreme Soviet. Indeed, effective authority had begun to migrate from party to state, even during the late communist years, as Gorbachev was elected first to the chairmanship of the Supreme Soviet Presidium in 1988, then to a newly established chairmanship of the Supreme Soviet in 1989, and then to the presidency itself in 1990.

Developments in Russia were part of a wider trend towards executive presidencies, not only in the former Soviet republics but throughout the post-communist world. Turkmenia and Georgia were the first to institute presidencies of this kind, in 1990 and 1991 respectively; in 1994, with the adoption of a new constitution and direct popular elections, Belarus became the last to do so. Most of Eastern Europe had moved towards executive presidencies by this time, with Hungary and the Czech Republic the main exceptions.[3] At the same time, the late 1980s had seen the development of a body of scholarship that 'took institutions seriously', and there were many indications, in this literature, that an executive presidency was unlikely to contribute towards the formation of a party system or political stability more generally.[4] Did the Russian experience, by the mid-1990s, bear out these gloomy forecasts? Had a working balance been found between an elected president, the government that he appointed, and a parliament that was also directly elected? And how did the institution of presidential government relate to a society that had rediscovered mass politics but become disillusioned by it within a few short years?

The emergence of presidential government

The creation of the new presidency had been among the radical proposals announced by Gorbachev at the Central Committee plenum in February 1990, at which the party's constitutionally guaranteed 'leading role' had been relinquished. The idea of presidential government, it appears, was under discussion in Gorbachev's immediate circle from late 1987 onwards, as a means of circumventing the central party bureaucracy, who were seen as the main obstacle to reform.[5] The idea of a Soviet presidency, in fact, was a good deal older than this. It had been under discussion at the time of the adoption of the 1936 Constitution, which introduced some other elements of separation of powers (Stalin, however, had opposed it and the idea made no further progress). It had also been considered in 1964 during preparatory work for the constitution eventually adopted in 1977. In 1988, during preparations for the Nineteenth Party Conference, the question of a presidency was once again examined before a decision was made to establish instead a chairmanship of the Supreme Soviet which should normally be held by the party general secretary.[6] The idea of presidential government surfaced once again in 1989, when it was suggested in the press and was formally proposed to the First Congress of People's Deputies – provided the choice was made by direct and competitive elections – by Andrei Sakharov.[7]

Gorbachev, and other members of the leadership, had originally opposed an elective presidency. He justified its introduction at this time as a means of ensuring that swift executive action could be taken in circumstances that required it, particularly where the economy, ethnic relations and public order were concerned.[8] Anatolii Luk'yanov, who presented the proposals to an extraordinary Congress of People's Deputies in March 1990 and then succeeded Gorbachev as chairman of the Supreme Soviet, argued that an institution of this kind would facilitate dialogue among the socio-political movements that had been brought into being by democratization and in turn would strengthen consensus and mutual understanding. The president could act quickly in the event of wars, disasters, social disorders or other extraordinary circumstances, and he could help to resolve the impasse that had developed between the Soviet government and the Congress and Supreme Soviet. Nor was there any reason to fear that the new presidency would lead to a new form of authoritarian rule: there was an 'entire system of safeguards' against this, including limits on age and tenure and the ability of Congress – if a sufficiently large majority decided accordingly – to recall the president and overrule his decisions.[9] As jurist Boris

Lazarev explained in an interview shortly before the vote was taken, laws were being adopted but they were rarely put into practical effect; and there was often a need to take decisions quickly, in a way that even the Presidium had not found possible.[10] In short, it was 'either a presidency, or chaos', as sources 'close to the government' told *Pravda* shortly after the vote had been taken.[11]

Understandably, perhaps, there were misgivings in some quarters that this was (whatever the intentions of those who had proposed the change) a step back towards personal dictatorship. Historian Yurii Afanas'ev, for instance, argued that the proposals were premature: the first step should have been the adoption of a new constitution. Another deputy pointed to the danger that a 'little father' figure would become increasingly popular as their difficulties deepened: what would protect them from a 'tsarist-style socialism' under such circumstances? Many of the republican leaders who spoke were concerned about the possible exercise of presidential power to suspend the operation of their own parliaments; and there was a majority, though not a sufficiently large one, in favour of a formal separation between the presidency and the party leadership.[12] Other speakers, however, accepted the proposals as a means of ending what was described as a 'vacuum of power', and in the end the establishment of the presidency was approved by 1,817 votes to 133, with 61 abstentions.[13] Gorbachev was duly elected to the new post on 15 March, although he received no more than 59 per cent of the votes of all the members of the Congress (or 71 per cent of those who took part) in an uncontested ballot.[14]

Any citizen aged between 35 and 65 could be elected to the presidency of the USSR for a maximum of two five-year terms. The president was normally to be elected by universal, equal and direct suffrage, although in the difficult circumstances that obtained it was agreed that Gorbachev – exceptionally – would be elected by the Congress itself (the 'father of the house', literary scholar Dmitrii Likhachev, carried the day on this point with an impassioned warning that if they did not elect a president without further delay – and he was old enough to have experienced the revolution of 1917 – there was a real danger of civil war).[15] The president, under the terms of the legislation, was to report annually to the Congress of People's Deputies and would brief the Supreme Soviet on the 'most important questions of the USSR's domestic and foreign policy'. He would propose candidates for the premiership and other leading state positions, he had a suspensory veto over legislation, and he could dissolve the government and suspend its directives. He could also declare a state of emergency, and introduce direct presidential rule. The president headed a new Federation Council, consisting of the presidents of the fifteen union republics, with responsibility for inter-republican issues; he also headed a Presidential Council, which was responsible for the 'main directions of the USSR's foreign and domestic policy'.[16]

A further law to 'protect the president's honour and dignity' was adopted in May; and in September 1990 these already impressive powers were extended by parliamentary vote, giving Gorbachev the right to institute emergency measures to 'stabilize the country's socio-political life' for a period of 18 months.[17] Several further changes were made by the Fourth Congress of People's Deputies in December 1990, completing the move to a fully presidential administration. The Council of Ministers was replaced by a more limited 'cabinet', headed by a prime minister who – together with his colleagues – would be nominated by the president and accountable to him. The president meanwhile became head of a new security council with overall responsibility for defence and public order, and he himself appointed its other members. He also appointed a new vice-president, responsible for carrying out the functions that were entrusted to him (Gennadii Yanaev, a member of the party secretariat who had formerly worked in the trade union movement, was elected to this position on 27 December after Gorbachev had intervened on his behalf).[18] The Presidential Council, formed the previous March, disappeared entirely, and a reconstituted Federation Council headed by the president became, in effect, the supreme state decision-making body.[19]

There was some concern among Soviet liberals that these still more extensive powers – greater than Stalin had ever commanded – could open the way to a new period of personal and dictatorial rule. For the reform-minded Inter-regional Group, once again, the proposals represented a 'usurpation of power', leaving too much authority in the hands of a single person. Boris Yeltsin went still further, complaining that the centre was 'seeking to constitutionalize an absolutist and authoritarian regime which could ultimately be used to provide a legal pretext for any high-handed act'.[20] Gorbachev himself drew attention to a cartoon in which he had been shown with a tsar's crown in his hands, trying it on for size.[21] There were, in fact, considerable limitations upon the powers of the new president, extensive though they undoubtedly were. He could be impeached by a two-thirds vote of the Congress of People's Deputies; his ministerial nominations required the approval of the Supreme Soviet, which could force the resignation of the cabinet as a whole if it voted accordingly; and he had himself to report annually to the Congress of People's Deputies upon the exercise of his responsibilities. In any case, as Gorbachev told a gathering of miners in April 1991, he had voluntarily surrendered the extraordinary powers that he possessed as general secretary of the CPSU. Would he have done so if he had been seeking unlimited personal authority?[22]

A Russian presidency

There was, in fact, an attempt to dismiss Gorbachev as president at the Fourth Congress of People's Deputies in December 1990; and his powers had already been undermined by the increasing reluctance of the union republics to accept the decisions of what they came to describe as 'the centre'. The republics were led by Russia, where Yeltsin had been elected parliamentary chairman in May 1990 following elections in which radicals in Democratic Russia had secured more than 20 per cent of the seats available.[23] In March 1991, as the Soviet population was voting in a referendum on the future of a 'renewed federation', voters in Russia were being asked in addition if they would support the institution of a directly elected presidency. At the elections that subsequently took place, in June 1991, Yeltsin was a clear winner on the first ballot, becoming (as Bill Clinton put it) Russia's first elected president in a thousand years. By the end of the year most of the other republics had moved in the same direction, towards a presidential system with an elected chief executive: among them Leonid Kravchuk in Ukraine, Nursultan Nazarbaev in Kazakhstan, and Islam Karimov in Uzbekistan. The Russian presidential elections were accordingly a decisive moment: in shifting legitimacy from the USSR to its republics, from Gorbachev and a still dominant CPSU towards

Yeltsin and the radical democrats who provided his most active supporters, and more generally from parliaments to presidents.

The decision to create the office of Russian president had not originally been controversial.[24] At the First Russian Congress of People's Deputies, in May and June 1990, the proposal had the support of deputies from all of the parliamentary factions. The Communists of Russia group, normally Yeltsin's most implacable opponents, were in favour of the change and themselves proposed amending the constitution in this sense. However, once Yeltsin had become parliamentary chairman and (in July 1990) resigned from the CPSU, the issue of the presidency became more partisan and the question of who might fill the position a bitterly contested one. At the Second Russian Congress, in December 1990, all that was agreed was that the Supreme Soviet and its constitutional committee should consider appropriate amendments to the Russian constitution.[25] As a constitutional amendment would require a two-thirds majority in the Congress, Yeltsin's hardline opponents seemed well placed to resist any change that would be to their disadvantage. The decision to call a referendum on the future of the USSR, however, altered the position once again. On 25 January 1991 the Presidium of the Russian Supreme Soviet proposed an additional question on the establishment of a directly elected presidency; its proposal was approved by the Supreme Soviet on 7 February; and then Russia's voters were asked to express their views. On a 75.1 per cent turnout a resounding 69.9 per cent approved the change.[26]

The Congress of People's Deputies had originally been called by deputies anxious to condemn the Russian president. The outcome of the referendum, and the open expression of public support throughout the republic, influenced the Congress in a different direction and on 5 April it was resolved that a presidential election would be held on 12 June 1991. The Supreme Soviet was asked to prepare a law on the presidency as well as any amendments that might be necessary to the Russian constitution; the Russian government, in the meantime, would exercise full law-making powers.[27] The changes concerned were duly approved by the Russian Supreme Soviet on 24 April and by the Fourth Congress of People's Deputies on 22 May. It was agreed that candidates for the Russian presidency must be citizens aged between 35 and 65, and that they could hold the office for no more than two five-year terms.

Nominations could be made by political parties, trade unions and public organizations, or by other groupings that were able to collect 100,000 signatures in their support. The president, for his part, could not be a deputy or a member of a political party; he enjoyed the right of legislative initiative, reported to the Congress once a year, and appointed the Russian premier with the consent of the Supreme Soviet.[28] Yeltsin's own standing was strengthened further when he headed the resistance to the attempted coup of August 1991 in the name of the Russian parliament (Gorbachev, meanwhile, lost his extraordinary powers), and in the discussions that took place later in the year to negotiate a looser association of sovereign republics it was the Russian president who was clearly the dominant figure.

Yeltsin owed much of his dominance to the fact that he had been directly elected, unlike Gorbachev, who had been chosen by Soviet parliamentarians. At the same time Yeltsin had to govern through a Congress of People's Deputies that had also been chosen by a popular vote, and which was able to claim the same right to represent the will of the electorate. The Congress had initially been supportive, electing Yeltsin as chairman, approving a declaration of Russian sovereignty in June 1991, and then granting him emergency powers the following November. Yeltsin, however, used his position to launch a programme of radical economic reform under the guidance of Yegor Gaidar, who was acting prime minister from June 1991; and parliamentary resistance strengthened as the consequences of those reforms became clearer. Gaidar was forced to stand down at the Seventh Congress in December 1992. At the Eighth Congress, in March 1993, the president was stripped of his emergency powers and ordered to act in accordance with the constitution, in terms of which the Congress was itself the 'supreme body of state power' and the president merely the 'chief official'.[29] Yeltsin's supporters had already talked of 'emergency measures', and on 20 March the president called publicly for a 'special form of administration' under which the Congress would continue to meet but would be unable to challenge his decrees. The Congress, hurriedly convened for an emergency session, voted to impeach the president but not by the necessary two-thirds majority; the outcome was an agreement that a referendum, originally agreed the previous December, would be held on 25 April 1993 to decide 'who rules Russia'.[30]

The referendum, in the event, did little to resolve a continuing impasse. Voters were asked if they 'had confidence' in Yeltsin as Russian president, and if they approved the policies that president and government had been conducting; they were also asked if they favoured early presidential or parliamentary elections. The turnout was a respectable 64.6 per cent. Of those who voted, 58.7 per cent supported the president and 53.1 per cent approved his policies; 49.5 per cent favoured early presidential elections, and a much more substantial 67.2 per cent early parliamentary elections, but in both cases this fell short of the majority of the electorate that was necessary for constitutional changes.[31] For Yeltsin and his supporters this was a verdict that justified pressing ahead with a constitution that provided for a 'presidential republic' with a much more limited legislature, and by the end of the year they had attained their objective. Only a strong executive, Yeltsin told the Congress, could preserve the integrity of Russia and with it the continuation of reform.[32] The Congress, he complained in December 1992, tended 'just to reject, just to destroy'. Too many deputies engaged in 'cheap populism and open demagoguery ... and in the final analysis, the restoration of a totalitarian Soviet-Communist system'.[33]

For parliamentarians and their speaker, Ruslan Khasbulatov, the issue was a rather different one: whether government should be accountable to elected representatives, and whether a broadly representative parliament should be allowed to act as a counterbalance to what would otherwise be an overwhelmingly powerful executive. For Khasbulatov, Russian history and then Marxism-Leninism had combined to exaggerate the power of a single 'tsar'. It was essential, in these circumstances, to establish a secure division of powers and then to develop the role of parliament as a 'representative organ' of the whole society. Parliament, in particular, could serve as a 'counterweight' to the executive, exercising its influence over public spending, legislation and the composition of government as parliaments did in other countries.[34] Opening the Russian parliament in March 1992, Khasbulatov accused the government of an 'attack on democracy' and complained that individual ministers had a dismissive attitude towards representative institutions in general.[35] He also insisted, in the confrontation between parliament and presidency, that government should be accountable to the Congress and Supreme Soviet rather than to the 'collective Rasputin' that surrounded the president.[36] And he argued more generally that a presidential republic was not appropriate for the particular circumstances of post-communist Russia, with its need to maximize consensus and public understanding.[37] These differences, in the end, were resolved by force, when parliament was dissolved by presidential decree on 21 September 1993 and then seized by the Russian army on 4 October following an attempt by parliamentary supporters to occupy the Kremlin and establish their own authority.

Yeltsin had produced his own draft of a new constitution in April 1993, on the eve of the referendum, and a constitutional conference which met in June and July with a number of Supreme Soviet deputies in attendance produced another version that was in Yeltsin's view 'neither presidential nor parliamentary'. Yeltsin had, however, predicted a 'decisive battle' between the supporters and opponents of his programme of reforms, and in the different circumstances that obtained after the suppression of what he regarded as a parliamentary insurrection it was a rather more authoritarian draft that was published in November 1993 and approved at a referendum the following month (see Figure 9.1).

There was, in fact, some doubt as to whether the constitution had been adopted constitutionally: the law on the referendum required a majority of the electorate, not just of voters, to indicate their support, and there was some evidence that the turnout had fallen below 50 per cent, which was the level that Yeltsin had specified in his decree.[38] It was difficult, however, to alter any of the provisions of the document that had now become Russia's first post-communist constitution, and it appeared to have shifted Russian politics decisively towards a system based upon strong executive authority or a 'super-presidential republic', as an *Izvestiya* journalist described it.[39]

Publics, parliaments and presidents

The powers of a Russian president are in part those of his office. But leadership, in all systems, is also a function of popular support for the president as an individual, and for the presidency more generally as an institution: particularly when the presidency is a

Under the December 1993 Constitution, the President of the Russian Federation is:

head of state (Art. 80:1);

the guarantor of the constitution (Art. 80:2), to which he swears an oath (Art. 82:1);

he 'defines the basic directions of the domestic and foreign policy of the state' (Art. 80:3) and represents the Russian Federation domestically and internationally (Art. 80:4);

he is elected for four years by direct, equal and secret ballot (Art. 81:1);

he must be at least 35 years old, and have lived in the Russian Federation for at least ten years (Art. 81:2), and may not be elected for more than two consecutive terms (Art. 81:3);

he 'appoints with the agreement of the State Duma the chairman of the Government of the Russian Federation', has the right to preside at government meetings and 'takes decisions on the resignation of the Government of the Russian Federation'; he nominates candidates for the chairmanship of the State Bank; on the recommendation of the prime minister, he appoints and dismisses deputy premiers and federal ministers; he nominates candidates for the Constitutional Court, the Supreme Court and the Procuracy General; he forms and heads the Security Council, appoints and dismisses his plenipotentiary representatives in the regions as well as the high command of the armed forces and diplomatic representatives in foreign states and international organizations (Art. 83); additionally, he calls elections to the State Duma, dissolves the Duma in appropriate circumstances, calls referenda, initiates legislation, and reports annually to the Federal Assembly on 'the situation in the country' and the 'main directions of the domestic and foreign policy of the state' (Art. 84);

he is Commander in Chief and can declare a state of war (Art. 87) as well as a state of emergency (Art. 88); he declares amnesties (Art. 89) and issues decrees that have the force of law throughout the territory of the Federation (Art. 90).

Figure 9.1   The Russian Presidency, December 1993

Source: Based upon *Konstitutsiya Rossiiskoi Federatsii. Prinyata vsenarodnym golosovaniem 12 dekabrya 1993 g.* (Moscow: Yuridicheskaya literatura, 1993).

directly elected one. The picture that emerged in the early post-communist years, in these respects, was a rather mixed one. Yeltsin, certainly, had a greater popular following than Gorbachev, even before the Soviet presidency had been overtaken by events. In 1989 it was the future Soviet president who was named 'man of the year', and by a wide margin (Sakharov came second, and Ryzhkov third);

by 1990 Yeltsin, with 32 per cent support among those surveyed, had moved ahead of Gorbachev, with 19 per cent. In early 1991 Yeltsin stood first in terms of popularity among all Russian leaders of the twentieth century, ahead of Lenin, Gorbachev and (by a wide margin) Nicholas II.[40] Yeltsin, in more qualitative terms, was seen as 'open and straightforward' (34 per cent), 'ambitious' (26 per cent) but also 'resolute' (24 per cent). Gorbachev, by contrast, was 'hypocritical' (28 per cent), 'weak and lacking in self-confidence' (20 per cent) and 'indifferent to human suffering' (19 per cent), although he was also 'flexible and capable of adapting to change' (18 per cent); just 7 per cent saw him as 'decisive'.[41]

In virtually all surveys from the time he was elected as Russian president, moreover, Yeltsin was first among the candidates in a hypothetical presidential contest. In early 1992 he was able to command 32 per cent support, as compared to Gorbachev with 4 per cent and all other candidates with 15 per cent; a substantial proportion, admittedly, did not intend to vote (16 per cent) or had not decided (32 per cent).[42] By the summer of 1993 Yeltsin was able to command 21 per cent of the vote if a presidential election were held; Gorbachev was down to 2 per cent, with Vice-President Rutskoi the only serious challenger on 16 per cent; again, 18 per cent intended not to vote and 35 per cent were uncertain of their loyalties.[43] By the summer of 1994 Yeltsin's support was down again, with just 11 per cent intending to support him in a presidential contest; but he was still in first place, ahead of the economist Grigorii Yavlinsky, Rutskoi and Vladimir Zhirinovsky, with a still more substantial 19 per cent intending not to vote and 38 per cent unsure.[44] Another poll, in June 1994, gave Yeltsin a more impressive 17.1 per cent, followed once again by Yavlinsky, Rutskoi and Zhirinovsky; once again, however, a greater proportion were undecided, and 40.5 per cent of those who were asked took a negative view of the Russian president, with only 20 per cent favourably disposed.[45]

So far as the political system in general was concerned, there was more support for a presidential republic (42.6 per cent) than for a parliamentary one (32.1 per cent).[46] And, in the case of a conflict, there was substantial support for the right of the president, if he thought it necessary, to dissolve the legislature. More than half (51 per cent agreed, in the summer of 1993, that the president should be 'able to suspend the Supreme Soviet and rule by decree if he thinks this necessary', with a third (34 per cent) taking the opposite view. At the same time a similar proportion agreed that the Supreme Soviet should 'have the power to stop the president taking actions that it objects to', and there was a still stronger preference for a government of experts rather than politicians (78 per cent agreed, 18 per cent disagreed), with a similar proportion favouring a role for the Supreme Court in resolving any dispute.[47] Later surveys produced a broadly similar result, with the president more widely supported than parliament (25 per cent as against 15 per cent), but with 38 per cent suggesting they should be equal in powers: a vote, in effect, for gridlock.[48] In another survey in the summer of 1994 a third thought the president should be supreme; 17 per cent thought it should be parliament, and 13 per cent the government, but still larger numbers (37 per cent) had no idea. Supporters of Russia's Choice were clearest in their support for the primacy of presidential power (62 per cent), with Communist Party supporters the firmest in their commitment to parliamentary government.[49]

In the conflict that developed in late 1993 there was more support for the president (41.2 per cent) than for his parliamentary opponents (18.6 per cent), with 28.8 per cent disinclined to support either side. Yeltsin's unconstitutional decision to dissolve parliament was approved by a majority (52.7 per cent), with 33.6 per cent taking the opposite view. And yet there were misgivings, if the polls were any indication. A modest 13.6 per cent thought the storming of parliament had been necessary; a much more substantial 43.6 per cent thought it could have been avoided; and for more than a third (36.9 per cent) the storming of parliament was unacceptable in any circumstances. Interviewed a month later, 25.4 per cent thought the parliamentary leadership had been mostly to blame for the tragic resolution of the crisis on 3–4 October, when more than a hundred people had died. Yeltsin was held responsible by 20.3 per cent; the largest proportion, however (46.9 per cent), blamed 'both sides in equal measure'. And asked if the president's actions had led to civil war or averted it, the jury was divided: 31.2 per cent thought Yeltsin had saved the nation from a fratricidal struggle but nearly as many (28.9 per cent) thought his actions had contributed towards such an outcome.[50]

There were nonetheless low levels of support for all political

Table 9.1 Trust in institutions, 1993–5 (percentages)

	June 1993	July 1994	February 1995
Trust zone			
Orthodox Church	48	46	47
Mass media	26	20	21
Armed forces	39	37	24
Distrust zone			
Security services	20	21	13
Local government	13	11	13
Regional government	10	8	13
Courts, police	16	14	9
Parliament	9	5	4
Government	18	7	6
Collapse			
President	28	16	8
Trade unions	13	8	8

Source: Adapted from *Ekonomicheskie i sotsial'nye peremeny: monitoring obshchestvennogo mneniya*, no. 2 (1995), p. 15 (based upon representative Russia-wide samples).

institutions, including the presidency and Yeltsin personally, and they declined steadily as the 1990s advanced (see Table 9.1). By late 1994, according to one survey, only 11 per cent of a large and representative Russia-wide sample trusted the new Russian parliament, and only 12 per cent trusted the government; Yeltsin's support was little better, at 19 per cent. Moreover, the president had many more convinced opponents (13.4 per cent) than he had active supporters (1.4 per cent).[51] In another survey in the summer of 1994, Yeltsin was trusted by 17 per cent of those who were asked but distrusted by a much more substantial 68 per cent, with the young as suspicious as the old.[52] This was symptomatic of a much more general cynicism towards politicians, and the parties in which they were organized. In the same study only 7 per cent were willing to trust the political parties, with 81 per cent distrustful: these were the lowest levels of trust that were reported in the survey, although all of the institutions that were mentioned (apart from the Church) had, on balance, a negative image.[53] And were politicians, as a

216 *Stephen White*

group, honest? Only 3 per cent answered affirmatively; 45 per cent thought there were very few of this kind, and 34 per cent thought there were none at all.[54]

Nor was there a great deal of confidence that the presidency, or any of the parties or their leaders, would be able to take Russia out of its crisis. Who, for a start, was responsible for the crisis? For a small minority, in the summer of 1994, it was 'Jews' (5 per cent) or 'foreign governments' (10 per cent). For much larger proportions it was the disintegration of the USSR (47 per cent) or 'the mafia' (46 per cent); but similar numbers blamed the Russian government (43 per cent) or the president himself (40 per cent).[55] So far as taking Russia out of its crisis, for the largest group (15 per cent) only the army or military structures could do so; for a further 12 per cent it was their local or regional authority; and then came the president and government, with 10 per cent and 7 per cent support respectively. The Federal Assembly, and politicians generally, each obtained 4 per cent support, with the largest group of all (32 per cent) unable to provide a positive response.[56] Other, somewhat earlier, polls found a higher level of confidence in the president (28.1 per cent); but 21 per cent were unsure, and the largest group of all (33.3 per cent) saw no political or social force that could take Russia out of what was already a protracted crisis.[57]

While Yeltsin was clearly the most popular choice in any future presidential contest, his supporters were a small and declining proportion of the electorate. In September 1994, for instance, just 14 per cent were Yeltsin enthusiasts; much larger proportions were unwilling to reveal their voting intentions (25 per cent) or had decided not to participate in any elections of this kind (27 per cent).[58] Yeltsin's support, moreover, was steadily diminishing (see Table 9.2).

In June 1991, at the time of his election, about 71 per cent were Yeltsin supporters with 29 per cent 'completely in agreement with [his] views and positions'. By November 1993 he had more opponents (47 per cent) than supporters (42 per cent), with only 7 per cent in complete agreement and a larger proportion (9 per cent) prepared to 'support anybody provided it's not Yeltsin'.[59] By April 1994 only 8 per cent were prepared to support the Russian president, but 30 per cent were in disagreement with some of his actions and 41 per cent thought he should resign.[60] A majority thought

The Presidency and Political Leadership 217

Table 9.2 Yeltsin's support, 1993–5 (percentages)

	July 1993	Feb. 1994	June 1994	Feb. 1995
Complete confidence	28	20	16	8
Partial confidence	32	34	34	31
No confidence	24	26	35	48

Source: *Ekonomicheskie i sotsial'nye peremeny: monitoring obshchestvennogo mneniya*, no. 2 (1995), p. 12.

Yeltsin should not stand again in a presidential contest; if he did stand in an early contest a majority would not support him.[61] As for the elections themselves, few (19 per cent) thought they should be postponed; many more (37 per cent) wished to observe the legal requirement that they take place in 1996, and 25 per cent thought the current administration should be 're-elected as soon as possible'.[62]

What, in fact, were the ideal characteristics of a Russian president? According to the surveys that were conducted in the summer of 1993, he or she should above all be highly educated (75 per cent). Next in importance was decisiveness (59 per cent), and then nationality (the same proportion thought any new president should be a Russian). Other requirements were that a new president should not have emerged from the communist *nomenklatura* (49 per cent), and that he should be a man (a requirement for 42 per cent, although 41 per cent thought a woman was equally acceptable). It was less important that the president should believe in God (for 75 per cent it had no significance, with 18 per cent in disagreement), or that the president be young (24 per cent were in favour with 18 per cent against), or that the president should have no prior association with the Communist Party (important for 29 per cent, but not for 38 per cent of those who were asked). For a substantial proportion (43 per cent) a future president should be beyond reproach in his personal life and 'without bad habits'; but 45 per cent were prepared to accept a president with the 'usual human weaknesses'.[63] Other studies confirmed that decisiveness was of the first importance (44.2 per cent), but added a 'concern to look after the interests of ordinary people' (40.6 per cent), a 'clear programme of activity' (39 per cent), and a willingness to 'observe the law' (36.3 per cent).[64]

The perils of Russian presidentialism

The experience of Russian presidentialism in its early years suggested a number of points that were general to presidential systems, but also a number of features that were distinctively Russian.

(1) All presidential systems depend heavily upon the person of the president. The Russian system did so more than many others, and in terms not simply of the president's policy choices but also of his physical health and personality. Yeltsin himself told interviewers that he relied more than anything else upon his intuition.[65] A close analysis of his speeches by three academics found that the Russian president was 'predictable only in one respect – his unpredictability'.[66] What impression did he make upon ordinary Russians? For the largest proportion, according to survey evidence, the Russian president was – once again – 'unpredictable' (28 per cent). For a further 26 per cent it depended entirely upon the people that surrounded him; another 19 per cent found it difficult to reply.[67] The president's occasional absences introduced a further element of uncertainty; so did reports of his periodic visits to hospital, even if it was for the relatively minor complaint of radiculitis.[68] There was some support for the idea that the president, as elsewhere, should be required to undergo a regular medical examination.[69] The 1993 Constitution added to these concerns by abolishing the position of vice-president; in the event of presidential ill-health, his functions would be performed by the prime minister until new elections had taken place (Art. 92 [3]).

Concerns about the presidential role were not allayed by repeated reports of alcoholism. President Yeltsin himself admitted, in an interview in 1993, that he 'sometimes' allowed himself a glass 'or maybe two' of cognac on a Sunday evening with his family, or some beer after visiting the bathhouse.[70] His parliamentary critics were more outspoken. 'It's time to stop the public drunkenness of our president,' a Communist deputy demanded after an unsteady performance during Yeltsin's first visit to the United States. 'When he's shown on television, he can't stand up without support.'[71] There was further criticism in early 1993 when the president, defending himself against impeachment, spoke uncertainly before the Russian parliament and had to be assisted from the hall (deputies agreed he had 'created a strange impression'), and later in the year when Russian troops withdrawing from Germany were treated to a 'stirring rendition of "Kalinka"' under the impromptu conductorship of the president.[72] A number of advisers who expressed their concern at his performance while in Germany were simply left at home during President Yeltsin's next foreign trip, which concluded with his controversial non-appearance at Shannon airport to take part in discussions with the Irish prime minister.[73]

(2) The complex and unsatisfactory relationship between president and parliament was a much more general feature of presidential systems. The December constitution had been intended to resolve any tensions of this kind in favour of the president. It certainly endowed him with extensive powers to nominate the prime minister and members of the government, to dissolve the Duma if it repeatedly refused to endorse his choices, and to issue his own decrees with the force of law. But there was no guarantee that the presidential administration would reflect majority opinion in the Federal Assembly, or that its decisions would find favour with the deputies of either house. The Duma, for its part, could adopt decisions entirely at odds with presidential policies, as it did in February 1994 when the conspirators of August 1991 and the parliamentary leaders of September–October 1993 were amnestied. The Duma could also hold a vote of no confidence in the government, as it did (but not with a sufficiently large majority to force its removal) in October 1994. Under the provisions of Article 117 this led either to the dismissal of the government by the president, or to the dissolution of the Duma itself. But there was, again, no guarantee that future elections would resolve the crisis, and no reason for the president to accept their outcome; and there could in any case be no dissolution of the Duma on this basis within the first year of its election (Art. 109[3]).

One of the ways in which presidents and parliaments were associated in other nations was through the party system. And this, again, was a weakness in the post-communist system. President Yeltsin had left the CPSU in July 1990 at the 28th Congress; later he took the view that, as an elected Russian president, he should remain independent of party affiliation. In the December 1993 elections Yeltsin again stood above the contest, as did Prime Minister Chernomyrdin. The electorate as a whole made their intentions clear by staying at home (the turnout was just 54.8 per cent), by voting for independents (the largest group in both houses), or by voting against all of the candidates on the paper (a record 17 per cent; in addition 7 per cent of the vote was declared invalid).[74] Parties themselves remained notoriously weak, with limited memberships, a constant tendency to divide, and a focus on leadership intrigue; just 3 per cent of adults were members of any of the parties, movements or political organizations that had come into being by 1994.[75] In these circumstances, the best way to influence public policy was not to secure a popular following but to become a presidential adviser, and if possible a member of one of the bodies by which he was surrounded, particularly the security council. It was notable, for instance, that the collapse of the rouble on 'black Tuesday' (11 October 1994) was first considered not by government itself but by the security council.

(3) Government itself was left in a difficult situation by the presidential system. The prime minister, wholly dependent upon the president's favour, could find his position usurped by other members of the presidential entourage, or by his own deputy (as when First Deputy Premier Oleg Soskovets, not Chernomyrdin, accompanied Yeltsin on his October 1994 visit to the USA and then negotiated on his behalf with the Irish government during their controversial stop-over). Presidential nominations, in their turn, required parliamentary approval, but this was not likely to be forthcoming so long as president and parliament represented different political philosophies. As a result, ministers and even prime ministers could spend a considerable time in an 'acting' capacity, nominated by the president (like Gaidar in June 1992) but not yet approved by the parliament. (Gaidar, in the end, withdrew his own candidature after failing to secure parliamentary backing in December.) There was no new finance minister, similarly, after the resignation of Boris Fedorov in January 1994, and the minister dismissed after 'black Tuesday', Sergei Dubinin, was simply acting in that capacity and not yet formally appointed. Matters were more difficult still with the chairmanship of the State Bank, nominated by the president but approved or dismissed by the Duma (it was clear that Viktor Gerashchenko, who resigned in late October 1994, would be difficult to replace with a candidate acceptable to president as well as to parliament).

The Soviet system had maintained an effective form of government by monopolizing political power in the hands of the Communist Party and, within the party, by concentrating authority in the hands of the leadership. The partly reformed system that existed after 1988 was an uneasy combination of party direction 'from above' and electoral control 'from below', a tension that was eventually resolved in favour of the voters. The post-communist system, however, introduced a new source of tension with the separate election of an executive president and a working parliament. The tension between the two led to a governmental impasse throughout 1992 and 1993; but the constitution that was introduced in December 1993 provided no long-term solution. There were suggestions that, for instance, the president should be chosen by a representative assembly, not directly by the people;[76] equally, it was widely argued that president and parliament should be elected on the same date so as to increase the chances that they would reflect a related choice of political alternatives and then provide a coherent programme of government for the future. It was more likely that a workable system would require a move to quasi-presidentialism: towards a system more like the French, in which the president enjoyed a popular mandate but the government required a parliamentary majority. The Russian tradition was strong in its attention to centralized direction; its future was likely to depend upon the extent to which it could incorporate other, more Western traditions of accountability and popular consent.

Notes

1 M.F. Nenashev, *Poslednee pravitel'stvo SSSR* (Moscow: Krom, 1993), p. 26.
2 *Izvestiya*, 6 April 1991, p. 1.
3 See for instance Ray Taras, 'Leaderships and Executives', in Stephen White, Judy Batt and Paul G. Lewis (eds), *Developments in East European Politics* (Durham, NC: Duke University Press, 1993), chapter 10. See also James McGregor, 'The Presidency in Eastern Europe', *RFE/RL Research Report*, vol. 3, no. 2 (14 January 1994), pp. 23–31.
4 For a representative selection of views, see for instance Arend Lijphart (ed.), *Parliamentary versus Presidential Government* (Oxford: Oxford University Press, 1992); Fred W. Riggs, 'Presidentialism in Comparative

Perspective', in Mattei Dogan and Ali Kazancigil (eds), *Comparing Nations* (Oxford: Blackwell, 1994); Giovanni Sartori, *Comparative Constitutional Engineering* (London: Macmillan, 1994), part 2; and Juan J. Linz and Arturo Valenzuela (eds), *The Failure of Presidential Democracy: Comparative Perspectives* (Baltimore: Johns Hopkins University Press, 1994), particularly the chapters by Linz (which is the origin of the contemporary discussion) and Stepan and Skach.
5 Fedor Burlatsky as quoted in Dusko Doder and Louise Branson, *Gorbachev: Heretic in the Kremlin* (New York: Viking, 1990), pp. 279–80. Burlatsky is also identified as the originator of the idea of presidential government by Boris Kurashvili in *Strana na rasput'e* (Moscow: Yuridicheskaya literatura, 1990), p. 105. On political change more generally during the late Soviet and early post-communist periods see Stephen White, *After Gorbachev*, revised 4th edition (Cambridge: Cambridge University Press, 1994), chapters 2 and 8; and White, Graeme Gill and Darrell Slider, *The Politics of Transition: Shaping a Post-Soviet Future* (Cambridge: Cambridge University Press, 1993), chapter 4.
6 *Sovetskoe gosudarstvo i pravo*, no. 7 (1990), pp. 3–4.
7 A.A. Protashchik (ed.), *Cherez ternii* (Moscow: Progress, 1990), p. 702; A.D. Sakharov, *Trevoga i nadezhda* (Moscow: Interverso, 1990), pp. 272, 274. Proposals for a 'firm hand' at the top in any transition from totalitarian to democratic rule had a similar logic: see for instance A. Migranyan in *Novyi mir*, no. 7 (1990), pp. 166–84, and Migranyan and I. Klyamkin in *Literaturnaya gazeta*, 16 August 1989, p. 10.
8 *Materialy plenuma Tsentral'nogo komiteta KPSS 5–7 fevralya 1990 g.* (Moscow: Politizdat, 1990), p. 19. For the earlier objections of Gorbachev, Ligachev, Medvedev and Vorotnikov see Protashchik (ed.), *Cherez ternii*, pp. 702–3.
9 *Vneocherednoi tretii s"ezd narodnykh deputatov SSSR 12–15 marta 1990 g. Stenograficheskii otchet*, 3 vols (Moscow: Izvestiya, 1990), vol. 1, pp. 17–18.
10 *Pravda*, 10 March 1990, p. 2.
11 *Pravda*, 1 April 1990, p. 2.
12 *Vneocherednoi tretii s"ezd*, vol. 1, pp. 45–6 (Afanas'ev), p. 126 (N.T. Dabizha), pp. 58–61 (Gumbaridze, one of those who advanced republican arguments), and pp. 395–6 (vote).
13 ibid., p. 193.
14 ibid., vol. 3, p. 55.
15 ibid., vol. 2, pp. 385–6.
16 For the text of the law see *Vedomosti S"ezda narodnykh deputatov SSSR i Verkhovnogo Soveta SSSR*, no. 12 (1990), item 189.
17 ibid., no. 22, item 487; and no. 40, item 802.
18 ibid., no. 1 (1991), art. 18. The position of vice-president disappeared later in the year: ibid., no. 37, item 1082.
19 For the text of the constitutional changes see ibid., no. 1, item 3.
20 *Pravda*, 16 December 1990, p. 2.

The Presidency and Political Leadership 223

21 *Pravda*, 1 December 1990, p. 4.
22 *Izvestiya*, 6 April 1991, p. 1.
23 *Pravda*, 26 March 1990, p. 2 (Vorotnikov's estimate).
24 On these developments see Michael E. Urban, 'Boris El'tsin, Democratic Russia and the Campaign for the Russian Presidency', *Soviet Studies*, vol. 44, no. 2 (1991), pp. 187–208; and Richard Sakwa, *Russian Politics and Society* (London: Routledge, 1993), chapter 2.
25 Urban, 'Boris El'tsin', p. 188.
26 *Izvestiya*, 26 March 1991, p. 2.
27 *Izvestiya*, 6 April 1991, pp. 1, 3.
28 For the text of the law see *Vedomosti S"ezda narodnykh deputatov RSFSR i Verkhovnogo Soveta RSFSR*, no. 17 (1991), item 512.
29 *Rossiiskaya gazeta*, 13 March 1993, p. 1.
30 See White, *After Gorbachev*, pp. 264–5.
31 *Rossiiskaya gazeta*, 6 May 1993, p. 1.
32 *Rossiiskaya gazeta*, 8 April 1992, pp. 1–4.
33 *Izvestiya*, 10 December 1992, p. 1.
34 *Narodnyi deputat*, no. 12 (1992), pp. 7–8, 13–14, and no. 13 (1992), pp. 7–8. For an extended statement of his views see R.I. Khasbulatov, *Vybor sud'by* (Moscow: Respublika, 1993), and idem, *The Struggle for Russia: Power and Change in the Democratic Revolution*, edited by Richard Sakwa (London: Routledge, 1993).
35 *Izvestiya*, 12 March 1993, p. 1.
36 *Izvestiya*, 9 February 1993, p. 1, and (for the 'collective Rasputin') 10 April 1993, p. 1.
37 *Izvestiya*, 5 June 1993, pp. 1–2; similarly *Rossiiskaya gazeta*, 2 June 1993, pp. 3–4.
38 See for instance *Moskovskii komsomolets*, 11 January 1994, p. 1.
39 *Izvestiya*, 12 October 1994, p. 4.
40 *Nezavisimaya gazeta*, 28 February 1991, p. 2; *Sem' s plyusom*, no. 12 (March 1991), p. 4.
41 *Nezavisimaya gazeta*, 28 February 1991, p. 1; similarly *Moscow News*, no. 15 (1991), p. 10. A fuller survey of the Gorbachev-Yeltsin relationship, with survey data, is provided in L.N. Dobrokhotov (ed.), *Gorbachev-El'tsin: 1500 dnei politicheskogo protivostoyaniya* (Moscow: Terra, 1992).
42 Irina Boeva and Viacheslav Shironin, *Russians between State and Market* (Glasgow: University of Strathclyde Centre for the Study of Public Policy, 1992), p. 32.
43 Richard Rose, Irina Boeva and Viacheslav Shironin, *How Russians are Coping with Transition* (Glasgow: University of Strathclyde Centre for the Study of Public Policy, 1993), p. 53.
44 Richard Rose and Christian Haerpfer, *New Russia Barometer III* (Glasgow: University of Strathclyde Centre for the Study of Public Policy, 1994), p. 39. According to a survey in *Segodnya* Yeltsin had 14 per cent support, Yavlinsky 8 per cent and Zhirinovsky 7 per cent (26 May 1994, p. 3).

45 *Argumenty i fakty*, no. 27 (1994), p. 2.
46 *Mir mnenii i mneniya o mire*, no. 6 (17) (March 1993), p. 1 (25.3 per cent were unsure). According to a survey reported in *Vek* the largest proportion (32.8 per cent) believed supreme power should belong to the president, but a larger 37.3 per cent were unsure (no. 39, 1994, p. 6).
47 Rose et al., *How Russians are Coping*, pp. 37–8.
48 Rose and Haerpfer, *New Russia Barometer III*, p. 38.
49 *Ekonomicheskie i sotsial'nye peremeny: monitoring obshchestvennogo mneniya*, July–August 1994, p. 13.
50 *Mir mnenii*, no. 1 (January 1994), pp. 1–3.
51 *Obshchaya gazeta*, 7–13 October 1994, p. 8.
52 Rose and Haerpfer, *New Russia Barometer III*, p. 31.
53 ibid., pp. 31–2. There were similar findings in *Argumenty i fakty*: only 1 per cent had confidence in political parties, as compared with 74 per cent that trusted the army (no. 22, 1994, p. 1).
54 *Moskovskie novosti*, no. 42 (1994), p. 7.
55 Rose and Haerpfer, *New Russia Barometer III*, pp. 17–18.
56 *Obshchaya gazeta*, 7–13 October 1994, p. 8.
57 *Mir mnenii*, no. 4 (24) (April 1993), p. 1.
58 Calculated from *Segodnya*, 13 October 1994, p. 3; similarly *Ekonomicheskie i sotsial'nye peremeny*, May–June 1994, p. 12 (16.5 per cent were for Yeltsin in such circumstances but 44.2 per cent were unsure or refused to indicate their opinion).
59 *Ekonomicheskie i sotsial'nye peremeny*, May–June 1994, p. 11.
60 ibid., July–August 1994, p. 13; similarly Rose and Haerpfer, *New Russia Barometer III*, p. 40 (43 per cent thought Yeltsin should resign, 30 per cent that he should continue in office).
61 *Mir mnenii*, no. 1 (January 1994), p. 9. According to a survey reported in *Moskovskie novosti* 29 per cent would vote for Yeltsin in an early contest, but 53 per cent would not (no. 30, 1994, p. 6).
62 *Moskovskie novosti*, no. 30 (1994), p. 6. On the decline in Yeltsin's electoral support see Stephen White, Ian McAllister and Olga Kryshtanovskaya, 'El'tsin and His Voters: Popular Support in the 1991 Russian Presidential Elections and After', *Europe-Asia Studies*, vol. 46, no. 2 (1994), pp. 285–303.
63 *Moskovskie novosti*, no. 33 (1993), p. A11.
64 *Mir mnenii*, no. 10 (76) (September 1993), p. 1.
65 *Izvestiya*, 11 June 1992, p. 3.
66 *Pravda*, 10 June 1991, p. 2.
67 *Mir mnenii*, no. 11 (November 1992), p. 8.
68 *Le Monde*, 11 September 1993, p. 11.
69 Tests of this kind are normal in France and the USA, among other presidential systems.
70 *Argumenty i fakty*, no. 16 (1993), p. 3.
71 *Nezavisimaya gazeta*, 16 May 1992, p. 2.
72 *Guardian* (London), 29 March 1993, p. 18, and 9 September 1994, p. 12.

73 *Argumenty i fakty*, no. 39 (1994), p. 2.
74 *Segodnya*, 21 December 1993, p. 2.
75 *Obshchaya gazeta*, no. 40 (1994), p. 8.
76 *Izvestiya*, 15 March 1994, pp. 1, 4.

10 *The Legacy of Leninist Enforced De-participation*

TROY McGRATH

> History does not repeat itself with precision. But the similarity of dangers is unmistakable. The vacuum left behind by the first formally secular messianism is unique, and not properly understood.
> *Ernest Gellner*[1]

> The strongest predictor of the first phase of post-Soviet politics is the last phase of Soviet politics.
> *Timothy Colton*[2]

In Russia, the introduction of multiparty elections, a principal source of power and legitimacy in any democratic political system, has inexorably led to a whole host of new problems for a (Cold) war-weary, economically shocked population. Indeed, the transition process has unleashed the traditional Russian battle between order and anarchy, as all institutions, old and new, continue to lose authority amid accelerating economic chaos and disintegration.[3] This has rendered Russia's democratic construction all the more difficult because neither the newly found 'democrats' nor the born-again communists entered the transition period with adequate sensitivity of the relationship between electoral laws, governing institutions and democratic outcomes. They are now challenged with the monumental tasks of designing and establishing a political incentive structure capable of encouraging political and economic elites to identify alternative peaceful approaches to solving pressing societal problems.

Such a system must also be able to adjust to shifting governing coalitions while being stable enough to withstand the pressures that are the inevitable products of fundamental change.[4]

One of the principal obstacles to creating these arrangements is the institutional legacy of the previous political order. True, the Leninist system was both discredited and discarded by a disenchanted Soviet population. Yet, however radical the departure from the past might seem, the course of post-communist institutional evolution has been conditioned strongly by the old regime. While the collapse of the Leninist system was brought about by the failure of its core institutions, especially the economic planning system, the ruling elite's degeneration and the decline of its internal discipline were equally important. The ultimate failure of the 'Soviet experiment' signified a rejection of the self-imposed rule of Lenin's 'combat party' organization, but it could not erase the deeply ingrained vestiges left by the Leninist system and its political practices, so that 'the mix of people and institutions that succeeded it showed a substantial measure of continuity.'[5] Thus, while Leninist rule in Russia disintegrated in tandem with its central institutions, it did not leave in its wake a *tabula rasa* upon which democratic institutions could easily be drafted.[6]

Leninist systems were dominated by a ruling communist party. In the former USSR, the leading role of the Communist Party of the Soviet Union (CPSU) was codified in Article 6 of its 1977 Constitution.[7] The party maintained control over society through censoring media, culture and the arts; prescribing educational curricula; maintaining party groups in all work places, state and educational institutions; supervising the economy through its departments in the Central Committee; controlling political appointments through the *nomenklatura* system, and dominating the electoral system – from announcing the campaign's commencement and nominating the candidates to publishing the (often falsified) vote counts. In addition, Soviet citizens were drafted into mass organizations 'transmitting' the CPSU's values and ideals. The party also had in its arsenal the threat of coercion to make sure that its objectives were implemented. In the political sphere, it was the party that made all major (and even minor) decisions. Its membership – which in 1989 constituted about 9.6 per cent of the adult population[8] – adhered strictly to its guidelines.

The party legitimated itself through its manipulation of the 'sacred texts' of Marxism-Leninism and its charismatic legacy of initiating and defending the socialist revolution. It established a further basis for legitimacy by entering into an implicit 'social contract' with society. The population would exchange silence and subservience to the party in the political realm for the party's provision of life's basic economic necessities (the CPSU still further legitimated itself by actually fulfilling this contract). However, the party also succeeded in reversing the legitimation flow. Rather than a sovereign people constituting the authority that verifies and bestows legitimacy, as in a democracy, legitimacy in the USSR was authenticated by the CPSU itself. By the 1980s, when it could no longer satisfy its own bases for social peace, the party, led by Mikhail Gorbachev, embarked on a project to strengthen the economy and re-establish the party's former role by having it prove its leadership-worthiness. Gorbachev's reforms – notwithstanding several important features such as the introduction of multiple-candidate elections, and the (albeit grudging) acceptance of alternative political parties and elites – could not overcome seven decades of single-party rule, strong patron-client political networks and popular passivity.

The population had opportunities to 'participate' in Soviet political life. However, the leadership attempted to control society via a strategy of mobilization which transformed the nature of participation so that partial adherence became total involvement. This objective was pursued by means of various techniques of indoctrination as well as through mass participation, which was channelled into a functionally distinct form of political activity called 'co-production'. This involved activities and behaviour designed to implement norms and policies via a dense network of 'transmission belts', or organizational adjuncts to administration, such as trade unions, residential committees and other public organizations. In this way, the Leninist approach identified vast new areas of political potential in what were usually thought to be non-political special-purpose social institutions and mass organizations. The forced participation of citizens in co-production kept them out of the political arena and relegated their input to rituals of pseudo-participation such as voting (and standing) in single-candidate elections and holding membership of sham commissions.[9]

The political effectiveness of the Leninist polity that emerged was based upon the successful forced *de*-participation of society in its own management. Although the Bolshevik regime rose to power largely due to the extensive mass political participation at the time of the October revolution, its success in maintaining dominance over society was achieved by suppressing public participation in decision-making and in the selection of decision-makers. Rather than institutionalizing popular participation in government (the task currently faced by Russian leaders), the CPSU seized exclusive control of the political, economic and social functions of Soviet society. This is a political obstacle which contemporary Russia has inherited.

Russia's point of departure

Russia's emerging electoral and party systems have been conditioned by the processes of power and authority legitimation that shaped the lives of the contemporary elite. In constructing a new (presumably democratic) political order, Russian politicians are drawing upon the only relevant experiences they have: the rules, norms and organizational structures of the obsolete Leninist *ancien régime*. Thus, Russian democracy's construction crew is composed of workers whose productivity is hampered by behavioural patterns resulting from the disincentives and bureaucratic restrictions of command economies. Leninist systems are the womb from which post-communist democracies must emerge, and consequently it is essential to consider their legacy.[10]

Clearly, the new conceptions, rules and institutional structures borrowed from Western political models have merged rather uneasily with the old norms of behaviour persisting in Russia. This is because the previous (Leninist) system was the antithesis of a liberal order, combining uncertain procedures with certain results. Procedures were capricious due to a veritable absence of the rule of law and of standard operating methods, while the hegemony of the CPSU party-state directorate dictated most (if not all) political, social and economic outcomes.[11] These old norms, in effect institutional remnants of the legitimation process of the Leninist system, are essentially antagonistic to the development of a Western party system and representative democracy, limiting the amount of real change in the new state's institutional arrangements. Indeed it is difficult to imagine how those political procedures and institutions necessary to stabilize and consolidate a democratic political order could rapidly materialize from such a political system.

Even sustained by hasty and ample doses of the magical elixir known as the market, the democratization of Russian politics has not yet been achieved. The popular disillusionment with the quasi-democracy that has emerged in Russia is now a trend characteristic of both opponents and supporters of basic economic reform, as wider circles of Russian citizens strongly object to the inherent social and economic inequalities inevitable in a market economy, and adhere to values of 'equal distribution' of wealth. Survey data from recent years indicate that for many in Russia 'markets lead to lower living standards and social conflict, [while] privatization leads to social and class division'. Consequently, 'a clear picture emerges of a population for whom an alternative normative rhetoric to markets and democracy is lacking but which has experienced the transition as divisive, disabling, and unjust'.[12]

Thus far the practice of democracy in Russia has proved to be a very difficult game, in which anti-market and anti-capitalist prejudices have become widespread in the face of the dreaded risks of the newly emerging social order. Unfortunately, many citizens have come to perceive the inequities and defects of the current system as characteristic of genuine democracy, and the democratic idea is being discredited.[13] The result is in many cases a longing to return to a more traditional past with an emphasis upon orthodoxy and order, with strong overtones of social and economic egalitarianism. Consequently, the ideological orientations of important groups of society have shifted towards restoration of the previous order with a nostalgic adherence to old forms of social guarantees, the economic certainties of state paternalism, and simple political formulae.[14] However, looking back to a romanticized (often imaginary) past tends to obscure present possibilities.

Three examples will serve to underscore this point. First, the desire for a 'strong hand' to take charge and enforce order (à la Yeltsin facing down a fractious and rebellious parliament and ruling by decree) is of course a double-edged sword. As was suggested in the pages of the influential daily *Nezavisimaya gazeta* (Independent

Newspaper), 'Yeltsin's actions have historical parallels with those of Nicholas II and Lenin, both of whom dissolved elected assemblies and moved toward authoritarianism and repression. The losers on both occasions were the Russian people.'[15] Second, the alleged egalitarianism of the Russian population is held out as one of the few beneficial aspects of the old order. This relates to a traditional political culture rooted in organic collectivism and a consensual approach to societal representation, known as *sobornost'*. Taken from the *sobor*, a proto-parliamentary ecclesiastical assembly of the sixteenth and seventeenth centuries, *sobornost'* encompassed a mystical notion 'whereby the (vicariously) assembled people (*sobor*) are united by an apprehension of religious truth that moulds them into a community united in harmonious variety.'[16] Unfortunately, the 'collectivism' that was cultivated under communism was generally 'not a brotherhood, not a selfless service to the good, but a dictatorship of indifference, a revelry of dependence, a cowardice of consciousness'.[17] Moreover, as a number of scholars have asserted, the incompatibility of this surviving overly collectivist mentality with new forms of social life and new political institutions constitutes a serious obstacle to the transition from a Leninist order to a more democratic system.[18]

Third, there is a proclivity among the Russians to cling to notions of orthodoxy and nation. Scholars such as John Hall have pointed out that the vacuum created by the collapse of the socialist project was always most likely to be filled by nationalism.[19] This is true for a variety of reasons, and particularly so in post-communist Russia. To begin with, the Soviet Union was never organized as a Russian nation-state, and because the Russian Republic itself was so instrumental in the destruction of the old order, many Russians hold the concept of the Russian nation aloft. In fact, despite their privileged position in some realms, Russians tended to consider themselves underprivileged by the old system, particularly within the Russian Republic.[20] In Russian eyes, both communism and the Soviet Union were destroyed, and Russia was the executor of their fate. Thus, Russians consider themselves heroes and democrats, i.e. not those responsible for the former empire.

But nationalism in this part of the world tends to be vicious, destructive and illiberal, given that nations are being constructed *ab initio*, that is from peasant bases rather than from extant high cultures.[21] Consequently, nationalism, in whatever form, is generally incompatible with democracy, since it elevates the rights of a particular community over the rights of all citizens. This process impedes the emergence of an authentic civil society in a Western understanding of the term.[22] Thus, any 'return' to the past, whether to an antiquated sense of the Russian nation, to the 'good old days' of law and order, or to the alleged egalitarian spirit of the previous social order, is tainted by Russia's long experience with communism. This legacy has produced a tendency to embrace sweeping, absolute solutions that obfuscate practical problems and real prospects, and a counter tendency to discard these same solutions just as readily as they were embraced when individual utilities so dictate.

Hence the vaunted promise of democracy has paled in the face of the unfulfilled expectations of a population accustomed to the cradle-to-grave security of a 'nanny state'. The manifest inability of the post-communist government to live up to these expectations has engendered the fragmentation and personalization of political life, in which confrontation takes precedence over compromise and leaves the electorate confused and alienated, a state of affairs which merely adds to the already disquieting strains on the democratization process.[23] 'The transition experience itself has reoriented public opinion away from utopian expectations about the market and democracy, which were characteristic of the period when the old system was collapsing, toward a more informed and certainly more cautious outlook.'[24] This means that *until and unless* the twin shocks of marketization and privatization produce more substantial and more stable class and sectoral differences, the politics of Russia's quasi-democracy are likely to be driven by other, much less manageable, cleavages, such as ethnicity, regionalism or charismatic demagogy.[25]

The result is that, in the absence of the coercive structures of the old order and with the ineffectual institutionalization of the rules governing competition in an electoral democracy, power struggles have continued to occur. This has contributed greatly to the conflict and political instability that have characterized the contemporary Russian political scene.[26] Thus, as a number of analysts have pointed out, despite the opening rounds of democratic elections in most countries of the region, the consolidation of a functioning political order is but *one* possible outcome of the political transition under way in this area. With regard to Russia, some posit that, due to the complexity of the current economic, political and social situation, as well as to certain aspects of Russian political culture, 'a transition towards another type of non-democratic political arrangement is more likely than genuine democratization'.[27] This is all the more plausible since contemporary Russia lacks a critical determinant of democratic consolidation, the inculcation of democratic (especially procedural) norms among contending elites such that they develop a stake in 'playing the game' of democratic politics and therefore come to value the rules of that game.[28]

Thus, while the old regime collapsed fairly rapidly and seemingly with little effort, the creation of a new order to replace it has proved an arduous task. The advent of 'bloc' politics and the threat of demagogues (Yeltsin no less than Zhirinovsky) has transformed the politics of the Russian Federation into a magnificent spectacle, though at present it seems unlikely to spawn a coherent ruling group with a viable governing programme. The result in the short term is that the successor to the Leninist political order in Russia is not a thriving democracy, but rather an inwardly divided and erratic regime, precariously presiding over a weakened state comprised of partially reformed bureaucracies and fragile, new institutional arrangements.

This is something which essentially has been ignored by many analysts of 'transition' and 'democratization' literature seeking to explain the Russian Federation's current political status. Indeed, these writers have failed to provide useful analytical frameworks for studying the Russian case. First, they focus largely upon authoritarian systems (Spain, Brazil) which lack the particular ideological and socialization characteristics of Leninist systems. Second, the existing typologies of democracy largely marginalize institutional factors, ignoring questions such as whether it makes a difference whether a presidential, parliamentary, unitary or federal system emerges.[29] Third, such approaches severely undervalue one particularly critical factor in the equation for instability for post-totalitarian regimes: their starting points. These are crucial because they strongly influence the paths of social and political change that emerge in the transition period. Just as the institutions and organizations of the early Bolshevik regime borrowed or copied much from the tsarist order, so too has the emerging 'democracy' in Russia been strongly influenced by its Leninist past.

Therefore, one must not underestimate the extent to which elements of the Soviet system remain firmly grounded in the population's lives and behaviour. Survey data from late 1992 suggested that Russians viewed socialism relatively favourably: 67 per cent largely or entirely agreed that socialism had its advantages, with only 10 per cent against. Another poll asked Russians when there had been a government that took into account the needs of the ordinary people in Russia, and 21 per cent claimed this was the case under Brezhnev. Moreover, an *Izvestiya* poll published in March 1993 found that most of its provincial respondents actually preferred the Soviet system as it existed up to 1991 to its post-communist successor. Probably a similar nostalgia for the 'better times' of the past explains why 49 per cent of the Russians asked in a separate survey still regarded Stalin as a great leader.[30]

The electoral implications of the Leninist legacy

As suggested at the beginning of the chapter, a major reason for the inability of the Russian political system to achieve the level of democratization possible when the CPSU was relegated to the ash-heap of history is the legacy of the Leninist political order itself. The most salient problems plaguing the democratization efforts in Russia reveal vestiges (intellectual and institutional) of the old system. These are most apparent in the battle between the executive and legislative branches of government, and in the problem of creating a viable party system. Indeed one of the major obstacles to the creation of a functioning government and workable party system is the traditional (tsarist and Leninist) fixation with the powerful leader who promises law and order. The problem is essentially twofold: one of presidents and one of parties. While the two dimensions of this problem are intertwined, they are best analysed separately, particularly in order to determine just how much they are relics of the past.

First, then, there is the problem of presidents: namely the Yeltsin factor. As Erik Hoffmann points out, presidential leadership can be decisive in creating a viable constitutional order, especially during the immediate post-authoritarian phase of transition that precedes democratic consolidation. The political and institutional decisions taken in the wake of a revolution can have enormous influence in determining the evolving political system. It is for this reason that many consider the two-year delay in calling for direct parliamentary elections and a constitutional plebiscite in Russia a crucial error which has carried considerable repercussions.[31]

Initially the reformers around Yeltsin believed that a market economy was an essential prerequisite for political stability; hence they concentrated on economic reform to the detriment of democratic political development. This meant creating an executive whose powers were unbounded by party hierarchies and policies, and barely restricted by parliamentary checks and balances, or by other constitutional guarantees on limiting power. Popularly elected but partyless, Boris Yeltsin naturally has been unable (and often unwilling) to democratize traditional political and legal cultures. In fact, his presidency may well have strengthened authoritarian elements of these cultures, intentionally or unintentionally.[32]

This inevitably leads to the oft-mentioned concept of the 'iron hand'. Leninist political orders (and tsarist Russia) greatly emphasized maintaining the leadership's stability and authority. This was particularly and ruthlessly true of the Soviet era, in which official policy was rigidly controlled and always presented in the form of unified, public utterances. Efforts to change or amend policy, except through strictly regulated internal channels, were generally prohibited.[33] Of course, this was not the case during the final, debilitating years of the Gorbachev regime, in which the government line resembled something akin to a wet noodle. In fact, it was the slow descent from order to disorder that most troubled the Russian population.

As the Russian public has observed firsthand, democracy without consensus or coercion becomes anarchy, and this fear of an absence of law and order is one of the greatest forces that drives Russian society. This is evidenced by the significant degree of support for the 'iron hand' that since 1991 has continued to exist in Russia.[34] Moreover, the programme content of some of the electoral associations (see this volume's Appendix) illustrates this point. The Liberal Democratic Party of Russia claimed in its programme that it would end crime within three months of assuming power. The

Communist Party of the Russian Federation and the Future of Russia – New Names bloc declared that they would introduce a state of emergency to eliminate the 'mafiya' and restore order in Russia. It is not surprising, then, that many favoured a strong and enlightened national leadership capable of enforcing its policies and laws, arguing that authoritarian leadership is necessary at least in the initial phases of the democratization process. It seems that this was not at odds with a large portion of voters' sympathies, as gauged by public opinion polls.[35]

This, naturally, has been a significant factor in the calculations of those involved in the institutional battles among the current leadership elite, since the desire for the return of strong leadership cannot be written off as merely a rationale or fantasy of a power-hungry executive branch. Thus, data continue to show a significant portion of the Russian population willing to accept restriction of freedoms by the state: more than a third (36 per cent) place order above freedom; an equal number (36 per cent) are prepared to allow restrictions on freedom of movement, and 45 per cent are willing to have force used against a potentially violent demonstration. As economic hardship limits the time and energy people have to devote to politics, and as the excitement of overthrowing a system begins to fade, many have returned to the traditional belief that individual actions can make no real difference and that a strong government is best.[36] Such views have become even more prevalent as constitutional restraints and divided powers, at least in the eyes of the public, seem to result merely in presidential-parliamentary gridlock and a degeneration of the usefulness and effectiveness of the state. In fact, as Daphne Skillen argues in Chapter 5 of this volume, and as Michael Urban has noted elsewhere, Zhirinovsky's leadership images – suggesting the need for an 'iron hand' – contributed to his party's surprising electoral success in the December 1993 elections.[37]

Of course, not everyone in the new political order harked back to the days of the strong hand. Some politicians (especially parliamentarians) feared that an overwhelmingly powerful executive could lead along the path to the past, where both Russian history and Marxism-Leninism combined to exaggerate the power of a single strong leader, whether tsar or general secretary. They emphasized the need to secure a true division of powers and to develop the role

The Legacy of Leninist Enforced De-participation 237

of parliament as the principal representative organ of the entire society. This was countered by the executive branch, in the person of Boris Yeltsin, who stressed that he could not guarantee the continuance of reforms, maintenance of order or Russia's integrity without a strong executive. In November 1991, not only was Yeltsin assigned the power to rule by decree until the end of 1992 by the Congress of People's Deputies, but he also appointed himself prime minister and began to name his own cabinet 'without having to bother with obtaining parliamentary assent'. After parliament had granted Yeltsin additional powers, he largely excluded important political actors like Ruslan Khasbulatov (Chair of the Presidium of the Supreme Soviet) and Vice-President Aleksandr Rutskoi from any major responsibility for reform.[38]

Thus, since the autumn of 1991 Russian politics has largely been the story of the Yeltsin government's behaviour and its relationship to other political actors and groups. Opposition to Yeltsin's actions solidified during 1992 because the government failed to create a firm reform alliance spanning the various shades of democrats. This deepened the divide in the reformist camp. The executive branch chose to remain on the ideological fringe, and therefore contributed to its own political isolation and embattled position.[39] The subsequent battle between the parliament (led by Khasbulatov and Rutskoi) and the president quickly spawned talk of the possible need for 'emergency powers' which would not necessarily be in line with the constitution, including the dissolution of parliament and the declaration of direct presidential rule. The resulting confrontation between the two branches of government involved bloody street battles that jeopardized the political legitimacy of the entire government.[40]

In December 1993 Russian voters elected a new parliament (bringing a different set of problems) and adopted a presidentially favoured draft constitution. Yeltsin supporters played partisan politics with the draft and the holding of the elections – tactics 'reminiscent of Soviet efforts to use Constitutions and elections to generate elite conformity and mass political indifference'.[41] Once again, this resembles past structures, because whether dominated by the tsar, the CPSU Politburo, or now the Russian president, the legislature has always occupied a subordinate role in the Russian political system. Indeed, for much of the post-communist period the boundary between executive and legislative power in Russia has been ill-defined, and competing claims to power have undermined the authority of the fledgling democratic state. The simple fact that parliament's dissolution entailed massive demonstrations and a military assault demonstrates that certain democratic norms of political competition have yet to be institutionalized. This is further evidenced by the nature of the elections held in the wake of the disastrous events of October 1993.

The combination of Russia's presidential system and its legacy of the 'iron hand' presents further potential obstacles to the country's transition process. Indeed, recent scholarship (and historical practice) demonstrates that transitional countries selecting parliamentary systems have better proven track records in consolidating a democracy than those choosing presidential regimes. Alfred Stepan and Cindy Skach argue that between 1973 and 1989:

> Parliamentary democracies had a rate of survival more than three times higher than pure presidential democracies. Pure presidential democracies were also twice as likely as pure parliamentary democracies to experience a military coup.[42]

Given these factors and Russia's current social, economic and political turmoil, Russia's choice of a presidential regime is certainly a factor for concern.

From the time that the Yeltsin government acquired real state power (reinforced by the strongly 'presidential' constitution), 'its actions directly opposed the preferences of all other ideological positions, from moderate reformers and centrists to the communists and nationalists'.[43] In general, conservatives see progressives as selling out to a corrupt and imperial West, while reformers view their opponents as the malignant residue of an old and discredited order. In such an atmosphere political cooperation is virtually impossible. Therefore, what we are witnessing in Russia is an erosion of the state while the bureaucratic apparatus formerly in charge of integration and allocation degenerates into an aggregate of conflicting corrupt interests and local ambitions. This is compounded by rising unemployment, soaring prices, a great surge in crime and the state apparatus's mafia-style regression. The (mostly negative) consequences of marketization further widen the schisms in Russian society.

The creation of a new entrepreneurial class, whose conspicuous consumption and often ill-gotten gains offend many, has not offset the deprivation now felt by the majority. The rise of the 'mafiya' is but one symptom of a public that has lost faith in the rule of law, since institutions of government seem only to benefit a small stratum of society.[44] In many ways, this is viewed as analogous to the corruption (*kormlenie*) of the Brezhnev years.[45] Consequently, Russians have simply got out of the habit of obeying the law. This lack of respect for the rule of law was further increased by the methods of governing of both Gorbachev and Yeltsin, in which rule by decree was the norm, and laws could (and still can) be changed overnight without parliamentary consent. The result is a disturbing level of social intolerance and lack of respect for the whole democratic process.[46]

Public desperation has also been reflected in the inability of the new order to establish a system of political parties which has the sufficient confidence of the populace. By the beginning of 1993 there were some 50 proto-parties in Russia, most of which were really personal followings of individual politicians who had emerged over the previous few years. Few have articulated comprehensive, serious party platforms or programmes. With the exception of the Communist Party of the Russian Federation, virtually no party has any real, nationally established organizational structure. They continue to shift, split and recombine according to the tactical whims of their leaders, who are more absorbed in the game of Moscow politics than with addressing the concerns of their constituents.[47]

The weakness of Russian parties has been addressed in greater detail by Richard Sakwa in Chapter 8 of this volume. However, I would like to suggest that it can also be explained by the limitations of the political elites attempting to create them, and that the mass of voters are disenchanted by them. Thus far, parties in post-communist Russia have developed around alternative images of political organization by elites who received their primary political education within the old Leninist political order. Because these elites were influenced to a considerable extent by their conceptualizations and understandings of the CPSU's nature, they have both intentionally and unintentionally replicated elements of the old order within the new parties in particular, and within the political environment in general. Clearly, the more deeply ingrained structures and procedures are, the greater the likelihood that those socialized within the old organizations will attempt to replicate these structural features when establishing new ones. Hence, even individuals with liberal-democratic beliefs often unwittingly contribute to sustaining elements of the old order.[48] In Chapter 6 of this book Wyman, Miller, White and Heywood demonstrate this fact with evidence that Russia's Choice supporters identify with a number of political beliefs and practices generally regarded as non-democratic.

Some have argued that the transference of the old rules of inner-CPSU competition to new political parties has resulted in leader-centred party organizations, which have become the norm in the new political system. Hence, parties are identified with, and seen as the creatures of, their leaders, such as Zyuganov, Gaidar and Zhirinovsky, who are viewed as the 'bosses' of their respective parties. This personalization of politics tends to encourage conflict within the political elite, a behavioural pattern which was cultivated within the CPSU and which lies at the root of the current factionalism of Russian political parties. In this sense the CPSU's legacy has entailed not a simple transfer of institutional elements into new organizations but a more complex process of organizational adaptation and innovation as new actors respond to a political order in transition.[49]

The most obvious vestiges of the past institutional environment's influence are found in the nationalist and communist parties, which have principally accepted or copied the CPSU's organizational structures. Arranged hierarchically, authority within them theoretically ascends from primary units to congresses, representative and executive committees, and finally to a chairperson. Various categories of membership are present in many of these parties, resembling the different levels of the CPSU's former structure: youth members, candidate and full members, as well as the distinction between inner-party officials and rank-and-file subscribers. The parties place a premium upon internal order and discipline, as opposed to inner-party democracy – though how effective this has been is yet unclear.[50]

The Russian liberal parties have taken a different tack, more in reaction to the Leninist experience than in emulation of it. In essence they are proto-parties and leadership support groups, not parties in the commonly recognized sense. Because they eschew the type of transformative vision found in the ideology of the nationalists and communists, and because social interests have yet to crystallize fully, they have developed as parties without coherent programmes. Hence the parties of this type that have come into existence were often based upon a small group of intellectuals, with original but abstract ideas.[51] Moreover, the anti-organizational character of many of these parties reflects a fear that any distinct political entity is likely to develop into a party similar to the CPSU. This viewpoint centres upon the notion that strong organization entails the reduction of intra-organizational democracy, leading to the loss of moral superiority, since the founders of these predominantly oppositional forces conceived of themselves not as electoral competitors and representatives of voters, but as liquidators of the old one-party system.[52]

Among the masses the entire notion of parties has been wholly discredited, to the extent that there is widespread hostility to the very idea of a political party, a concept that has been deeply compromised after so many years of a single-party dictatorship. Political parties generally have bad reputations, and politicians are seen as opportunists on the make for power and privilege. Partly because communist political systems have tended to create cults of personality, Russians harbour deep suspicions of all political leaders.[53] Indeed, it is not entirely clear to the Russian population just who is in charge now.[54]

Hence, poor regime performance, the lack of electoral legitimacy, and the extent of official corruption and privilege have led to a widespread contempt for 'democratic' institutions. This is endemic of the dual-track nature of the transition in Russia: the simultaneous attempt to construct both a pluralist democracy and a market economy, which while generally seen as mutually supportive in the long term, are proving in the present stage to be mutually obstructive.[55] As the initial post-communist leadership took its first, tentative steps in managing the Russian Federation, it found that the new visions of political freedom and individualism conflicted with the residual expectations of 'cradle-to-grave socialism'; that is, that issues like state-supported housing, education, health care and job security were taken for granted.

The problem is that civil society's ability to ensure the continued success of a democratic order assumes the existence of a web of autonomous political and social organizations, as well as their capacity to act more or less responsibly within an established institutional framework. Without that framework and the implied willingness of groups to play by an agreed set of rules, the result is cacophony and political paralysis, leaving society susceptible to new forms of demagogy.[56] The reactionary mentality witnessed in Russian society today exists not only as a legacy of the Leninist system. The current social experience is both contributing to its development and creating the potential for its extension, particularly among those social groups able to exert a significant influence on political developments.[57] Such a situation could have far-reaching consequences for the development of the new political order in Russia.

Notes

1. Ernest Gellner, 'Homeland of the Unrevolution', *Daedalus*, vol. 122, no. 3 (Summer 1993), p. 153.
2. Timothy Colton, in Timothy Colton and Robert Legvold (eds), *After the Soviet Union: From Empire to Nations* (New York: Norton, 1992), p. 22.
3. Thomas Remington, 'Regime Transition in Communist Systems: The Soviet Case', in Frederic J. Fleron and Erik P. Hoffman (eds), *Postcommunist Studies and Political Science* (Boulder: Westview, 1993), p. 288.
4. Brendan Kiernan, *The End of Soviet Politics* (Boulder: Westview, 1993), p. 9.
5. Stephen White, *After Gorbachev* (Cambridge: Cambridge University Press, 1993), p. 262.
6. Judith S. Kullberg, 'In the Ruins of the CPSU: Elites and Party Formation in Russia', Paper delivered at the 1994 APSA Meeting in New York, September 1994, p. 2.
7. *Konstitutsiya (Osnovnoi Zakon) Soyuza Sovetskikh Sotsialisticheskikh Respublik* (Moscow: Politizdat, 1977).
8. See membership figures in *Izvestiya TsK KPSS*, no. 4 (1990), pp. 113, 115.
9. Philip G. Roeder, 'Modernization and Participation in the Leninist Developmental Strategy', *American Political Science Review*, vol. 83, no. 3 (September 1989), pp. 858–64.
10. Robin Alison Remington, 'Democracy and the Market in East Central Europe: Hard Choices', in Gary Wekin et al. (eds), *Building Democracy in One-Party States* (Westport: Praeger, 1993), pp. 140, 149.

11 Valerie Bunce and Maria Csanadi, 'Uncertainty in the Transition: Post-Communism in Hungary', *East European Politics and Societies*, vol. 7, no. 2 (Spring 1993), pp. 244–5.
12 Stephen Whitefield and Geoffrey Evans, 'The Russian Election of 1993: Public Opinion and the Transition Experience', *Post-Soviet Affairs*, vol. 10, no. 1 (1994), pp. 47–8. In fact, anti-market responses to a variety of questions in this study ranged from 57 per cent to 72 per cent, while anti-democracy responses consistently outpolled pro-democracy responses. See Table 5, 'Attitudes to Markets, Privatization and Democracy', p. 48.
13 Grigory Vainshtein, 'Totalitarian Public Consciousness in a Post-Totalitarian Society', *Communist and Post-Communist Studies*, vol. 27, no. 3 (1994), pp. 255–6.
14 According to a 1993 survey, 47 per cent of Russians polled strongly agreed that 'no reforms should lead to unemployment'. See *RFE/RL Research Report*, vol. 2, no. 22 (May 1993), p. 47. Similarly, another survey found that 52 per cent of Russians believed that 'the state should guarantee that people's basic needs are met' (Monitor-5 survey, March 1993, based on sample of 10,577 respondents from urban and rural areas of Russia). Both polls are cited in Vainshtein, 'Totalitarian Public Consciousness', pp. 253–4.
15 Vitalii Tretyakov, 'Ikh vsekh nuzhno ostanovit', *Nezavisimaya gazeta*, 23 September 1993, p. 1, as cited in Paul Kubicek, 'Delegative Democracy in Russia and Ukraine', *Communist and Post-Communist Studies*, vol. 27, no. 4 (1994), p. 435. In 1992, Yeltsin issued 1,727 decrees and 811 directives, and in the first half of 1993 the respective figures were 955 and 460. Meanwhile, the Supreme Soviet only passed 112 laws in 1992. See Dominic Gualtieri, 'Russia's New War of Laws', *RFE/RL Research Report*, 3 September 1993.
16 Michael Urban, 'The Politics of Identity in Russia's Postcommunist Transition: The Nation Against Itself', *Slavic Review*, vol. 53, no. 3 (Fall 1994), p. 741. Also see idem, 'Contending Conceptions of Nation and State in Russian Politics', *Demokratizatsiya*, no. 4 (1993).
17 Vladimir Pankov, 'Propoved' o nashikh grekhakh', *Nezavisimaya gazeta*, 25 December 1991, p. 5, as cited in Urban, 'The Politics of Identity', pp. 746–7.
18 See Viktor Sergeyev and Nikolai Biryukov, *Russia's Road to Democracy: Parliament, Communism and Traditional Culture* (Aldershot: Edward Elgar, 1993). A short discussion of their views is found in Erik Hoffmann, 'Challenges to Viable Constitutionalism in Post-Communist Russia, 1991–1993', *The Harriman Review*, vol. 7, nos 10–12 (November 1994), p. 31.
19 John Hall, 'Nationalisms: Classified and Explained', *Daedalus*, vol. 122, no. 3 (Summer 1993), p. 20.
20 See, for example, Rogers Brubaker, 'Nationhood and the National Question in the Soviet Union and Post-Soviet Eurasia: An Institutionalist Account', *Theory and Society*, vol. 23 (1994), pp. 47–78.
21 Hall, 'Nationalisms', p. 20.

22 Sarah Meiklejohn Terry, 'Thinking About Post-Communist Transitions: How Different are They?', *Slavic Review*, vol. 52, no. 2 (Summer 1993), p. 335.
23 ibid., pp. 335–6.
24 Whitefield and Evans, 'The Russian Election of 1993', p. 58.
25 Philippe Schmitter with Terry Lynn Karl, 'The Conceptual Travels of Transitologists and Consolidologists: How Far to the East Should They Attempt to Go?', *Slavic Review*, vol. 53, no. 1 (Spring 1994), p. 180.
26 See White, *After Gorbachev*, chapter 8.
27 Grzegorz Ekiert, 'Democratization Processes in East Central Europe: A Theoretical Reconsideration', *British Journal of Political Science*, vol. 21 (Autumn 1991), p. 288.
28 See Dankwart Rustow, 'Transitions to Democracy: Toward a Dynamic Model', *Comparative Politics*, vol. 2, no. 2 (April 1970), pp. 337–63, esp. pp. 358–9.
29 According to Juan J. Linz, such questions should be of critical interest to those studying transitions. Juan J. Linz, 'Transitions to Democracy', *Washington Quarterly*, no. 13 (Summer 1990).
30 *Mir mnenii i mneniya o mire*, no. 9 (1992), *Izvestiya*, 28 September 1992 and 27 March 1993, cited in White, *After Gorbachev*, pp. 281–5.
31 Hoffmann, 'Challenges to Viable Constitutionalism', pp. 37–46.
32 ibid., p. 36.
33 Philip Selznick, *The Organizational Weapon: A Study of Bolshevik Strategy and Tactics* (New York: McGraw-Hill, 1952), p. 32.
34 Matthew Wyman, 'Russian Political Culture: Evidence from Public Opinion Surveys', *Journal of Communist Studies and Transition Politics*, vol. 10, no. 1 (March 1994), p. 43 (tables 8–10).
35 See data from *Nezavisimaya gazeta*, 4 April 1992, and *Moskovskie novosti*, no. 33 (1992), cited in ibid., p. 44 (tables 12–13) and pp. 47, 49 (tables 18, 22).
36 ibid., pp. 32–5.
37 See Daphne Skillen's contribution to this volume and Michael Urban, 'December 1993 as a Replication of Late-Soviet Electoral Practices', *Post-Soviet Affairs*, vol. 10, no. 2 (1994), p. 145.
38 Neil Robinson, 'From Coup to Coup? The Post-Communist Experience in Russia, 1991–1993', *Coexistence*, vol. 31 (1994), esp. pp. 298–9.
39 Judith S. Kullberg, 'The Ideological Roots of Elite Political Conflict in Post-Soviet Russia', *Europe-Asia Studies*, vol. 46, no. 6 (1994), pp. 947–8.
40 White, *After Gorbachev*, pp. 262–6.
41 Hoffmann, 'Challenges to Viable Constitutionalism', p. 47.
42 Alfred Stepan and Cindy Skach, 'Constitutional Frameworks and Democratic Consolidation: Parliamentarianism versus Presidentialism', *World Politics*, vol. 46, no. 1 (October 1993), pp. 1–22, p. 10.
43 Kullberg, 'The Ideological Roots of Elite Political Conflict', pp. 947–8.
44 See Stephen Handelman, 'The Russian "Mafiya"', *Foreign Affairs*, vol. 73, no. 2 (March/April 1994), pp. 83–96, and idem, *Comrade Criminal: The*

Theft of the Second Russian Revolution (London: Michael Joseph, 1994).
45 Under the medieval principle of *kormlenie*, centrally appointed officials were permitted to rule an area or province for a certain period in order to enrich themselves through taxes, rent collections and any abuse of local power they might devise. See William E. Odom, 'Soviet Politics and After: Old and New Concepts', *World Politics*, vol. 45, no. 1 (October 1992), esp. p. 81.
46 In one survey after another a high degree of intolerance for 'social deviance' can be noted, particularly regarding homosexuals, AIDS victims, the homeless and the physically handicapped. See Wyman, 'Russian Political Culture', p. 46 (table 16).
47 Daniel Yergin and Thane Gustafson, *Russia 2010 and What it Means for the World* (London: Brealey Publishing, 1994), p. 89.
48 Kullberg, 'In the Ruins of the CPSU', pp. 9, 14.
49 ibid., p. 14.
50 ibid., pp. 13–14, 16.
51 White, *After Gorbachev*, p. 268.
52 Kullberg, 'In the Ruins of the CPSU', p. 10.
53 Remington, 'Democracy and the Market', p. 149.
54 See, for instance, the poll results in 'Komu prinadlezhit vlast' v Rossii', *Izvestiya*, 2 July 1994, p. 1.
55 Meiklejohn Terry, 'Thinking About Post-Communist Transitions', p. 334.
56 ibid., p. 335.
57 Vainshtein, 'Totalitarian Public Consciousness', pp. 249, 253.

11 *Conclusion*

PETER LENTINI

The contributors to this volume have consistently argued that elections in pre-revolutionary Russia, the Soviet period and the contemporary Russian Federation have been hindered by some form of politically interventionist institution – either tsar, CPSU or president. Elected assemblies have been subordinated to other institutions. The present author, in his chapter 'Overview of the Campaign', has suggested that, despite the fact that the new electoral provisions provided several innovations, so that, for example, new political organizations could now begin to play a role in post-Soviet government, there were numerous deficiencies that hampered the poll from achieving the status of what could be considered a 'free and fair election'. The campaign was conducted over a brief period of time. Many political organizations found it difficult to develop strategies that would enable them to gain enough signatures, select leading candidates, develop comprehensive programmes and devise electoral tactics. The media were biased heavily in favour of those electoral associations closely allied with the Russian government, in particular the Russia's Choice bloc. Contestants with adequate financial means and assistance also found the Russian media receptive to their custom. Yeltsin's supporters designed the rules of the campaign, oversaw the drafting of the constitution and supervised the conducting of the plebiscite. In addition, there was evidence of widespread ballot fraud.

The elections and plebiscite, however, should be considered historically significant despite their shortcomings. Contemporary Russia may not be classified as a well-established liberal democracy, but nor is it totalitarian like the Soviet Union was. The Russians are presently governed by popularly elected executive and legislative bodies. Despite falsified vote counts and state interference in their design and supervision, the elections and plebiscite yielded Russia's first new constitution since 1978 and a post-Soviet parliament. The dubious status of these institutions is now irrelevant given the fact that no state body has sought to inquire into their nature, nor have any political organizations felt compelled to withdraw from their seats in protest. Parties and movements now play a somewhat larger role in the country's political life: the Electoral Statute has provided them with a possibility to compete for seats in the legislature and their representatives are playing important roles as chairs of committees. Hence they are participating in the governing process. Nevertheless, Russian voters demonstrated that they are sceptical of these organizations, preferring instead representatives with whom they are familiar and whom they can trust to promote their interests in Moscow. They are less willing to put their faith in members of political organizations who espouse ideological lines. Because of its experience under CPSU rule the Russian electorate harbours negative attitudes towards political parties. Moreover, given that they are largely leadership-oriented, engaging more in personal struggles than in policy-crafting, parties and other political organizations have not shown their best faces to the electorate. In addition, with the possible exception of the Communist Party of the Russian Federation, Russian political organizations largely lack party discipline to any significant degree and this fact further weakens their potential appeal.

There are two main points that I seek to address in order to conclude this volume. First, I wish to analyse the 'fruit' of the elections, the Russian Federal Assembly, and how it has performed in the period since it was elected, focusing particularly on its relationships with the Russian president and government. It is hoped that this can provide a better picture of whether or not the elections produced an institution capable of curbing the Russian presidency and implementing the voters' will. Second, I will present a brief overview of local elections held since 1994 and assess the importance of the franchise in current Russian politics.

The Russian Federal Assembly

The Russian Federal Assembly elected by Russian voters is a body which differs greatly from any of its Soviet predecessors. Russian parliamentarians possess backgrounds that vary significantly from those of their Soviet counterparts, particularly regarding sex, age, level of education and occupation. Soviet legislatures were intended to be microcosms of society; their deputies were chosen to emphasize this quality, rather than for their political skills. Thus, during the Stalin to Chernenko periods, party officials went to great pains to select more women, young people (aged 30 and under), elderly people and people without higher education than would normally be found in a Western legislative organ.[1] Soviet voters elected a more 'professional' corps of deputies as a result of the reform measures enacted during the Gorbachev years at the elections to the USSR Congress of People's Deputies and to republican-level legislatures. Deputy compositions were more likely to be dominated by men, managers, middle-ranking party officials and those with higher education. However, there remained, particularly in the USSR Congress, a number of deputies who were typical of the 'old style' representation norms.[2]

The Russians elected an extremely 'professional' parliament on 12 December 1993. For instance, the typical Duma deputy was a man in his forties (the average age of list deputies was about 47 years and the characteristic constituency deputy was about 43.7 years old), a graduate of an institution of tertiary education (424 out of 444, or 95.5 per cent elected on 12 December), a professional politician (minister, administrator or political party official), white-collar manager or academic researcher.[3] The archetypal Federation Council 'senator' was a man aged 47.7 years, who had received a higher education (169 out of 171, or 98.8 per cent elected on 12 December) and was a professional politician.[4] Nevertheless, Russian analysts are worried that, like their Soviet predecessors, who were mainly party members and bound to adhere to CPSU directives through democratic centralism, and therefore unable or perhaps unwilling to assert their independence as legislators and constituency representatives, contemporary Duma deputies – particularly those elected through party lists – and senators may be hindered from advocating voters' interests given their links and loyalties to the Yeltsin administration, regional elites or political organizations.[5]

There are examples of this point being effectively challenged. For instance, Duma deputies Yegor Gaidar and Boris Fedorov resigned from their posts in the Russian government in early 1994 to protest Yeltsin's backtracking on reform. More recently, the pro-government Russia's Choice faction was split. Key figures supporting the administration's line in Chechnya, such as Foreign Minister Andrei Kozyrev, left the group after Yegor Gaidar openly entered into opposition to Yeltsin in response to the president's campaign there. The 'opposition' – the Communist Party of the Russian Federation, the Agrarian Party of Russia and the Liberal Democratic Party of Russia – has also shown that among its 'list' deputies it has been difficult to maintain internal discipline. For instance, the Liberal Democratic Party of Russia has suffered from disputes since early 1994. Leading deputies including the faith healer Anatolii Kashpirovsky, and numbers two and three on the party list, Viktor Kobelev and Vyacheslav Marychev,[6] have deserted its fraction, largely over disputes with party leader Vladimir Zhirinovsky. Kobelev has joined former Vice-President Aleksandr Rutskoi's Derzhava (Great Power) movement.

There were many fears that the new institutional arrangements would be destabilizing for Russia's democracy. For instance, the Russian Constitution greatly favours the Russian president. This is a significant factor in transitional regime construction. Alfred Stepan and Cindy Skach argue convincingly that countries that select parliamentary rather than presidential frameworks for their institutional design have greater chances of consolidating democracy.[7] However, Yeltsin's constitutional powers are potentially challenged by a parliament that could be considered extremely hostile to reforms.[8] Indeed, the fact that the opposition holds more seats than reformist forces clearly reinforces that proposition.[9] Therefore, it is necessary to evaluate to what degree the two institutions have been able to work *with* as well as *against* each other since the elections. In addition, it is essential to analyse the extent to which Yeltsin has allowed the parliament to perform and, moreover, to what extent the legislature has been able to thwart presidential powers.

Authors argue that there are indications that the elections have initiated major strivings towards democratic consolidation and political institutionalization. Anders Åslund provides perhaps the most optimistic account:

> The Russia emerging today ... is not falling apart but coming together. The new political institutions function. Strikes are rare, and no serious social unrest is on the horizon ... In short, Russia has undergone fundamental changes and appears to be on the right track.[10]

Moreover, he argues that:

> The new State Duma has proved far more responsible and moderate than expected. The most common complaint is that it does not adopt more laws ... A vital improvement is that the deputies of the Duma are disciplined by 11 political parties, which act in coordination. Single deputies can no longer be bought, as the parties check vested interests.[11]

Indeed, Richard Sakwa has argued in this volume that with the exception of Zhirinovsky's occasional outbursts, even the Liberal Democratic Party of Russia has become 'parliamentized'.

There are numerous examples which point to hostilities between the executive and legislative branches. However, they are occurring within constitutionally adopted guidelines. For instance, among its first legislative activities, the Duma enacted a general amnesty for those accused of participating in the August 1991 coup which attempted to place the USSR under the control of a State Committee for the State of Emergency, and for the imprisoned supporters of the parliamentary forces from the events of September–October 1993. Yeltsin could have viewed this measure, which led to the release of his opponents from prison, as a defeat. However, by allowing the amnesty to remain in place, he made a significant tactical move. Among those released was his potentially strongest nationalist opponent, former Vice-President Aleksandr Rutskoi. It was believed that a free Rutskoi would help neutralize the nationalist opposition by presenting Vladimir Zhirinovsky with another contender for leadership within the movement.

The Federation Council has also shown its unwillingness to allow the president to make certain appointments to key positions of power. Yeltsin's attempts to staff the Constitutional Court illustrate this point. The Russian Constitutional Court, the judicial body empowered to determine whether legislative acts comply with the constitution, was dissolved in autumn 1993. Despite its potential importance in the Russian political system – especially at a time when the country is undertaking a transition away from a system in which one institution, the CPSU, made and interpreted the law – the Russian Constitutional Court was only fully staffed in February 1995 after 'an endlessly drawn-out appointment procedure'.[12] The Court is considered hard to predict in terms of its political position as its members do not have political records. Nevertheless, they can be classified in three groups: those considered loyal to Yeltsin (Ernest Ametisov, Tamara Morshchakova, Nikolai Vitruk, Anatolii Kononov, Vladimir Tumanov, Ol'ga Khokhryakova, Yurii Danilov, Vladimir Yaroslavtsev and Marat Baglai); those who cannot be considered fully loyal to Yeltsin (Gadis Gadzhiev, Boris Yebzheev, Nikolai Seleznev, Oleg Tyunov, Vladimir Oleinik, Yurii Rudkin and Vladimir Strekozov), and those in open opposition to Yeltsin (Nikolai Vedernikov, Valerii Zor'kin and Viktor Luchin).[13] The Court elected two allegedly pro-Yeltsin judges as its chair (Tumanov) and deputy chair (Morshchakova).[14] According to the Law on the Constitutional Court of the Russian Federation, the Court cannot consider cases on its own; rather at least 20 per cent of the Federation Council's members are required to agree whether or not the Court may judge a case. Despite this limitation, the Court's decisions are not subject to appeal and legislation which it rules as unconstitutional will be automatically invalidated.[15]

Other aspects of presidential–parliamentary relations have been strained. For instance, the two branches exhibited a conflict of opinions over declaring 12 December a non-working public holiday. On 12 September 1994 Yeltsin decreed 12 December a new national holiday, to be celebrated as Constitution Day to mark the new constitution adopted on 12 December 1993.[16] However, on 8 December the Duma rejected the proposal. By voting to retain 12 December as a working day, the Duma broke a tradition dating back to 1936. Stalin and Brezhnev marked the dates of the 1936 and 1977 constitutions (respectively 5 December and 7 October) as public holidays. Moreover, as Julia Wishnevsky argues, the vote suggests that a majority of the deputies have doubts over whether the constitution is 'an entirely legal document'.[17] Nevertheless, Yeltsin overruled the Duma's decision and issued a decree making 12 December a state holiday.[18]

The issue of confidence in the government is another problem area between the executive and the State Duma. According to the constitution adopted in December 1993 the Duma may conduct votes of confidence in the government (Article 103).[19] However, the president has the ultimate decision whether or not to dismiss the government. The constitutional procedures mandate that the Duma must first issue a proclamation of no confidence in the government which must be supported by a majority of its deputies. After the Duma expresses no confidence in the government, the president has the option of either dismissing it or not agreeing with the lower house's decision. If, within a three-month period, the Duma expresses another vote of no confidence in the government, the president can either dismiss the government or disband the Duma and call for new elections (Article 117).

On 11 October 1994 the Russian rouble fell a record 845 points to 3,926 to the US dollar; a Central Bank injection of 80 million dollars prevented the currency from plummeting to over 4,000 to the dollar.[20] At the insistence of the centrist Democratic Party of Russia faction, a motion of no confidence in the government was placed on the Duma's agenda. On 12 October Duma deputies voted 230 to 2 with numerous abstentions to hold a ballot of confidence in the government.[21] The proposal on 19 October by the nationalist Russia's Path faction leader Sergei Baburin that the performance of Prime Minister Viktor Chernomyrdin's government be discussed 'immediately' was voted down; subsequently deputies scheduled the vote to take place on 27 October 1994.[22]

The Duma's initiative fell short on the day. Of the 450 Duma deputies, 194 voted against the government, 54 supported it, 55 abstained and 147 were absent. Therefore, the Duma was 32 votes short of the majority it needed to pass a vote of no confidence in the government.[23] Victor Yasmann argues that the result can be considered 'a personal victory' for Yeltsin, who:

> managed to split the opposition by appointing Aleksandr Nazarchuk, a member of the Agrarian Party, as the new minister for agriculture before the vote was taken. As a result, the Agrarians, who generally work with the Communists, vowed not to vote against the government.[24]

Nevertheless, the following day the Duma adopted, 'by an overwhelming majority a resolution branding the performance of Prime Minister Viktor Chernomyrdin's government "unsatisfactory"'.[25]

At the time of writing, the Duma was considering another vote of no confidence in the government, which its deputies claimed was linked largely with a move to restructure Ukraine's debt. However, Deputy Prime Minister Yurii Yarov considers that their initiatives had more to do with 'pre-election manoeuvring'.[26] The motion was dropped from the Duma's agenda after Zhirinovsky's Liberal Democratic Party of Russia faction withdrew its support.[27]

In other matters Yeltsin has certainly faced challenges from the legislative branch. For instance, according to the constitution, the Federation Council implements presidential decrees of a state of emergency (Article 102). Twice in February 1995 the Federation Council rejected Yeltsin's decrees for states of emergency in Ingushetia and North Ossetia.[28] Moreover, in mid-January 1995 the upper house considered proposals to begin impeachment proceedings against Yeltsin – for which they are empowered under Article 93 of the constitution – and to prosecute him for violating the constitution by dispatching the army to Chechnya without declaring either military or emergency rule.[29] The vote fell far short of the 90 required (61 voted in favour).[30]

Executive–parliamentary relations have been rather stormy during the 1994–5 period. According to the constitution, the president retains an overwhelming amount of political power. Indeed, in particular matters, such as the Chechen crisis, his exercise of power has been wide-ranging. Nevertheless, the parliament has made attempts to make itself heard and has on several occasions mounted effective challenges to presidential initiatives and to the Russian government, and has demonstrated that it is a viable contender for political power in its own right. Moreover, executive–legislative differences have been settled by discussions and legal procedures rather than by violence and the staging of large-scale demonstrations.

The future of elections in Russia

During 1994 elections were held to local government legislatures. Based on their results, there is very little which supporters of political change through elections and supporters of further reform may find assuring. The initial rounds of the elections were consistently plagued with low turnout figures, often resulting in their being postponed until the autumn. As Tat'yana Mikhalskaya argues, for instance, in Novgorod, where 25 per cent of voters were required to participate in order for the elections to be valid, none of its eight districts produced a legitimate result. Moreover, in the regions where valid elections were held – Nizhnii Novgorod, Irkutsk, Bryansk, Voronezh and Samara *oblasti* and Sakhalin – the legislatures invariably met for the first time without full deputy corpuses.[31]

Opposition forces benefited in the local elections. For instance, in Penza *oblast'* many democratic candidates campaigned very hard, but the population voted against them. Forty out of 45 seats in the province's legislative assembly were won by members of the former *nomenklatura*. *Izvestiya* reporter Aleksandr Kislov notes the conservativeness of the voting behaviour of Penza's residents at these elections: these same voters voted against the constitution in December 1993, and Viktor Ilyushenko, former leader of the National Salvation Front, hails from the area. Moreover, Kislov contends that redistricting efforts clearly worked to benefit the rural areas: 30 of the 45 seats in the legislature represent these localities. Even more significant were the differences in the number of voters in districts, which ranged between 100 and 200 per cent, despite the fact that the election statute demands no more than a 10 per cent variance.[32]

Nikolai Medvedev, Head of the Administration for Work with Geographic Areas, noted that democratic forces would be seriously disadvantaged in the local elections. He claimed that 'no matter what propaganda efforts the [democrats] make, opposition representatives will receive at least 43 per cent in the elections'.[33] By his estimations Lipetsk, Tambov, Orel, Ryazan' and Voronezh *oblasti* were the areas where democratic canvassing would be 'most hopeless'. This was largely due to the 'blunders the reformers committed'. In order to rectify the social situation, economic policies had to be reoriented to take the population's conditions into account.[34]

In subsequent rounds of elections held in autumn 1994, results were generally very bad for democratic forces. For instance, it was noted in *Izvestiya* that in the ten regions that conducted elections on 27 November 1994:

the results eloquently indicate that, for the most part, victory was celebrated by representatives of pro-Communist and nationalist forces. The democrats suffered a fiasco almost everywhere.[35]

Boris Fedorov, former finance minister and current leader of both the liberal Union of 12 December faction in the State Duma and the business-oriented Forward Russia Party, noted similar results, yet stressed that there were some positive lessons that democratic forces could learn from these elections. He argued that the victories of the Communists and 'Zhirinovskyites' could be attributed to three major factors. These were, firstly, the weakness, lack of will and corruption of the local authorities, all of which led to votes for the opposition forces; secondly, the democrats' inability to dissociate themselves from those in power, and, finally, the democrats' lack of organization, commitment, action, meetings with voters and specific programmes.[36] These conditions contributed to the opposition's victories in Krasnodar, for example. However, Fedorov claims that democratic forces were successful in Sochi, where State Duma deputy V. Boiko was able to organize a united bloc of progressive candidates for the city's offices, where they won 9 out of 26 seats (35 per cent). Moreover, Fedorov stresses that victory in the elections could be achieved if contestants developed a clear-cut programme and commitments, a 'team' atmosphere and an energetic, business-like approach.[37]

These factors will certainly be essential in future campaigning, because Russian politicians and their supporters will need to encourage voters to participate in subsequent votes. Indeed, recent public opinion surveys indicate that there is a high degree of political apathy among the Russian electorate. For instance, a Russia-wide poll conducted by the All-Russian Centre for the Study of Public Opinion and published in *Segodnya* in early November 1994 indicated that 40 per cent of Russians would not participate in elections to the State Duma if they were held the next Sunday.[38] Similarly, 42 per cent of respondents in a poll conducted in Novgorod indicated that they did not intend to participate in elections anymore. This reply came as a result of 77 per cent of those surveyed considering that the reform process is heading in a negative direction (as opposed to 18 per cent who viewed it positively), and 51 per cent seeing their situation deteriorating from the previous year (compared to 33 per cent who felt there was no change and 6 per cent who considered their lot in life better). The Novgorod respondents did not have faith in politicians: only 6 per cent supported Yeltsin's policies, while 78 per cent opposed them.

Moreover, they had more trust in the Church (26 per cent) and in the army (20 per cent) than in the Provincial or State Dumas (respectively 5 per cent and 1 per cent).[39]

Conclusion

These factors – lack of enthusiasm for elections, support for neo-communist and nationalist forces – create difficult dilemmas for those designing future Russian electoral guidelines. According to the established legislation, new Russian presidential elections are to be conducted in June 1996. In agreement with the concluding section of the constitution, voters are scheduled to elect the Federal Assembly in December 1995. There has been much speculation in the Russian and Western scholarly and popular press, virtually since the Federal Assembly began meeting, concerning whether or not elections will be held, who the main contestants will be and what possible scenarios will emerge after the polls. It is not my intention to engage in political forecasting at this time; therefore I will avoid any prognosis of future elections. At the time of writing there are still no approved laws to govern the election of either the president or the parliament. Reports appearing at present focus on, for instance, the number of Duma deputies to be elected through party lists: Yeltsin favours 150, while Duma deputies prefer the established total of 225. Moreover, there have been particularly acute shortcomings in the drafts of laws on presidential elections. Leonid Kirichenko argues that under one of the earlier drafts there was a possibility that both candidates could lose because they polled less than 50 per cent of the votes. The elections would have to be conducted again with two potentially more unpopular candidates. If, after two rounds of elections, there was still no president elected, Kirichenko postulates, 'many politicians may have a pretext for demanding an annulment of direct elections of the president by the people ... and their replacement by presidential election by a narrower circle, for instance by the Federal Assembly'.[40] Flaws in legislation notwithstanding, candidates have begun their campaigns for the presidency. They include the current frontrunner, Yabloko leader Grigorii Yavlinsky, and former Vice-President Aleksandr Rutskoi. At present, Yeltsin has not officially declared whether or

Conclusion 257

not he will make a re-election bid; however it was reported that 'the President's staff is working as if Yeltsin will seek a second term'.[41]

Competitive politics in Russia is still in its infancy: both Russia's politicians and its citizens are learning the procedural norms and practices as the situation develops. The contributors to this volume have suggested that there have been many impediments blocking free and fair elections in Russia. Despite these hindrances, Russian voters have been able to score isolated victories in getting their representatives elected. However, these efforts have also been overshadowed by social conditions which militate against further democratic developments. Indeed, the unexpected success of the opposition forces in the December 1993 elections and the poor fate of the democrats in subsequent elections illustrate this point. As was argued in this volume's Introduction, with these elections Russia has taken only the first step in its political marathon of democratic consolidation and institutionalization. The contemporary Russian Federation's political system has certainly seen many significant developments on those of its Soviet and pre-revolutionary ancestors. Nevertheless, it still possesses some of their traditions and practices, such as its manner of conducting elections. It remains to be seen whether or not this will change after these new institutions become more firmly rooted in Russian politics.

Notes

1 See, for instance, 'Soobshchenie Tsentral'noi izbiratel'noi komissii ob itogakh vyborov v Verkhovnyi Sovet SSSR odinnadtsatogo sozyva sostoyavshikhsya 4 marta 1984 goda', *Vedomosti Verkhovnogo Soveta SSSR*, no. 11 (14 March 1984), item no. 2241, pp. 199–203.
2 See, for instance, the lists of deputies that appear in *Izvestiya* on 5 April, 16 April, 21 May, 25 May and 26 May 1989; A. Nazimova and V. Sheinis, 'Vybor sdelan', *Izvestiya*, 6 May 1989, p. 3; *Narodnye deputaty SSSR* (Moscow: Vneshtorgizdat, 1990), *Spisok narodnykh deputatov RSFSR* (Moscow: Vneshtorgizdat, 1991), and Darrell Slider, 'Political Elites in the Republics', in David Lane (ed.), *Russia in Flux: The Political and Social Consequences of Reform* (Aldershot: Edward Elgar, 1992), pp. 41–61.
3 Based on author's database compiled from 'Spisok deputatov Gosudarstvennoi Dumy Federal'nogo Sobraniya Rossiiskoi Federatsii, izbrannykh po obshchefederal'nomu izbiratel'nomu okrugu' and 'Spisok deputatov Gosudarstvennoi Dumy Federal'nogo Sobraniya Rossiiskoi

Federatsii, izbrannykh po odnomandatnym izbiratel'nym okrugam', *Rossiiskaya gazeta*, 28 December 1993, respectively pp. 2–3 and 3–5, and Dmitrii Orlov, 'Portret Dumy v tsifrakh', *Rossiiskie vesti*, 10 January 1994, p. 1.

4 Based on author's database compiled from 'Spisok deputatov Soveta Federatsii Federal'nogo Sobraniya Rossiiskoi Federatsii izbrannykh po dvukhmandatnym izbiratel'nym okrugam', *Rossiiskaya gazeta*, 28 December 1993, pp. 5–6.

5 Yurii Buida, 'Russkii noyabr': oppozitsionnost' vkhodit v modu', *Nezavisimaya gazeta*, 2 December 1993, pp. 1, 3.

6 Robert Orttung, 'Marychev Leaves LDP', *OMRI Daily Digest*, no. 51, part I (13 March 1995).

7 Alfred Stepan and Cindy Skach, 'Constitutional Frameworks and Democratic Consolidation: Parliamentarianism versus Presidentialism', *World Politics*, vol. 46, no. 1 (October 1993), pp. 1–22.

8 Pre-election summaries of voting records of the list candidates who were previously RSFSR People's Deputies were published in 'Stepen' podderzhki politicheskikh i ekonomicheskikh reform', *Argumenty i fakty*, no. 49 (1993), p. 4.

9 See, for instance, the article by Nikolai Troitsky in *Megapolis Express*, no. 1 (5 January 1994), p. 16, cited as '"Senators" and Duma Members Don't Promise a Quiet Life', in *Current Digest of the Post-Soviet Press*, vol. XLVI, no. 1 (1994), pp. 1–2.

10 Anders Åslund, 'Russia's Success Story', *Foreign Affairs*, vol. 73, no. 5 (September/October 1994), pp. 58–71, at p. 58.

11 ibid., p. 60.

12 See, for instance, Sergei Parkhomenko, 'Sovet Federatsii otverg novuyu partiyu kandidatov v chleny v KS', *Segodnya*, 16 November 1994, p. 2.

13 See for instance, *Kommersant" daily*, 8 February 1995, and *Izvestiya*, 9 February 1995, cited in Analytica Moscow, *Politica Weekly Press Summary: Electronic Mail Version*, vol. II, no. 5 (4–10 February 1995).

14 See Julia Wishnevsky, 'Constitutional Court Elects Pro-Yeltsin Leaders', *OMRI Daily Digest*, no. 32, part I (14 February 1995), and Analytica Moscow, 'Dossier: Background of Newly Elected Chairman of the Constitutional Court, Vladimir Tumanov', item 4B, *Politica Weekly Press Summary: Electronic Mail Version*, vol. II, no. 16 (11–17 February 1995).

15 *Kommersant" daily*, 8 February 1995, cited in Analytica Moscow, *Politica Weekly Press Summary: Electronic Mail Version*, vol. II, no. 5 (4–10 February 1995).

16 Julia Wishnevsky, 'Yeltsin Declares 12 December "Constitution Day"', *RFE/RL Daily Report*, no. 179 (12 September 1994).

17 Julia Wishnevsky, 'Duma Rejects Proposal to Declare 12 December a Holiday', *RFE/RL Daily Report*, no. 232 (12 December 1994).

18 Julia Wishnevsky, 'Yeltsin Overrules Duma on Constitution Day', *RFE/RL Daily Report*, no. 233 (12 December 1994).

Conclusion 259

19 *Konstitutsiya Rossiiskoi Federatsii prinyata vsenarodnym golosovaniem 12 dekabrya 1993 g.* (Moscow: Yuridicheskaya literatura, 1993).
20 Penny Morvant, 'Ruble Collapse Continues', *RFE/RL Daily Report*, no. 194 (12 October 1994).
21 Penny Morvant, 'State Duma Schedules Vote of No Confidence in Government', *RFE/RL Daily Report*, no. 195 (13 October 1994).
22 Julia Wishnevsky, 'No Early Vote of Confidence in Government', *RFE/RL Daily Report*, no. 200 (20 October 1994).
23 Victor Yasmann, 'Government Survives No-Confidence Vote', *RFE/RL Daily Report*, no. 206 (28 October 1994).
24 ibid.
25 Julia Wishnevsky, 'Duma Brands Government's Performance "Unsatisfactory"', *RFE/RL Daily Report*, no. 207 (31 October 1994).
26 Robert Orttung, 'Minister Says No-Confidence Vote Will Fail', *OMRI Daily Digest*, no. 70, part I (7 April 1995).
27 Interfax, cited in Robert Orttung, 'Duma Drops No-Confidence Vote From Agenda', *OMRI Daily Digest*, no. 71, part I (10 April 1995).
28 Interfax, cited in Robert Orttung, 'Federation Council Rejects State of Emergency', *OMRI Daily Digest*, no. 28, part I (8 February 1995).
29 Julia Wishnevsky, 'Attempt to Impeach Yeltsin Fails', *OMRI Daily Digest*, no. 15, part I (20 January 1995).
30 ibid.
31 Tatyana Mikhalskaya, in *Moskovskie novosti*, no. 13 (1994), p. A7, cited as 'Local Authorities: No New Faces', *Current Digest of the Post-Soviet Press*, vol. XLVI, no. 13 (1994), p. 14.
32 Aleksandr Kislov, 'Nachalis' vybory v mestnye organy vlasty. V penzenskoi oblasti manipulyatsii s okrugami obespecheli oppozitsii bezgovorochnuyu pobedu', *Izvestiya*, 2 February 1994, p. 1.
33 Valerii Vyzhutovich, 'Vozvrashchenie "partkhoznomenklatury" k vlasti na mestakh mozhet vynudit' El'tsin k otstupleniyu', *Izvestiya*, 3 February 1994, p. 1.
34 ibid.
35 'Vybory pokazyvayut: demokraticheskie sily teryayut pozitsii v regionakh', ibid., 29 November 1994, p. 2.
36 Boris Fedorov, 'Krasnodar–Sochi–Moskva', *Izvestiya*, p. 2.
37 ibid.
38 Interfax report, '40% rossiyan ne zainteresovany v novykh deputatakh Gosdumy', *Segodnya*, 11 November 1994, p. 2.
39 Tat'yana Shchipanova, 'Bol'shinstvo novgorodstev ne khotyat vybirat'', *Segodnya*, 24 November 1994, p. 3.
40 Leonid Kirichenko, 'Presidential Law Absurd', *Moscow News*, no. 3 (1995), p. 4.
41 NTV, 10 April 1995, cited in Robert Orttung, 'Filatov Says Yeltsin's Staff Preparing for Campaign', *OMRI Daily Digest*, no. 72, part I (11 April 1995).

Appendix: Electoral Associations and their Programmes

PETER LENTINI

This Appendix contains information on the electoral associations that participated in the elections to the Russian State Duma in December 1993.[1] What follows is a listing of their origins, programmatic orientations and leading candidates; the social groups that they sought to represent and that comprised the largest part of their membership, and the political organizations and citizens' groups which formed them. The 1993 elections were the first 'proto-party' or 'multiparty' elections in Russian history in over seventy years. Nevertheless, independent candidates were still very important in these elections, winning nearly 130 of the State Duma's 450 seats.

The information contained herein highlights the fact that, although parties and political movements participated in the elections, the Russian party system is still at an early stage of development and parties are still not a major link between state and society. Nevertheless, parties are playing a somewhat stronger role in Russian politics than they were in the 1990–93 period. Richard Sakwa has claimed that during that period nine factors hampered the development of a stable Russian party system:

(1) an unstable ideological basis, reflected in indistinct programme differentials;
(2) a problematic relationship between leaders and parties resulting in *krugovshchina* (the tendency for parties to fracture around their dominant personalities);
(3) a political and social atmosphere which was decidedly anti-party;

(4) the emergence of a presidential system and, moreover, of a president who has not allied himself with any political parties or movements, claiming to be above politics, and the election of a non-party parliament in 1990;
(5) the cooptation of the most able individuals into government rather than into political parties;
(6) small party memberships reflecting an anti-party stance among the Russian population;
(7) the absence of reliable social bases from which parties could draw support;
(8) the importance of regional politics, which hampered the effectiveness of a national base for party development;
(9) the breakup of the Soviet Union, which 'weakened the coherence of the parties and challenged them to find a new synthesis of the national idea and democratic principles'.[2]

Therefore, Sakwa's categorization of Russia's political configurations as not *proto-party* but *pseudo-party* has significant grounding.[3] What the programmatic information presented below demonstrates is that these deficiencies are in the process of being overcome, although only to a small extent.

In the following I refer to the blocs that competed in the elections as 'electoral associations'. I do so for several reasons. First, I follow a juridical principle. The Central Electoral Commission (abbreviated to Tsentrizbirkom) registered all parties and blocs participating in the elections as electoral associations (*izbiratel'nye ob"edinenniya*). My second reason for referring to these blocs as electoral associations rather than parties is that few parties (i.e. groups actually calling themselves parties) participated in the elections and put forward their own slates of candidates. Those that did included the Agrarian Party of Russia, the Democratic Party of Russia, the Communist Party of the Russian Federation, the Liberal Democratic Party of Russia and the Party of Russian Unity and Accord.

However, even the party lists that the aforementioned electoral organizations put forward were not filled solely with their party members or with members only of that organization. Overall, 69 out of 225 list deputies (30.7 per cent) did not belong to political parties or movements as members, but, nonetheless, won their seats in this manner. For instance, of the 21 deputies elected to the Agrarian Party of Russia's list, five (23.8 per cent) did not belong to the party. Similarly, five of the Democratic Party of Russia's 14 deputies (35.7 per cent); two of the Communist Party of the Russian Federation's 32 deputies (6.3 per cent); two of the Party of

Russian Unity and Accord's 18 deputies (11.1 per cent); six of Russia's Choice's 40 deputies (15 per cent); 15 of the Yavlinsky-Boldyrev-Lukin bloc's 20 deputies (75 per cent) and ten of the Women of Russia bloc's 21 deputies (47.6 per cent) were not members of political parties or movements. Most surprising, however, is the fact that the Liberal Democratic Party of Russia – which won the greatest number of seats through the party list (59) and, as is argued below, claims to have quite a substantial membership and numerous regional support centres – had a surprisingly high number of independent candidates elected as its deputies (24, or 40.7 per cent). Moreover, two of its deputies belonged to other political parties. Deputy Vitalii Zhuravlev is registered as a member of the Party of Social Justice and Viktor Vishnyakov is listed as a member of the Communist Party of the Russian Federation.[4] Therefore, these parties in effect had a much broader appeal than their original membership, and the term 'electoral association' is, in my opinion, more appropriate than the term 'party'.

Another factor which should be noted in referring to the weakness of the party system in Russia pertains to its absence of strong regional bases of support. Although some of the associations listed in this Appendix claim to have widespread support in some regions of Russia, and are established on an all-Russian basis, none of them fielded candidates in every one of the 225 single-seat constituencies.

This piece is not an exhaustive exposition of all the programmatic objectives that the electoral associations put forward in the 1993 elections. However, I hope that it illustrates how the electoral associations began to break away from the difficult position of having similar programme structures and objectives by undertaking more clearly defined stances. Richard Sakwa has noted that in the period before the elections 'thirty-eight significant parties all had much the same sort of programme and amorphous policies'.[5] Nevertheless, excluding Russia's Choice, which was the only electoral association supporting extensively pro-market principles, most of the competitors favoured common themes. These included a socially based market economy or state-guided transition to the market, the implementation of strong law and order policies, strengthened links with the states of the former USSR and the protection of the rights of Russians living in the 'near abroad' (the republics of the former USSR). Indeed, it has been noted that even a week before the elections were held, Russian voters were still unclear about the major differences between the electoral associations. Moreover, the voters claimed that the candidates' 'acting skills' were the main determinants on which they made their choices.[6] Therefore, it is worth noting these major limitations when studying the programmatic objectives set out below.

Programmatic information on the electoral blocs[7]

Blok 'Vybor Rossii'
Russia's Choice Bloc (VR)

This bloc was organized as an association supporting the course of reform after the April 1993 referendum. Russia's Choice collected 150,000 signatures supporting its bid for the Federal Assembly and fielded 234 candidates. The bloc included Democratic Russia, the Association of Private Farm Workers (AKKOR), the Peasants' Party of Russia, the 'Living Ring' Union, the Association of Privatized and Private Enterprises, 'Shchit' (Shield), the Democratic Initiative Party and others. Its founding congress was held on 16–17 October 1993. VR's all-federal list of candidates was headed by former first deputy chairman of the Council of Ministers, Yegor Gaidar, chairman of the President's Human Rights Commission, Sergei Kovalev, and former social defence minister Ella Pamfilova. The bloc's symbol was a statue of Peter the Great on a horse; its slogan was 'freedom, property and legality'. Leading bloc figure and key presidential supporter Gennadii Burbulis presented an explanation of VR's slogan in the newspaper *Megapolis Express*:

> Freedom is serious hard work for surmounting the totalitarian heritage and all that is connected with the communist dictatorship ... There will be nothing for us without property as a means of achieving freedom. It is absorbed as the holy right of private property, while there is still the little-realized right of intellectual property ... Legality for us is not an incantation, but a condition in which the formation of a valuable middle-class person is possible. It is a condition which must protect us from the bandit, the ... bureaucrat and from power evading the guarantees of the security of the country and citizens.[8]

Among the bloc's aims was the rebirth of the great traditions of the country based on patriotism, morality, democracy and the distinction of labour. The bloc supported a new parliament based on the accountability of deputies before their electoral associations and their electors. It sought to promote a new federalism as the foundation for the construction of the state of the Russian Federation. The bloc opposed separatism and advocated fusing the national idea with the idea of democracy of a European orientation combined with national traditions. VR advocated a federalism that would not be connected with the national question, but would rather be one in which the supremacy of federal law would be guaranteed.

In its economic programme VR foresaw a reform of the budgetary system and a gradual lowering of taxes. VR supported stimulating tax resource savings and liquidating import subsidies. The bloc circulated the slogan, 'Not the salvation of the weak, but assistance to the strong'. VR was concerned particularly with overcoming the limitations in the military-industrial complex. The fundamental provisions of its privatization programme promoted the 'real inclusion' of all citizens of Russia in land privatization, strengthening the financial responsibility of enterprises, the legislative defence of joint stockholders' rights and support for entrepreneurs. In its agrarian policy, VR supported overcoming the subsidized character of seasonal credit and implementing a change from compulsory state orders.

After the 1993 elections VR had the largest number of deputies in the State Duma, with 70 (15.6 per cent). This number comprised 40 deputies from their federal list and 30 from the single-seat constituencies. Russia's Choice also took four committee chairs: Defence (Sergei Yushenkov), Health Protection (Bela Denisenko), Information Policy and Communications (Mikhail Poltoranin) and Organization of the State Duma (Vladimir Bauer).

Rossiiskoe dvizhenie demokraticheskikh reform
Russian Movement for Democratic Reforms (RDDR)

This movement was formed in 1992 and was drawn largely from the membership of the Inter-regional Deputies' Group of the USSR Congress of People's Deputies. The RDDR collected 135,000 signatures before submitting its list to the Tsentrizbirkom for registration. Its leader was former mayor of Moscow Gavriil Popov (who, incidentally, did not compete for a place in the Federal Assembly). Heading its 153-candidate list were St Petersburg mayor Anatolii Sobchak, physician and entrepreneur Svyatoslav Fedorov and people's artist Oleg Basilashvili. The RDDR failed to clear the 5 per cent threshold for the party-list seats. Four of its deputies were elected to the Duma in the constituencies. Its symbol was the astrological Taurus.

Among the democratic camp the RDDR considered itself different from, for instance, VR or the Party of Russian Unity and Accord (PRES) because neither the movement nor its members were striving to achieve power either collectively or individually. Rather, by participating in the elections the RDDR hoped to stimulate what it considered the most important political development for Russia – the development of two democratic camps. In the first there would be a core of democrats 'from within' (i.e. bureaucrats). The second grouping would be comprised of those who wanted to contribute to democracy by working 'outside' the system. This is where the RDDR saw itself.[9]

The RDDR placed a priority on individual human rights over the rights of the nation and of the state. Its formula for the state's configuration was a broad federalism with 'deeper decentralization' and a limitation of the rights of the federal centre, while simultaneously maintaining Russia's integrity.[10]

Its economic programme had several distinctive features. For instance, the movement supported making the state's priority the finance of manufacturing. It also advocated reducing taxes, cutting federal expenditure, reviewing privatization decisions, making state sector management more precise, issuing land vouchers (no less than 1,000 free to each person) and declaring the right of each person to receive up to 40 hectares of private land 'close to home' for his or her own agricultural use. No less than 10 per cent of the land fund would be distributed for the creation of private farms; any kolkhoz or sovkhoz 'working normally' would have the right to receive state subsidies.

The RDDR also put forward some points for a military programme. It supported transferring from conscript-based armed forces to a professional military subordinate to federal powers. 'Regional forces' such as militias or national guards would be allowed. However, they would complement the conscript forces and be financed from local budgets.

The association claimed that several factors impeded its campaign progress. Its problems included the fact that RDDR branches were not active in all of Russia's regions. Another factor raised by Popov was that originally the RDDR was listed on the back page of the ballot paper and voters would have to turn the document over to see their listing.[11]

Blok 'Yavlinsky-Boldyrev-Lukin'
'Yavlinsky-Boldyrev-Lukin' Bloc (Yabloko)

This bloc was formed at the end of October 1993 primarily from three political forces: the Republican Party of Russia, the Social Democratic Party of Russia and the Russian Christian Democratic Union–New Democracy party. Several other lesser-known and less influential organizations also participated in the bloc's formation. Yabloko collected 170,000 signatures and put forward a 172-candidate list which included a range of well-known economists, lawyers, academics, entrepreneurs and diplomats. The bloc advocated 'fundamental democratic values, freedoms and market economics' and at the same time repudiated 'explosive' measures in the economy and politics. According to its leaders' self-evaluation the bloc considered itself an 'independent democratic constructive opposition' to the economic policies pursued by the Gaidar and Chernomyrdin government. Many of its list deputies were affiliated with the Yavlinsky-directed Tsentr Ekonomicheskikh i Politicheskikh Isledovanii (Centre for Economic and Political Research, abbreviated as

EPITsentr), based in Moscow. Heading the list were the highly respected reform economist Grigorii Yavlinsky, former USSR people's deputy Yurii Boldyrev, and diplomat and former permanent ambassador to the US Vladimir Lukin.

Yabloko's economic bases revolved around introducing institutional changes in the economy without making it impossible to achieve financial stabilization. The bloc placed an emphasis on reform 'from below'. It advocated close economic interrelationships between Russia and the USSR's former republics, a system of demonopolization, the development of competition, and a review of budgetary policies and tax regulations. Yabloko was decidedly against the voucher privatization process which, in its estimation, was not moving enterprises into private hands. Rather the bloc considered it the 'collectivization of industry'.

Corruption was another area to which the bloc was extremely sensitive, feeling its existence was perhaps a result of the inheritance of previously accepted and adopted economic policies. Therefore, the bloc advocated honesty in politics, openness and publicity in the operations of those in power.

Occupying 5.1 per cent of the overall seats in the Duma following the elections, Yabloko was represented by 23 deputies, 20 of whom were elected through its federal list. Bloc deputies chaired two committees: Mikhail Zadornov was put in charge of the Budget, Taxes, Bank and Finance Committee and Vladimir Lukin became chair of the International Affairs Committee.

Partiya Rossiiskogo edinstva i soglasiya
Party of Russian Unity and Accord (PRES)

The process of the party's formation began in May 1993, and on 6 August 1993 a committee in support of the party was registered. The party's founding congress was held in Velikii Novgorod on 17 October 1993 and the PRES Moscow city organization held its founding conference on 23 October 1993. About 222,000 voters supported the PRES's Tsentrizbirkom registration. The party was called the 'party of the regions' and entered into the elections with a political platform 'reflecting the aspirations of millions of Russians, residents of large and small cities and villages of the Russian "depths" (*glubniki*), to live in peace, harmony and prosperity'.

Its programmatic aims included the association of Russian land and the maintenance of the Russian state. To achieve this task the PRES advocated uniting the general interests of the regions. It claimed that although Russia calls itself a federation, the actual creation of a federation stands before Russia. During the election the PRES stressed that two models of federalism existed in Russia – national and territorial – and the party saw this as contradicting Russia's state configuration. What was necessary, in its view, was a transition period (which would take some time) in which elements of the old model would be retained in order to usher in a new federal model. Once this had occurred, the party would determine the strategy and tactics necessary to resolve the problem of the distribution of powers between the centre and the regions, between state power and local self-administration.

The PRES favoured continuing the course of economic reform, however, through a socially oriented market economy, which it considered a means for speeding up the exit of the country from its crisis and the creation of civilized market relations. In the process, the PRES advocated decentralizing power, granting more latitude to the subjects of the federation and to local organs, significantly broadening their rights, first of all in the areas of taxation, privatization, state property management, entrepreneurial support and the population's social defence. The party maintained a positive attitude towards private property, while supporting different forms of property within society.[12] Other objectives included the revival of the institution of legislative power in Russia as an active democratic organ; the creation of conditions which would make the repetition of violent outbursts of a political or any other nature impossible in Russia; a continuation of economic and political reform in the conditions of social and national peace, taking into account the interests of all society's strata, without violence and on an evolutionary path. In other economic matters the PRES supported the defence of Russian entrepreneurs' interests, particularly in manufacturing and services. Its concerns in national politics included the reform of Russian statehood based on the unity and aspirations of Russia, taking into account the opinions of all nations populating it, the defence of the life and interests of Russians in the 'near' and 'far' abroad. Finally, the PRES advocated the spiritual rebirth of Russia, and the revival of its historical distinctiveness based on a strong economy and common sense policy.

Heading its 143-candidate list were its leader, deputy chairman of the Russian Council of Ministers Sergei Shakhrai, Aleksandr Shokhin and Konstantin Zatulin. Despite the fact that it was called the 'party of the regions', its main drawback was that it operated on the basis of a state structure, and its 48 regional organs had few rank-and-file members. The PRES was allocated 19 seats in the Duma, 18 of which resulted from its success on the federal list. Three of its deputies were given committee chairs in the Duma: Sergei Shapovalov (Federation Affairs and Regional Policy), Konstantin Zatulin (Commonwealth of Independent States and Links with Compatriots) and Anatolii Sliva (Local Government).

'Dostoinstvo i miloserdie'
Dignity and Charity (DiM)

This bloc was formed on 20 October 1993, when the All-Russian Council of Veterans (Pensioners) of War, Labour, the Armed Forces and Law Enforcement Organs joined forces with the All-Russian Society of Invalids and the 'Chernobyl' Union. DiM collected 130,000 signatures. Their 58-candidate federation-wide list was headed by academic Konstantin Frolov, actor and former culture minister Nikolai Gubenko and president of the 'Chernobyl' Union Vyacheslav Grishin. The competitors were mainly representatives of all-Russian and large regional organizations of veterans of war and labour, invalids, Chernobyl victims and administration bureaucrats concerned with the problems of invalids and veterans.

Grishin, in an interview published in *Moskovskie novosti*, stated that DiM participated in the elections because the government had not fulfilled its promise to solve social policy problems. For instance, it had not controlled inflation, improved medicinal and medical services, strengthened the struggle with crime and corruption or paid stipends and pensions in good time. The bloc also supported industrial entrepreneurship and land reform. Its electoral slogans were 'For conditions of life suitable for the person'; 'For humanitarianism and the spiritual birth of the person', and 'Reform for the person but not at the person's expense'.[13] Two of its deputies were elected to constituency seats.

Konstruktivnoe ekologicheskoe dvizhenie Rossii
Constructive Ecological Movement of Russia (KEDR)

The KEDR began organizing itself in March 1993 and achieved an all-Russian status on 2 August 1993. On 7 October 1993 the KEDR's leader Anatolii Panfilov and leaders of several ecological and other movements signed an agreement on joint political activity. The KEDR's list to the Tsentrizbirkom was supported by approximately 150,000 voters. Its all-federal list of 44 candidates was headed by Lyubov' Lymar', chairwoman of the 'Soldiers' Mothers of Russia' movement, Vladimir Chubaraev, chief of the administration of Gossanepidnadzor (State Supervisory Committee on Sanitation and Epidemics), and Stanislav Baranov, general director of a light metal-design factory.

The KEDR favoured the formation of a legal base and a truly active mechanism for guaranteeing the health of the people of Russia. It cited as its main tasks the guaranteeing of legislative and ecological bases for the maintenance and development of native scientific-technological and intellectual potential; the development of a system of environmental education, and the creation of 100 non-state regional ecological funds.

With its underlying principles of constructiveness, awareness, humanity, realism, independence and openness, the KEDR advocated constructing a democratic, rule-of-law state, strengthening the development of private property, defending Russian national interests and maintaining a socially oriented state. The KEDR failed to clear the 5 per cent hurdle; therefore none of its candidates won seats in the Duma.

Zhenshchiny Rossii
Women of Russia (ZhR)[14]

ZhR was formed in the middle of October 1993, when three women's organizations joined forces: the Union of Women of Russia (the successor to the Soviet Women's Committee), the Union of Women Entrepreneurs and the Union of Women of the Navy. The movement's support base included the Union of Women of Russia's cells, uniting over 100 organizations representing the interests of home-makers, soldiers' mothers and women in the creative professions. ZhR collected 127,000 signatures. The movement's chairwoman, Alevtina Fedulova, a former first deputy chairwoman of the Soviet Women's Committee and CPSU Central Committee member,[15] in an interview published in *Izvestiya*, stated that ZhR is not a party but a political movement, and that it has no intention of becoming a party. ZhR does not advocate policies solely on the basis of sex; however, it has acknowledged that in Russia policies are drawn up in a single-sex manner – by men. Fedulova, after studying thirty of the programmes of Russia's parties and political organizations, came to the conclusion that none of them 'formed their own opinions towards the women's question'. She mentioned further that 'half the country are women and it is impossible to build a democratic society, to form a new parliament, without taking this circumstance into account'. It is important to note that ZhR is not a feminist organization and is against what it considers 'extremism' in all its forms.

The movement considered that there were certain issues affecting the lives of Russian women which needed to be addressed in the State Duma. First, ZhR was concerned with unemployment: women at this time constituted 73 per cent of the unemployed. There were also three million single women in Russia who might be able to count only on their personal earnings. Earlier, women received nearly 70 per cent of men's earnings, whereas by December 1993 this figure had been reduced to about 40 per cent of male salaries. Another issue of great concern to women which was not handled by other parties and movements was the reduction of maternal and infant mortality and high levels of illness.

ZhR did not consider its participation in the elections as part of a power struggle. Rather the movement viewed its electoral activities as a means of achieving peace and agreement in society. The movement advocated reform, but not at any cost. It placed an emphasis on social policy, claiming that 'a market economy is not an aim but a means of improving a person's life'. Moreover, the movement felt that 'social policy is not [simply] a populist promise'.

Although Fedulova admitted that the movement did not have a formally developed programme 'as, for example, Gaidar-led "VR"', ZhR possessed well-constructed views of societally problematic target areas. In the economy, the movement promoted policies to develop those spheres in which there are high degrees of 'personal' labour, such as agriculture, housing, construction, foodstuffs and light industries. ZhR also believed that tax policies should be reviewed and that producing goods was unprofitable if 70–80 per cent of the state budget was derived from personal earnings. As its basis for a state configuration ZhR favoured a united country in which all subjects would be equal. The bloc also sought to promote further both primary and secondary education. It maintained that health care should be made available for everyone. When it decided to participate in the elections the government was not making any guarantees on health issues and ZhR was concerned to reduce the number of services for which Russians were being forced to pay. ZhR promoted a family policy, enabling those who could work to maintain a dignified lifestyle while those who were unable to engage in labour would be able to have some social security. The bloc supported the principle of land being 'turned over to its masters', but felt that land should be transferred on the basis of life-long rent with inheritance rights.

Women of Russia's 36 candidates were led into the elections by Fedulova, presidential adviser Yekaterina Lakhova and actress Natal'ya Gundareva. Of the three leaders, Fedulova and Lakhova had been appointed on 15 November 1993 to the President of the Russian Federation's Commission for Questions of Women, the Family and Demography, Lakhova as its chairwoman.[16] ZhR's list was supported by 8.1 per cent of the electorate and was allocated 21 seats. Two of its candidates won in the constituencies. Galina Klimatova was elected chair of the Duma committee on Women, the Family and Youth. Fedulova was elected a deputy chair of the Duma.

'Budushchee Rossii – novye imena'
Future of Russia – New Names (BRNI)

This bloc was formed in October 1993 from members of the Youth Movement in Support of the People's Party of Free Russia and the politico-economic association Civic Union. BRNI's registration list was supported by about 109,000 voters. Its all-federation leaders were Vyacheslav Lashchevsky, secretary of the Russian Union of Youth, Oleg Sokolov, chairman of the youth movement 'Free Russia', and Vladimir Mironov, director of the Institute of Politics.

In its programme, BRNI considered it essential to prioritize the recognition of personal freedoms and creation of conditions conducive to fulfilling personal aspirations; the elevation of the prestige and needs of society over those of the state, and an emphasis on law. It entered the elections under the slogan 'To live in our country without fear, in prosperity, and to have pride in Russia'. The electoral association supported legislation which would allow the imposition of states of emergency in order to combat crime; supervision of the power structures; the integrity of Russia; the adoption of laws defending the rights of property holders; the formation of a conscript army, and the adoption of the constitution.

In its economic policies, BRNI was directed towards a market economy which prioritized stimulating industry, reducing expenditure, supporting the export branches of industry, struggling with monopolism and false competition, working out legislation to defend private property on land, giving legislative guarantees for the socially defenceless groups of the population, creating the conditions for youth's self-realization, preventing unemployment and raising the salaries of the intelligentsia in order to make 'an investment in societal development'. Its foreign policy goals included changing the system of national security and placing an emphasis on developing relations with the countries of the CIS. As a result of the elections the bloc gained one representative in the Duma, Nikolai Gen.

Grazhdanskii soyuz vo imya stabil'nosti, spravedlivosti i progressa
Civic Union in the Name of Stability, Justice and Progress (GS)

This bloc was formed in October 1993 largely from the structures of the old Civic Union (previously comprised of Arkadii Vol'sky's 'Renewal' Union, Nikolai Travkin's Democratic Party of Russia and Aleksandr Rutskoi's People's Party of Free Russia). It also included the Russian Union of Industrialists and Entrepreneurs, the All-Russian 'Renewal' Union, the Russian Social Democratic Centre, the Association of Industrialists and Entrepreneurs of Russia, the Trade Union of Timber Industry Workers of the Russian Federation, the Trade Union of Construction and Industrial Building Materials Workers of the Russian Federation, and the movement 'Veterans of War for Peace'. GS's registration bid was supported by about 150,000 voters. Its all-federal list was headed by Arkadii Vol'sky, president of the Russian Union of Industrialists and Entrepreneurs; Nikolai Bekh, chairman of the KamAZ Joint-Stock Company, and Aleksandr Vladislavlev, leader of the 'Renewal' Union. Overall, GS put forward 184 candidates on its list, which was supported by only 1.9 per cent of the electorate. Therefore, none of its candidates were elected through the party seats. However, the association captured one constituency seat.

Civic Union participated in the elections because it felt that the Yeltsin leadership had 'lost power, authority, professionalism and careful planning of activity, works without perspective and is undisciplined and corrupt'. In addition GS sought to introduce measures to bring in greater 'control over local officials'. Its programme – according to Vol'sky developed long before the elections – strove to create a socially oriented market in which the social rights of the poor members of society would be protected; to struggle with inflation by stimulating manufacturing; to preserve the scientific potential of the country; to withdraw from shock therapy, and to stave off destitution and unemployment. Its fundamental principles for reform were concerned with the country's own resources and placed a priority on the development of the domestic market. GS also supported the maintenance of historically developed ties and traditional markets for Russian goods; state control over the foreign trade of raw materials and energy, and economic equality for urban and rural areas. It also advocated an unbroken federative state in accordance with established democratic and legal norms, the cooperation of peoples of the former USSR, a military doctrine able to satisfy the country's geopolitical interests and a reduction in the armed forces, which would, however, be compensated by a growth in the quality of weapons and military technology.[17]

Demokraticheskaya partiya Rossii
Democratic Party of Russia (DPR)

The DPR, one of Russia's longest-standing and active political parties, was organized between April and May 1990 and held its first congress in December 1990.[18] In December 1992 it claimed to have about 50,000 members.[19] In October 1993, it signed a statement supporting the activities of Khasbulatov and Rutskoi in relation to the 'October Days'. The DPR submitted its registration list to the Tsentrizbirkom with 109,000 signatures.

At its Fifth Congress, the DPR nominated 167 State Duma deputy candidates. Its three national list leaders were party chairman Nikolai Travkin, a former USSR and Russian Federation people's deputy and head of the administration of Moscow's Shakovskii district (who was expelled from the party in early 1995), film director Stanislav Govorukhin, and former USSR people's deputy and academician of the Russian Academy of Sciences Oleg Bogomolov.

Among its programmatic principles, the DPR supported Russia as a federative state, the limitation of the president's powers through parliamentary institutions, and the introduction of barriers in the buying and selling of land which would condition its use for industrial purposes ('land must be used for the same [purposes] for the first twenty years after it is received or sold'). In addition the DPR considered it necessary for various forms of management to exist. It proposed to invest in the economy in order to curb inflation, and named protectionism as its fundamental foreign economic policy component. The party supported stronger integration within the borders of the CIS and the upholding of Russia's interests 'everywhere they exist'.

The DPR's list was supported by 5.5 per cent of the electorate, and the party was allocated 14 seats in the Duma; none of its candidates were successful in the constituencies. Sergei Glaz'ev was elected chair of the Committee on Economic Policy.

Agrarnaya partiya Rossii
Agrarian Party of Russia (APR)

The APR, which put forward 145 State Duma candidates, held its first congress in February 1993 and was registered on 9 April 1993.[20] The party collected 500,000 signatures supporting its bid for the Federal Assembly, the largest number of any party or electoral bloc. Heading its all-federal list were former Russian people's deputy and chairman of the deputy fraction 'Agrarian Union', Mikhail Lapshin; chairman of the Central Committee of the Trade Union of Workers in the Agro-Industrial Complex of Russia, Aleksandr Davydov, and deputy chairman of the Russian Federation Council of Ministers, Aleksandr Zaveryukha. Its candidates were primarily former Russian and USSR people's deputies, former kolkhoz chairmen, directors in the agro-industrial complex, officials from soviets of different levels and CPSU officials, representatives of the scientific and creative intelligentsia and representatives of joint-stock companies.

The APR contended the elections in the interests of 'all rural dwellers and also urban dwellers ... taking in the needs and pains of the countryside as its own'. Its programme's fundamental thesis was that 'the rebirth of Russia must begin from its first point – the village'. The Agrarian Party supported guaranteeing social rights, first and foremost of which was the right to labour. They also advocated social justice, and state support for producers and the lowest-earning strata of the population.

Naturally the APR had a definite attitude towards land policies and Russia's future economic development. It believed that 'the land is for those who work it', and felt that plots should be distributed freely as property to 'all residents of the town and country'. However, it opposed categorically the buying and selling of land. It supported a state-regulated transition towards market relations and the creation of a socially oriented market.

The party won 7.3 per cent of the seats in the Duma. It received 7.9 per cent of the party-list votes and as a result was awarded 21 mandates. An additional 12 deputies were elected in the constituencies. Three of its deputies were given key posts in the Duma. Ivan Rybkin was elected Speaker of the Duma, receiving 233 of the votes.[21] Aleksandr Nazarchuk and Vladimir Isakov respectively headed the Committee on Agricultural Issues and the Committee on Legislation and Judicial and Legal Reform.

Kommunisticheskaya partiya Rossiiskoi Federatsii
Communist Party of the Russian Federation (KPRF)

The Second Extraordinary Congress of the KPRF, held 13–14 February 1993 in Moscow, following the November 1992 Russian Constitutional Court ruling that Yeltsin had exceeded his constitutional powers by banning the entire party (the Court did, however, declare that he was within his powers to disband its leading organs), served as the party's *de facto* founding congress.[22] The KPRF was registered on 24 March 1993, receiving the registration number 1618.[23] The party considered itself the legal successor of the Communist Party of the RSFSR (KP RSFSR). It collected 187,000 signatures supporting its registration with the Tsentrizbirkom.

The KPRF was led by the chairman of its executive committee Gennadii Zyuganov who, before being elected to this position, was a member of the KP RSFSR's Central Committee, Secretariat and Politburo, and after 1991 was active in the national-patriotic forces of Russia, having served as a co-chairman of the National Salvation Front and the Duma of the Russian National Assembly.[24] Zyuganov, along with instructor/cosmonaut/test pilot for the Energiya association, Vitalii Sevast'yanov, and lawyer Viktor Ilyukhin, headed the KPRF's national list in the elections. The party is undoubtedly the largest in the present-day Russian Federation. In April 1993 it claimed to have more than 600,000 members.[25] Also included on its list of 151 candidates were former Russian Federation people's deputies and members of the fraction 'Communists of Russia';

former *obkom* (provincial committee) and *gorkom* (city committee) secretaries of the CPSU, the Komsomol (Young Communist League) and the All-Union Central Council of Trade Unions, and rank-and-file communists.

The party's pre-election platform was 'An appeal to communists, workers and all patriots of Russia' seeking to correct the wrongs of the 'anti-popular course' of Boris Yeltsin. Despite the fact that the KPRF participated in the elections, it considered the contest for the State Duma to be 'illegal and unconstitutional'. It did not shun participation since it believed that a boycott would have been a 'withdrawal from the struggle'. The KPRF considered the APR and 'other opposition organizations' its allies in the pre-election struggle. The party operated under the slogan 'Resistance to violence and illegality', and it advocated the creation of 'a forceful and consistent opposition'. In its 'programme for establishing civic peace and legality', the KPRF envisaged three stages: first, the establishment of the activities of the three branches of power 'on a legal basis'; second, economic and political stabilization and the election of a 'new popular government'; third, the drafting of a new constitution 'and making it active'.

The KPRF's economic programme and state configuration policies included the following key points. First, it advocated a 'withdrawal from shock therapy'. Second, it supported state regulation of production. Third, it sought to eliminate the 'unrestrained growth of prices and the mass pauperization of the people'. Fourth, the KPRF favoured introducing states of emergency to conduct a struggle with crime, speculation and corruption. The party proposed two main planks in its platform on state construction. First, it supported a separation and coordination of government powers. Second, it preferred legislative supremacy over the executive branch of power.

The KPRF gained control of 10.7 per cent of the seats in the lower house, comprised of 32 deputies elected from the party list and 16 from the constituencies. Before the Duma met, KPRF deputy Anatolii Luk'yanov was appointed to coordinate the work of the parliament's fractions.[26] In addition, the committee chairs on Security and on Social and Religious Organizations were taken respectively by KPRF representatives Viktor Ilyukhin and Viktor Zorkal'tsev.

Liberal'no-demokraticheskaya partiya Rossii
Liberal Democratic Party of Russia (LDPR)

The Liberal Democratic Party of Russia, originally the Liberal Democratic Party of the Soviet Union (until 1992), held its first congress on 31 May

1990 in Moscow and was registered by the USSR Justice Ministry on 12 April 1991.[27] The Russian Justice Ministry annulled its registration in August 1992,[28] because the party falsified its membership data. However, the party re-registered with the Russian Ministry of Justice in October 1992 under the name of the Liberal Democratic Party,[29] and it was registered once again on 14 December 1992.[30] After its Third Congress (April 1992) the party claimed to have between 80,000 and 83,000 members,[31] and in December 1992 its leaders boasted that there were between 80,000 and 100,000 members.[32] The party claimed several strong centres of support within (and in some places outside) the Russian Federation.

The LDPR collected 153,000 signatures supporting its list for the 1993 elections and was registered to compete on 10 November 1993, fielding 147 candidates. It also competed in 66 single-seat districts. Heading the list were its chairman, Vladimir Zhirinovsky, Viktor Kobelev and Vyacheslav Marychev.

The LDPR was the most successful of the 13 electoral associations on the party list, receiving 22.8 per cent of the votes and as a result being allocated 59 deputies. It also won seats in five constituencies, including Zhirinovsky's Shelkovo district in Moscow *oblast'*.[33] Sociological data compiled after the election indicate that the LDPR was supported by two distinct groups: young males aged 25–40 and older and less educated males. Most were blue-collar workers in state-owned industrial enterprises earning higher than average wages. They voted for the party because of concerns over 'anarchy' and 'weak government'.[34] LDPR deputies were also put in charge of the largest number of committees, with five: Ecology (Mikhail Lemeshev), Geopolitics (Viktor Ustinov), Industry, Construction, Transportation and Energy (Vladimir Gusev), Labour and Social Support (Sergei Kalashnikov), and Natural Resources and the Exploitation of Nature (Nikolai Astaf'ev). Following the elections, however, the LDPR suffered from severe internal conflicts and deputies left the party's fraction and the party itself.

According to its pre-election programme, 'What we offer', the LDPR proposed a programme minimum and a programme maximum. Its programme minimum made three main provisions. First, it promoted the discontinuation of all foreign aid (claiming that this had more to do with concerns of economic expediency than a lack of compassion). Second, it sought to end military to civilian conversion and, more importantly, to put Russian arms back on the international markets. Third, it intended to conduct a 'decisive struggle' against organized crime.

The LDPR proposed the following items in its programme maximum. First, it sought to end the flow of Russian refugees from other regions of the former USSR by taking a strong stand (politically and economically) against those governments who were threatening Russians on their soil. Second, the party advocated prohibiting non-Russian citizens from trading in Russian cities. Third, in order to stimulate Russian industrialists, the party proposed introducing a tax system favourable to producers (no rates would be higher than 40 per cent). Fourth, the LDPR felt it necessary to strengthen the state sector, to introduce state orders and to establish ties between enterprises. Fifth, the party advocated holding back payments on foreign debts, especially in those cases where it would not lead to any complications with foreign agencies. Moreover, the party firmly believed that under no circumstances should Russia assume for itself the responsibility of the shares of the debts of the other countries of the former USSR. The LDPR's sixth point stressed increasing state and entrepreneurial support for Russian science. Seventh, the party proposed halting the export of those goods and raw materials which Russia desperately needs: timber, oil, metals, foods and furs. Its eighth point included ending state support to foreign students. Point nine involved reducing bureaucrats' privileges and advantages in order to make life easier for invalids, families with many children, single mothers, the elderly and those persons suffering from some illness. Finally, the LDPR advocated reducing the military. However, rather than pensioning off its personnel, it preferred to transfer them to the forces of the Ministry of Internal Affairs, to the law enforcement organs and the system of the Ministry of Security.[35]

The party also had definite attitudes towards state construction. It supported a return to Russia's borders of 1900. Failing this achievement, it would settle for the lands which comprised the USSR in 1977. In addition, the LDPR wanted to restructure Russia from its present territorial configuration into 40 to 50 *gubernii* (provinces) with complete self-management powers.[36]

Notes

This chapter is an extensively revised and condensed version of a paper which appeared under the title 'Electoral Associations in the 1993 Elections to the Russian State Duma' in *Journal of Communist Studies and Transition Politics*, vol. 10, no. 2 (December 1994), pp. 1–36. Reprinted by permission of Frank Cass & Co. Ltd., London.

1 The author is grateful to Troy McGrath, Richard Sakwa and Stephen White, who provided useful criticisms of an earlier version of this paper and supplied several key documents.

2 Richard Sakwa, *Russian Politics and Society* (London: Routledge, 1993), pp. 166–72.
3 ibid., p. 171.
4 Figures were derived from the author's personal database compiled from 'Spisok deputatov Gosudarstvennoi Dumy Federal'nogo Sobraniya Rossiiskoi Federatsii, izbrannykh po obshchefederal'nomu izbiratel'nomu okrugu', *Rossiiskaya gazeta*, 28 December 1993, pp. 2–3.
5 Richard Sakwa, *Russian Politics and Society*, p. 166.
6 Nugzar Betaneli, 'Tsentrizbirkom dezorientiroval izbiratelei, zapretiv publikatsiya sotsiologicheskikh dannykh', *Izvestiya*, 15 December 1993, p. 4.
7 Information for this section is derived primarily from the exposition on the blocs compiled by Yana Meteleva, Dmitrii Orlov and Lyubov' Tsukanova, 'Izbiratel'nye bloki: kto est' kto', *Rossiiskie vesti*, 11 December 1993, p. 2. Preliminary information on parties and blocs which originally intended to compete is found in 'Kto pretenduet na mesta v novom parlamente', *Izvestiya*, 28 October 1993, p. 4, and in 'Bitva za izbiratelei nachalas'', which appeared in two parts in *Izvestiya*, 13 October 1993, p. 4, and 14 October 1993, p. 4. Other programmatic information sources are noted in this section. Further information on the blocs' and parties' leading candidates in the elections is drawn from *Izbiratel'nyi byulleten' po vyboram deputatov Gosudarstvennoi Dumy Federal'nogo Sobraniya Rossiiskoi Federatsii Obshchefederal'nyi Izbiratel'nyi Okrug: Gorod Moskva* (official ballot paper no. 2). Data on the number of signatures collected by the blocs in support of their bids to present federal lists to the electorate are from Interfax, 'Bloki i partii, predstavivshie spiski kandidatov v Tsentrizbirkom', *Izvestiya*, 9 November 1993, p. 2. Other major sources of programmatic information include the Party of Russian Unity and Accord's *Edinstvo i soglasiye dlya Moskvy* (Moscow, 1993), and the Liberal Democratic Party of Russia's pre-election documents which are contained in *Yuridicheskaya gazeta*, nos 40–41 (1993). Election data are from 'The Final Tally', *The Economist*, 8 January 1994, p. 30, and ITAR-TASS, 25 December 1993, cited in *RFE/RL Research Report*, vol. 3, no. 2 (14 January 1993), p. 3. Information on committee chairs is from *Rossiiskaya gazeta*, 26 January 1994, cited in *RFE/RL Research Report*, vol. 3, no. 7 (18 February 1994), p. 8. In addition to the posts that are listed here it should be noted that independent deputies, members of the fraction New Regional Policy, were elected chairs of the committees on Education, Culture and Science (Lyubov' Rozhkova), Nationalities' Affairs (Bair Zhamsuev), and Property, Privatization and Economic Activity (Sergei Burkov).
8 Yelena Petrushkina, 'Sobchak stoit pervym v poslednem spiske', *Megapolis Express*, no. 48 (8 December 1993), p. 17.
9 Andrei Krivov, 'V upryazhke smennykh loshadei', *Russkaya mysl'* (Paris), 25 November – 1 December 1993, p. 6.

10 See also Anatolii Sobchak's interview in the 'Ot pervogo litsa' column in *Moskovskie novosti*, no. 49 (1993), p. A8. See also the movement's ads appearing in *Moskovskii komsomolets*, 4 December 1993, p. 4, *Vechernyaya Moskva*, 6 December 1993, p. 2, and *Izvestiya*, 10 December 1993, p. 5.
11 Krivov, 'V urpazyake'.
12 ibid., p. 8.
13 'Ot pervogo litsa', *Moskovskie novosti*, no. 49 (5 December 1993), p. A9.
14 Programmatic information on Women of Russia is derived from Tat'yana Khudyakova's interview with ZhR's chairwoman Alevtina Fedulova, 'Alevtina Fedulova: Nashe dvizhenie sledovalo by nazvat' "Zhenshchiny dlya Rossii"', *Izvestiya*, 2 December 1993, p. 4.
15 See her biography in 'Sostav Tsentral'nogo Komiteta Kommunisticheskoi Partii Sovetskogo Soyuza izbrannogo XXVIII s"ezdom KPSS', *Izvestiya TsK KPSS*, no. 12 (1990), p. 44. For a discussion of women in the Central Committee, see Peter Lentini, 'A Note on Women in the CPSU Central Committee, 1990', *Europe-Asia Studies* (formerly *Soviet Studies*), vol. 45, no. 4 (1993), pp. 729-36.
16 See 'Ukaz Prezidenta Rossiiskoi Federatsii o Komissii po voprosam zhenshchin, sem'i i demografii pri Prezidente Rossiiskoi Federatsii', and 'Sostav komissii po voprosam zhenshchin, sem'i i demografii pri Prezidente Rossiiskoi Federatsii', *Rossiiskaya gazeta*, 1 December 1993, p. 4.
17 'Grazhdanskii soyuz vo imya stabil'nosti, spravedlivosti i progressa', *Kommersant" daily*, 1 December 1993, p. 4.
18 There exists quite a large literature on the history and official documents of the Democratic Party of Russia. See, for instance, the DPR's entry in V.F. Levichev and A.A. Nelyubin, 'Obshchestvenno-politicheskie organizatsii, partii i dvizheniya v SSSR', *Izvestiya TsK KPSS*, no. 8 (1990); V.P. Davydov, 'Demokraticheskaya partiya Rossii', *Sotsial'no-politicheskie nauki*, no. 11 (1990), pp. 66-74; V.N. Berezovsky, N.I. Krotov and V.V. Chervyakov, *Rossiya: partii, assotsiatsii, soyuzy, kluby: spravochnik* (Moscow: RAU Press, 1991), vol. 1, part 2, pp. 91-2 and pp. 325-6; Vladimir Pribylovsky, *Slovar' novykh politicheskikh partii i organizatsii Rossii* (Moscow: Panorama, December 1992), 4th edition, pp. 16-18; idem (edited by Dauphine Sloan and Sarah Helmstadter), *Dictionary of Political Parties and Organizations in Russia* (Washington, DC: Center for Strategic and International Studies; Moscow: Postfactum/Interlegal, 1992), pp. 19-22; V.G. Gel'bras, L.B. Dormidontova, T.G. Zagladina, N.B. Il'ina, V.V. Kuznetsova, L.M. Lysyakova, V.G. Rupets, B.G. Stopovsky, V.A. Sycheva and N.I. Sharova, *Kto est' chto: politicheskaya Moskva, 1993* (Moscow: Catallaxy, 1993), pp. 187-95, and A. Ostapchuk, E. Krasnikov and M. Meier, *Spravochnik politicheskie partii, dvizheniya i bloki sovremennoi Rossii* (Nizhnii Novgorod: Leta, 1993), pp. 10-13. See also 'Programnye tezisy Demokraticheskoi partii Rossii', in V.Ya. Zalmanov, B.N. Kondrashev and O.P. Simkina (compilers), *Politicheskie partii i ob"edineniya Rossii* (Moscow: Ivan, 1993), pp. 19-21; 'Ustav Demokraticheskoi partii Rossii', ibid., pp. 21-8, and I.I. Linkov,

'Prilozheniya: O nekotorykh rossiiskikh politicheskikh partiyakh i dvizheniyakh', in A.S. Barsenkov, V.A. Koretsky and A.I. Ostapenko, *Politicheskaya Rossiya segodnya: Ispolnitel'naya vlast', Konstitutsionnyi sud, lidery partii i dvizhenii* (Moscow: Moskovskii rabochii, 1993), pp. 401-3.
19 Linkov, 'Prilozheniya', p. 402.
20 The party's programme and rules are available respectively in 'Programma Agrarnoi partii Rossii', in Zalmanov, Kondrashev and Simkina, *Politicheskie partii*, pp. 7-11, and 'Ustav Agrarnoi partii Rossii', ibid., pp. 11-18.
21 Interfax, cited in Wendy Slater, 'Rybkin Elected Speaker of Lower House', *RFE/RL News Brief*, vol. 3, no. 4 (10-21 January 1994), p. 6.
22 Information on the KPRF's revival can be found in Viktor Trushkov, 'Eto tol'ko udavshiisya start', *Pravda*, 16 February 1993, pp. 1-2; Gennadii Zyuganov's interview with Boris Slavin, 'Splotim i vozrodim Rossiyu', ibid., 17 February 1993, p. 1; 'II s"ezd kommunistov Rossii: Informatsionnoe soobshchenie', *Glasnost'*, no. 7 (18-24 February 1993), p. 1, and V. Markov, 'II s"ezd Kompartii Rossii', ibid., pp. 2-4.
23 Valentina Nikiforova, 'Partiya zaregistrirovana', *Pravda*, 31 March 1993, p. 1. The party's official documents are contained in 'Programnye zayavlenie', in Zalmanov, Kondrashev and Simkina, *Politicheskie partii*, pp. 56-62, and 'Ustav Kommunisticheskoi partii Rossiiskoi Federatsii', ibid., pp. 63-70.
24 'Gennadii Andreevich Zyuganov', *Glasnost'*, no. 7 (18-24 February 1993), p. 2; Barsenkov, Koretsky and Ostapenko, *Politicheskaya Rossiya segodnya*, pp. 302-3, and Boris Slavin, 'Splotim i vozrodim Rossiyu'.
25 Valentina Nikiforova, 'KPRF ishchet soyuznikov', *Pravda*, 2 April 1993, p. 2.
26 Vera Tolz, 'Lukyanov Gets Temporary Post in New Parliament', *RFE/RL News Brief*, vol. 3, no. 3 (27 December 1993 - 4 January 1994), p. 2.
27 Linkov, 'Prilozheniya', pp. 404-5, at p. 404. See also the Liberal Democratic Party of the Soviet Union's entry in Levichev and Nelyubin, 'Obshchestvenno-politicheskie organizatsii'; B.F. Fedorov, 'Liberal'no-demokraticheskaya partiya (LDP) Sovetskogo Soyuza', *Sotsial'no-politicheskie nauki*, no. 1 (1991), pp. 97-9; Berezovsky, Krotov and Chervyakov, *Rossiya*, vol. 1, part 1, pp. 58-9, and ibid., vol. 1, part 2, pp. 317-18; Pribylovsky, *Slovar'* . . ., p. 42, and his *Dictionary*, pp. 44-5; Gel'bras et al., *Kto est' chto*, pp. 233-9, and Ostapchuk, Krasnikov and Meier, *Spravochnik*, pp. 84-6. See also 'Programma Liberal'no-demokraticheskoi partii Rossii', in Zalmanov, Kondrashev and Simkina, *Politicheskie partii*, pp. 93-6 and 'Ustav Liberal'no-demokraticheskoi partii Rossii (LDPR)', ibid., pp. 97-9.
28 The date of its registration annulment is listed as 11 August 1992 in Gel'bras et al., *Kto est' chto*, p. 233, and as 10 August 1992 in Ostapchuk, Krasnikov and Meier, *Spravochnik*, p. 86.
29 ibid.
30 Linkov, 'Prilozheniya', p. 405.

31 Gel'bras et al., *Kto est' chto*, p. 233.
32 Linkov, 'Prilozheniya', p. 405.
33 For a discussion of the LDPR's performance in the poll see Peter Lentini and Troy McGrath, 'The Rise of the Liberal Democratic Party and the 1993 Elections', *Harriman Institute Forum*, vol. 7, no. 6 (February 1994).
34 Vladimir Shokaraev, 'Kto golosoval za LDPR', *Izvestiya*, 30 December 1993, p. 4, and Elizabeth Teague, 'Who Voted For Zhirinovsky', *RFE/RL News Brief*, vol. 3, no. 3 (27 December 1993–9 January 1994), p. 5.
35 ibid., pp. 4–5.
36 ibid., p. 5.

Index

Accord for Russia, 181
Afanas'ev, Yurii, 205
agitation, fair play in, 73-4
agitvecher (agitational evening), 78
Agrarian Party of Russia (APR), 70, 110, 178, 181, 182, 249, 252, 261
  attitudes, 127, 130, 133, 134, 136, 139
  candidates, 76
  programme, 273-4
  proposed ban on, 80
  seats, 86
Agrarnaya partiya Rossii see Agrarian Party of Russia (APR)
Aleksandrov, Aleksei, 78
Alksnis, Viktor, 47, 75, 179
All-Russian Congress, Central Committee, 29, 30
All-Russian Council of Veterans of War, Labour, the Armed Forces and Law Enforcement Organs, 268
All-Russian Society of Invalids, 268
All-Union Central Council of Trade Unions, 275
All-Union Communist Party (Bolsheviks), and the 1936 Constitution, 30, 31-32
Ametisov, Ernest, 251
Andronov, Iona, 179
APR *see* Agrarian Party of Russia
Arbitration Tribunal, 80
Arkhangel'sk *oblast'*, 83
Armenia, 44
Åslund, Anders, 250
Association of Private Farm Workers (AKKOR), 263
Association of Privatized and Private Enterprises, 263
Astaf'ev, Mikhail, 69
Astaf'ev, Nikolai, 276
Astrakhan district no. 62 , 74
August regime (1991-3), 170, 172-5, 192, 250
authoritarianism, 233-9

Avak'yan, Suren, 47, 48, 49, 50
Avgust (August) bloc, 69
Aviastar, 155-6
Azerbaijan, 44, 116

Baburin, Sergei, 69, 180, 252
Baglai, Marat, 251
ballot fraud, 246
ballots, secret, 37, 44, 82
Baltic states, 51
Baranov, Stanislav, 268
Barghoorn, Frederick C., 4
Basilashvili, Oleg, 264
Bauer, Vladimir, 264
Bekh, Nikolai, 272
Bektabekova, O., 52
Belarus (Belorussia), 49, 203
Belov, Vasilii, 179
Belyaev, Aleksandr, 73
Berezkin, A.V., 47-8
Berlusconi, Silvio, 101
bloc politics, 177, 181, 186, 190, 233
blocs *see* electoral associations
Blok 'Vybor Rossii' see Russia's Choice (VR)
Bogomolov, Oleg, 273
Boiko, V., 255
Boldyrev, Yurii, 69, 100, 266
Bolshevik Party, 19, 22-4, 27-30, 188
  elections in the, 28-30
Bolshevik revolution, 172
Bolshevism, 191, 229, 233-4
  revulsion against, 184
Borovoi, Konstantin, 69, 182
Bragin, Vyacheslav, 100, 122
Brakov, Yevgenii, 45
Brezhnev, Leonid Il'ich, 251
Brezhnev regime, 171, 234, 239
  constitution, 32, 66-7, 204
BRNI *see* Future of Russia - New Names
Bryansk, 254
Budushchee Rossii - novye imena see Future of

Russia - New Names
Burbulis, Gennadii, 263
Butler, David, 2, 3, 39

candidates
　eligibility requirements (1993), 75-6
　popularity of, in Ul'yanovsk 148 Fig., 7.1
　pre-election meetings with the electorate, 49-50
　reasons for voting for, in Ul'yanovsk 153 Fig., 7.2
　single, 37-8
capitalism, market, 193
Central Electoral Commission (Tsentrizbirkom), 68, 71-2, 74, 77, 80, 82, 83, 85, 104-7, 115-16, 119
　Decree on Mass Information, 83
　registration of parties, 261
'centrists', 70
Chair of the Government of the Russian Federation *see* Prime Minister
Chair of the State Bank of the Russian Federation, 66
Chamberlain, William, 24
Charter for Civic Accord (1994), 181
Chechnya, Russian intervention in (1994), 6, 87, 192, 249, 253
Chelyabinskii rabochii, 120
Chernenko, Konstantin, 37, 248
'Chernobyl' Union, 268
Chernomyrdin
　Viktor, 76, 87, 114, 143, 177, 252
　as prime minister, 219, 220
Chiesa, Giulietto, 50
Christian democracy, 193
Chubais, Anatolii, 76, 113
Chubaraev, Vladimir, 268
Chukhrai, Pavel, 109
Chuvash, 155
citizens' rights, 66-7, 134
Civic Accord, 181, 183, 187
civic culture, consolidation or rise of extremist politics, 160-1, 162
Civic Forum, Czechoslovakia, 189
Civic Union (in the Name of Stability, Justice and Progress) (GS), 70, 72, 100, 109, 110, 115, 173, 179, 189, 271
　proposed ban on, 80
　programme, 271-2
civil society, 232, 241-2
　democratic tendencies in, 15-22
　and political parties, 189, 194
Clark, Terry D., 84, 86
Clinton, Bill, 207
collectivism, 231
Colton, Timothy, 226

commune, 15-16
decrees, 15-16
communism, 232, 240
　opposition to the regime, 171-2
Communist Party of the RSFSR, 274
Communist Party of the Russian Federation (KPRF), 70, 109, 110, 134, 139, 187, 188, 214, 261
　ban almost imposed, 68, 104-5
　discipline in, 239, 247, 249
　finance, 72
　number of seats, 86
　programme, 133, 136, 236, 274-5
　relationship to CPSU, 127, 174, 191
　turn to social democracy, 180-1
Communist Party of the Soviet Union (CPSU), 1, 8, 193
　Central Committee, Institute of Social Problems, 52
　end of rule, 64, 88, 170, 171-2, 184
　and Gorbachev's reforms, 40, 42-3, 45, 47, 50
　Gorbachev's relations with, 207
　leading role in Leninism, 227-9
　legacy of, 240
　monopoly, 3-4, 37, 39, 63, 64
　Yeltsin resigns from, 208
communists, 86, 255, 256
Communists of Russia group, 208, 274
Congress of Soviets of the USSR, 26
　Central Executive Committee, 26
Constituent Assembly (1917), 22-5
　dispersal of (1918), 24, 26
Constitution (1918), 26
Constitution (1924), 26
Constitution (1936), Stalin's, 8, 30-2, 204
Constitution (1977), 32, 66-7, 204
　Article 6 on status of CPSU, 3, 227
　amendment to, 47, 50
　Chapter VII, 66
Constitutional Democratic Party - People's Freedom Party, 69, 191
Constructive Ecological Movement of Russia (KEDR), 69-70, 146
　programme, 268-9
corporatism, 169, 197
corruption, 239, 241, 246
Council of Collective Farms, 43
Council of Ministers, 206
Council of Nationalities, 30-1
Council of Union, 30
coup, August (1991), 250
CPSU *see* Communist Party of the Soviet Union
Czechoslovakia, 189
Czech Republic, 203

Dagestan, 83
Dahl, Robert A., 2
Danilov, Yurii, 251
Danilov-Danil'yan, Viktor, 76
Davydov, Aleksandr, 273
Degtyarev, Ivan, 82-3
demagogues, threat of, 233, 242
Demidov, A., 52
democracies, parliamentary versus presidential, 238, 249
democracy, 133, 162
  'by design', 76
  continuum of, 3
  institutional factors in, 233
  and poverty, 194
  representative, 230
  television and, 97-8
Democratic Centralists, 29
Democratic Choice of Russia, 178
Democratic Initiative Party, 263
Democratic Party of Russia (DPR), 70, 72-3, 103-4, 110, 116, 179, 252, 261, 271
  attitudes, 127, 130, 136, 139
  programme, 272-3
Democratic Russia, 172, 173, 174, 177-8, 184, 187, 207, 263
Democratic Union (1988), 171
democratic values, 134-6
democratization, 131, 140, 204, 230, 234
  and liberalization, 36-7, 46, 54
'democrats', 69, 254-5
  and the media, 100-1
demographic imbalance, 47-8
Demokraticheskaya partiya Rossii see Democratic Party of Russia
Denisenko, Bela, 264
deputies, 67-8, 75, 248-9
  not belonging to parties, 261-2
  number in Duma, 256
  pre-1989, 38-9
Derrida, Jacques, 194
Derzhava (Great Power) organization, 180, 249
Dibrov, Dmitrii, 107
Dignity and Charity (DiM), 69
  programme, 268
DiM *see* Dignity and Charity
disenfranchisement, 20-1, 48
disillusionment with new democracies, 161, 230, 232
Dobryi vecher Moskva, 77
Dostoinstvo i miloserdie see Dignity and Charity
DPR *see* Democratic Party of Russia
Dubinin, Sergei, 220
Duma, 18-22
  elections to First (1906), 19-20

  elections to Second (1907), 19-20
  elections to Third (1907), 20-1
  elections to Fourth (1912), 20-2
  Fifth, 188
Duverger, Maurice, 172

Eastern Europe, 40, 203
  party formation, 190-1
Echo Moscow, 120
economic reform, 40, 173, 230
  attitudes to 133, 136, 137 Table, 6.5
  IMF directed, 86
  Yeltsin's, 209, 235
Election 79 , 38
election overload, and voter weariness, 157-8
elections
  in the Bolshevik Party, 28-30
  'by acclamation', 4-5, 36, 39, 54
  criteria for free and fair, 2, 36, 87, 133, 140, 246
  draft law on forthcoming presidential, 256
  function of, 2-3, 6
  future in Russia, 253-6
  history of Russian and Soviet, 15-35
  impact on future political process, 157-61
  Law of 11 December (1905) on, 18
  Law of 3 June (1907) on, 20-1
  limited choice variant, 40-6, 54
  multi-party, 63, 226, 260
  pre-reform Soviet (pre-1989), 36, 37-9
  Soviet (1937-87), 4-5
electoral associations, 9, 69, 77
  programmes, 260-81
  rather than parties, 261-2
electoral blocs, programmes, 263-77
electoral campaigns, study of, 52-3
electoral commissions
  (1936), 30
  (1993), 71-2
  soviets, 26-7
electoral commissions *see also* Central Electoral Commission (Tsentrizbirkom)
Electoral Law, USSR (1988), 75
electoral reform, 36-59, 86
  Soviet debates on (1989-91), 46-54
  under Gorbachev, 31, 32, 37, 40-6, 63
Electoral Statute, 247
elitism, 184, 239-41
Emerson, Michael, 82
environmental movements, 173
Espersen, Ole, 82
ethnic relations, Ul'yanovsk, 155
European Parliament, 82
European Russia, 19, 21
European Union, 72
Evans, Geoffrey, 86

Index

Evenkii district no. 224, 74-5
executive branch, 234, 235, 237

February Revolution (1917), 22
Federal Information Centre, 76
Fedorov, Boris, 76, 114, 220, 249, 255
Fedorov, Svyatoslav, 264
Fedoseev, Anatolii, 69
Fedulova, Alevtina, 70, 269, 270
Filatov, Sergei, 187
first-past-the-post system, 70, 74, 86, 176
Forward Russia Party, 255
franchise
   (1918), 26-7
   as coercion and control, 39
   pre-1989, 37
Friedgut, Theodore, 81
Frolov, Konstantin, 69, 268
Fukuyama, Francis, 193
Fund for Support of the Russian Movement for Democratic Reforms, 78
Future of Russia - New Names (BRNI), 70, 110, 236
   programme, 270-1
   proposed ban on, 80

Gadzhiev, Bagavutdin, 83
Gadzhiev, Gadis, 251
Gaidar
   Yegor, 69, 74, 76, 77, 87, 99, 109-10, 120, 124, 177-8, 185, 249, 263
   as prime minister, 193, 209, 220
   public image, 83, 103, 113-14, 240
Ganapolsky, Matvei, 107
Gdlyan, Tel'man, 69
Gellner, Ernest, 226
Gen, Nikolai, 271
general secretaryship, 203
geography, electoral, 47-8, 74-5
Georgia, 203
Gerashchenko, Viktor, 220
Germany, 27, 29
Getzler, Israel, 26
Glaz'ev, Sergei, 273
Golik, Yurii, 179
Gorbachev Mikhail, 48, 75, 209
   and the CPSU, 43, 228
   election as president, 203-7
   electoral reforms, 8, 31, 32, 37, 40-6, 63, 248
   leadership, 202-3
   standing in popularity, 212, 213
Gorbachev regime, 8, 235
Goryachev, Yu.F., 147, 149, 150, 152, 157, 158-9
government, confidence in the, 219, 251-2

Govorukhin, Stanislav, 102-3, 114, 273
Grazhdanskii soyuz vo imya stabil'nosti, spravedlivosti i progressa see Civic Union
Grishin, Vyacheslav, 268
GS *see* Civic Union (in the Name of Stability, Justice and Progress)
Gubenko, Nikolai, 268
Gubernskie vedomosti, 150
Gundareva, Natal'ya, 270
Gusev, Vladimir, 276

Hahn, Jeffrey W., 39
Hall, John, 231
Hankiss, Elemer, 36-7
Hanson, P., 145
Hansson, O., 151
Harrop, Martin, 2, 5, 39
Havel, Vaclav, 189
Heywood, Paul, 8, 66, 75, 240
Hincks, Darron, 30
Hoff, Magdalena, 82
Hoffmann, Erik, 234-5
Hofstadter, Richard, 185
Hungary, 171, 203
Huntington, Samuel P., 1, 7

ideology, 2-3, 230
Ilyukhin, Viktor, 274, 275
Ilyushenko, Viktor, 254
information for voters, 79-80
Ingushetia, 253
institutions
   failure of, 227
   trust in 215 Table, 9.1
insurgency, democratic, 170-2, 184
Inter-regional Deputies' Group, 45, 206, 264
interest groups, 69-70, 187
Irish government, Yeltsin and, 219, 220
Irkutsk, 254
Isakov, Vladimir, 274
Italy, Christian Democratic Party, 190
Itogi, 121
Ivanchenko, Aleksandr, 50
Ivanov, N., 156
Izvestiya, 74, 77, 82-3, 85, 116-17, 118, 211, 234, 254, 269

Japan, 125, 182-3
Japanese Liberal Democratic Party, 183, 190, 196
Jews, 131, 136
journalism, 101, 105, 117-18, 119-20

Kadets, 17, 19, 20, 21, 22
Kalashnikov, Sergei, 276
Kalinin, Vitalii, 78

Kalmykov, Yurii, 76
Karimov, Islam, 207
Kashpirovsky, Anatolii, 249
Kazakhstan, 49, 50, 207
KEDR *see* Constructive Ecological Movement of Russia
Khabarovsk *krai*, 82
Khasbulatov, Ruslan, 170, 186, 210-11, 237, 272
Khokhryakova, Ol'ga, 251
Kim, Jae-On, 125
King, Anthony, 3
Kirichenko, Leonid, 256
Kirgizia, 50
Kislov, Aleksandr, 254
Klimatova, Galina, 270
Kobelev, Viktor, 249, 276
Kollontai, Aleksandra, 29
Kolosov, V.A., 47-8
Komi-Permyak Autonomous District, 69
Kommunist, 29
Kommunisticheskaya partiya Rossiiskoi Federatsii see Communist Party of the Russian Federation
Komsomol, 275
  competitive elections within, 40-1
Komsomolskaya pravda, 112
Kononov, Anatolii, 251
Konstruktivnoe ekologicheskoe dvizhenie Rossii see Constructive Ecological Movement of Russia
Kostikov, Vyacheslav, 104
Kovalev, Sergei, 263
Kozyrev, Andrei, 76, 187, 249
KPRF *see* Communist Party of the Russian Federation
Krasnaya zvezda, 117, 118
Krasnodar territory, 151, 255
Krasnoyarsk, 26
Kravchuk, Leonid, 207
Kronstadt, 26
  suppression of rebellion (1921), 28
krugovshchina, 260
Kulik, A., 187

Lakhova, Yekaterina, 270
Lapshin, Mikhail, 70, 273
Lashchevsky, Vyacheslav, 70, 271
Latsis, Otto, 117
Latvia, and ethnic Russians, 47
Lazarev, Boris, 204-5
LDPR *see* Liberal Democratic Party of Russia
leadership, 234
  collective, 203
  and presidency in post-communist Russia, 202-25

League for Female Equality, 17
legislature, 234, 237-8, 248-53
legitimacy of governments, 2-3, 6, 237
Lemeshev, Mikhail, 276
Lenin, Vladimir Il'ich, 23, 64, 213, 227, 231
Leninism
  legacy of, 9, 106, 154-5
    electoral implications, 234-42
    enforced de-participation, 226-45
Levin, Alfred, 20
Lezhankin, P.P., 147, 150
Liberal Democratic Party of Russia (LDPR), 143, 186, 188, 249, 250, 253, 261
  attitudes, 127, 131, 134, 136-9
  independent candidates, 262
  media campaign, 102, 107-10, 116, 121-2
  number of seats, 85
  programme, 235, 275-7
  trends in support, 124, 128-9, 160, 180
  ultra-nationalism, 32, 70, 97
Liberal Democratic Party of the Soviet Union, 275
liberalism, 193, 240-1
liberalization, 36-7, 46, 54
Liberal'no-demokraticheskaya partiya Rossii see Liberal Democratic Party of Russia
Ligachev, Yegor, 41
Likhachev, Dmitrii, 205
Lipetsk region, 151, 254
list system, 5 per cent hurdle, 176-7
'Living Ring' Union, 263
local elections
  (1994), 157-8, 253-6
  Gorbachev's experimental, 41-2
Luchin, Viktor, 251
Lukin, Vladimir, 69, 100, 266
Luk'yanov, Anatolii, 204, 275
Luzhkov, Yurii, 177
Lymar, Lyubov', 70, 268
Lysenko, Nikolai, 69
Lyubarsky, Kronid, 85, 189-90

McGrath, Troy, 9
Mackenzie, W.J.M., 2-3, 4-5, 39
'mafiya', rise of the, 239
Makhachkaliya, 83
management elections, 40, 41
marketization, 230, 232, 238
Marxism-Leninism, 210, 228
Marychev, Vyacheslav, 249, 276
Mayakovsky, Vladimir, 97
media
  access of candidates to, 74
  bias, 246
  coverage of 1993 elections, 83, 85, 97-123
  effect on politics, 194

Regulations on Ways of Implementing the (1993), 107
role in 1993 elections, 8, 77-9, 148-51
satire, 112-13
media *see also* press
Medvedev, Nikolai, 254
Medvedev, Roy, 38
Megapolis Express, 263
Melik'yan, Gennadii, 76
Mensheviks, 19, 22, 27, 28
Michels, Robert, 172
Mikhailov, V.V., 147, 150
Mikhalskaya, Tat'yana, 253-4
Miller
  Bill, 8, 66, 75, 240
  William L., 2, 5, 39
Minkin, Aleksandr, 85
minority rights, 136
Mironov, Vladimir, 271
Mironova, Svetlana, 120
Mityukov, Mikhail, 186
modernization theory, 144
Mordvins, 155
Morshchakova, Tamara, 251
Moscow, 30, 82, 176, 192
Moskovskie novosti, 102, 117, 118, 268
Moskovskii komsomolets, 85, 118
Mostovshchikov, Sergei, 112
multiparty system, 144, 160
  evolution of, 169-201
municipal government, 16-18
Municipal Statute (1870), 16
Murphine, Ralph, 52

Narodnaya gazeta, 150
Narodnyi deputat, 51, 52
National Front of Latvia, 47
National Republican Party of Russia, 69
National Salvation Front, 179
nationalism, 173, 179-80, 231-2, 240, 256
  extreme, 131-3, 136-9
  values 138 Table, 6.6, 139
NATO, 87
Navstrechu vyboram, 77
Nazarbaev, Nursultan, 207
Nazarchuk, Aleksandr, 252, 274
neformaly, 170, 171
Nevzorov, Aleksandr, 103
New Russia bloc, 69
newspapers
  central compared with regional, 117-20
  coverage of 1993 elections, 116-21
Nezavisimaya gazeta, 103, 117, 230-1
Nicholas II, 31, 213, 231
Nie, Norman H., 125
Nizhnii Novgorod, 254

nomenklatura, 41, 177-8, 187, 192
  in 1993 election, 115
  after dissolution of CPSU, 184
  system, 3, 9, 227
nomination meetings, 49-50
nomination rights
  (1989), 44, 46, 49
  (pre-1989), 38
Nove, Alec, 15
Novgorod, 253-4, 255
Novgorodskie vedomosti, 119
Novodvorskaya, Valeriya, 171
Novosibirsk, 151
NTV (Independent TV), 107, 121

October crisis (1993), 214
October manifesto (1905), 17-18
October Revolution (1917), 26, 229
Octobrists, 17, 19, 20, 21, 22
Oleinik, Vladimir, 251
Omel'chenko, Elena, 8, 86
Omsk *oblast'*, Tsentral'nyi district no. 130, 69
opinion polls, 108-9, 124, 234, 236, 255-6
  'halo effect', 127
'opposition', 70, 249
order, enforcement of, 230-1
Orel, 254
Orenburg, 115
Orgburo, 29
Ossetia, North, 253
Ostankino TV, 77-8, 98, 99, 100, 101, 102, 109, 122

Pamfilova, Ella, 76, 263
Panfilov, Anatolii, 268
parliament, 186, 188, 196
  fragmentation, 85-6
  and presidency, 158, 173, 219-20, 237
  relative support for, 175, 213-14
  professional character of Russian (1993), 248-9
  public opinion and, 211-17
  role of, 210-11
  Yeltsin's dissolution of Russian (1993), 6, 63, 124, 211, 214, 238
parliamentary committees, 186
participation, 247
  characteristics of, 125-7
  mass, 228
  political interest and electoral 126 Table, 6.1
  in Ul'yanovsk elections, by age and profession 154 Fig., 7.3
Partiya Rossiiskogo edinstva i soglasiya see Party of Russian Unity and Accord
Party of Economic Freedom, 69, 182

Party of Peaceful Restoration, 19
Party of Russian Unity and Accord (PRES), 69, 100, 109, 110, 178, 182, 261
  candidates, 76, 83
  programme, 266-7
party system, 219-20
  development of, 9, 169-201
    periodization, 170-82
  factors hampering a stable Russian, 260-1
Pavlov, Nikolai, 179, 180
Pavlovskaya, M.E., 47-8
Peasants' Party of Russia, 263
Penniman, Howard, 2, 3
Penza *oblast'*, 254
People's Party of Free Russia, 68, 265, 271
People's Party of Free Russia *see also* Russian Social Democratic People's Party
perestroika, 170, 171
personalities, 114-15, 177, 182, 240-1
  and presidency, 218-19
Petrograd, 25
  soviet (1917), 25
Petrov, N.V., 47-8
Pilkington, Hilary, 8, 86
Pipes, Richard, 16, 17
Pochinok, Aleksandr, 76
Poland, 171, 172, 189
  Catholic Church in, 193
political attitudes, of party voters and non-voters 135 Table, 6.4
political order, meanings of, 7-8
political parties, 2, 9
  1993 election, 124-42
  banned (1993), 68-9
  common themes, 262
  concept parties, 189
  the general crisis of, 190-4
  negative attitudes to, 247
  proto-parties, 195, 239-41, 260
  pseudo-parties, 173-5, 195-6, 261
  role in representative democracy, 169
  sources of finance, 102
  status in new conditions, 51
politics
  patterns of, 185-7
  viewed as a market, 53-4
Politika, 53
Poltoranin, Mikhail, 76, 264
Ponomarev, Lev, 178
Popov, Gavriil, 83, 114, 120, 173, 177, 264, 265
Poptsov, Oleg, 106, 107
power relations, 1, 232-3
  shift from centre to republics, 51, 54
Pravda, 117, 205
PRES *see* Party of Russian Unity and Accord
presidency, 9, 66

characteristics of Russian, 217
elections to the USSR, 205-6
law on (1991), 208-9
and parliament, 158, 173, 219-20, 237
  relative support for, 213-14
and political leadership in post-communist Russia, 202-25
  problem of, 234-9
  public opinion and, 211-17
Russian, 207-12 Fig., 9.1
Presidential Council, 206
presidential elections, Russian (1991), 207-9
presidential government, 185-6, 210-11
  the emergence of, 203-7
  perils of Russian, 218-21
press, arbitration court, 100, 102-3, 105, 106
press *see also* media
Prime Minister, 66, 203, 220
privatization, 230, 232
Prizyv, 120
Probst, Fritz, 82
Public Associations, Law on (1991), 50
Public Chamber, 182, 183
public opinion, 108, 124-5
  presidents and parliaments, 211-17
  surveys in Ul'yanovsk, 157, 158, 159, 160
Public Opinion Foundation, 108

radio
  coverage of 1993 elections, 120-1
  free and paid air time, 101-16
Radio Russia, 101, 120-1
Ranney, Austin, 2, 3
RDDR *see* Russian Movement for Democratic Reforms
referendum
  on economic reform, presidency and Russian parliament (1993), 64, 209-10
  on future of USSR (1991), 208
Referendums, Russian Law on (1990), 66
regime politics, 169, 172, 174, 177, 182-94, 195-6
regional interests, 65
regional politics, 8, 86, 143-66, 192, 262
regions
  relationship with the centre, 158, 207
  stabilization, or stagnation, 143-66
  strengthening of the, 158-60
Reich, William, 111
religion, 192-3
'Renewal' Union, 271
representation
  population-based, 67-8, 86
  proportional, 17, 67-8, 86, 176
Republican Party of Russia, 265
republics

Index   289

and the centre, 207
differing electoral codes, 51
Reznikov, Mikhail, 98
Rokkan, Stein, 183, 192
Rossiiskoe dvizhenie demokraticheskikh reform see Russian Movement for Democratic Reforms
Rossiya television channel, 78, 79-80
Rossiya TV *see also* Russian TV
rouble
  in 1994, 252
  'black Tuesday', 220
RSFSR Congress of People's Deputies, 64, 77, 208-9
  elections (1990), 172
Rudkin, Yurii, 251
rule by decree, 185, 230-1, 234-9
Russia
  emergence of electoral and party systems, 229-34
  future of elections in, 253-6
  transition process, 226-9
Russian All-People's Union (ROS), 69, 179-80
Russian Christian Democratic Union - New Democracy party, 265
Russian Communist Workers' Party, 68
Russian Constitutional Court, dissolved (1993), 250-1
Russian Federal Assembly, 175, 219, 248-53
Russian Federal Assembly elections (1993), 2, 5-7, 8, 60-166
  attitude changes during campaign, 131-3
  attitudes of voters and non-voters, 133-9
  campaign, 77-81
  campaign trends, 127-31
  contestants, 67-71
  electoral provisions, 71-7
  evaluation of results, 83-5
  financing of, 71-3
  foreign observers, 82
  foul play during campaign, 82-3
  media coverage, 83-5, 97-123
  outcomes of, 6-7
  parties and voters, 124-42
  regional perspective, 143-66
  turnout, 125-7
  voting process, 81-3
Russian Federation, 1
  Constitution
    adopted in plebiscite (1993), 175, 218
    criticism of, 80-1, 104-5
    legal status, 85
    draft constitution (1993), 65-7, 75, 76-7, 211-12, 237-8
Russian Federation Council, 65, 75, 176, 248, 250-1

candidates, 70-1
decrees for states of emergency, 253
election of regional governors to, 158
seat allocation 84 Table, 4.1
Russian Movement for Democratic Reforms (RDDR), 69, 100, 109-10, 120, 177
  concert, 78-9
  programme, 264-5
Russian Orthodox Church, 193
Russian People's Deputies, 71
Russian Public Opinion and Market Research (ROMIR), 124-5
Rusian Security Council, 6
Russian Social Democratic Labour Party (RSDRP), 17, 19, 20, 21
Russian Social Democratic People's Party, 180
Russian Social Democratic People's Party, *see also* People's Party of Free Russia
Russian Supreme Soviet, Presidium of, 208
Russian TV (Rossiya channel), 99, 101, 102, 109, 110
Russian Union of Industrialists and Entrepreneurs, 179
Russian Union of Youth, 70
Russian Unity, 69
Russian-American Press and Information Center, 109
Russia's Choice (VR), 69, 124, 134, 139, 177-8, 187, 214, 240
  candidates, 76-7
  media campaign, 98, 99-101, 108-16
  media coverage, 77, 82, 120
  number of deputies, 85
  programme, 262, 263-4
  split in, 249
  trends in support, 87, 130-1
Russia's Path, 252
Rutskoi, Aleksandr, 113, 180, 181, 213, 237, 250, 256, 271, 272
Ryabov, Nikolai, 71, 80, 104, 176
Ryazan', 254
Rybkin, Ivan, 274
Rybkin, Viktor, 143
Ryzhkov, Nikolai, 202, 212

St Petersburg, 73, 176, 192
  Duma electorate, 17
  elections to soviet (1905), 26
  TV, 74, 78, 101, 109
Sakhalin, 254
Sakharov, Andrei, 45, 204, 212
Sakwa, Richard, 9, 68, 74, 86, 239, 250, 260-1, 262
Saltykov, Boris, 76
Samara *oblast'*, 254

Saratov *oblast'*, 26
  Engel'skii district no. 158 , 69
Sedze, Adzum, 82
Segodnya, 117, 118, 255
Seleznev, Nikolai, 251
Selivanova, Ol'ga, 53-4
Semenov, Yurii, 107
Serbia, 87
Sestanovich, Stephen, 86
Sevast'yanov, Vitalii, 274
Shakhrai, Sergei, 69, 73, 76, 100, 110, 114, 121, 178, 182, 267
Shapovalov, Sergei, 267
Shchipanova, Tat'yana, 120
'Shchit' (Shield), 263
Sheinis, Viktor, 176
Shelkovo district, Moscow *oblast'*, 276
Shokhin, Aleksandr, 76, 267
Shumeiko, Vladimir, 77, 80, 104-5, 143
Sidorov, Yevgenii, 76
Simbirsk *see* Ul'yanovsk
Simbirskii kur'er, 150, 151
Skach, Cindy, 238, 249
Skillen, Daphne, 8, 77-8, 236
Sliva, Anatolii, 267
Slovo Zhirinovskogo, 117
Smirnov, V., 51
Smiryagin, L.V., 47-8
Sobchak, Anatolii, 45, 69, 79, 100, 120, 264
sobornost' approach, 231
Sochi, 116, 255
social democracy, 193
Social Democracy of the Kingdom of Poland and Lithuania, 19
social organizations, provision, 42-3, 48-9
social stratification, and voting patterns, 151-4
socialism, attitudes to, 228, 234, 241
Socialist Revolutionaries (SRs), 17, 20, 22, 27
Sokolov, Oleg, 271
Soldiers' Mothers of Russia Movement, 70
Solidarity, 171, 172, 178, 189, 193
Solzhenitsyn, Aleksandr, 6, 158
Soskovets, Oleg, 220
sovereignty, declaration of Russian (1991), 209
soviets (councils)
  as democratic institutions, 25-8
  disbanded by Yeltsin (1993), 25
  elections to the, 25-6
Soyuz faction, 75
Stalin, Joseph, 4, 30, 31, 32, 37, 203, 204, 206, 234, 248, 251
Stalin's Russia, 15
  Constitution (1936), 8, 30-2
state
  erosion of the, 238
  paternalism, 230

State Duma, 65, 66, 175, 176, 186, 196, 250
  seat allocation 84 Table, 4.1
  Statute on Elections of Deputies, 67-8
  vote of no confidence in the government (1994), 219
State Enterprise, Law on (1987), 40-1
Statute on Federal Organs of Power in the Transitional Period, 65-6
Stepan, Alfred, 238, 249
Strekozov, Vladimir, 251
Surgh, Gerald D., 26
Sychev, V.A., 147, 150, 152

Tambov, 254
Tatars, 155
Tatarstan, 192
Tatarstan Social Centre (TOTs), 192
television, 97
  avoidance of public debate, 105-7
  coverage of 1993 elections, 77-8, 97-116
  free and paid air time, 101-16
  paid advertising during elections, 115-16
  time allotments, 74
Thatcher, Ian D., 8
Tikhonov, Vladimir, 179
Timofeev, V., 38
totalitarianism, 187-90
Town Government, New Statute (1892), 17
trade union movement, 173
trade unions, competitive elections within, 40-1
transition theories, 144
Travkin, Nikolai, 70, 102-3, 117, 127, 130, 179, 186, 271, 272
Trotsky, Leon, 15, 30
Trudoviks, 20
Tsarist government, 1, 15-22, 188, 234
Tsentrizbirkom *see* Central Electoral Commission
Tsipko, Aleksandr, 80
Tula, 82
Tumanov, Vladimir, 251
Turgai *oblast'*, 20
Turkestan, 20
Turkmenia, 50, 203
turnout figures
  (1989), 44
  (1993), 70, 74, 125-7
  (1994) local elections, 253-4
  (pre-1989), 39
Tyunov, Oleg, 251

uezd zemstvo assembly, 16
Ukraine, 207
  restructuring of debt, 253
Ul'yanovsk
  election process in (1993), 8, 144-57

role of the media, 148-51
voting patterns in 145-7 Table, 7.1, 151-7
Ul'yanovskaya pravda, 150
Union of 12 December faction, 255
Union of October 17, 19
Union of Russian People, 19
Union of Women Entrepreneurs, 269
Union of Women of the Navy, 269
Union of Women of Russia, 269
United States, 115, 125, 185, 190
  Yeltsin's visit to, 220
Urban, Michael, 5, 76-7, 82, 87, 236
USSR Congress of People's Deputies, 64, 75, 207, 264
  composition, 42-3
  draft electoral law (1988), 42-4
  elections (1989), 37, 42-6
  legislative acts, 45
  structure and practices, 49
USSR Federation Council, 206
USSR Security Council, 206
USSR Supreme Soviet, 4, 106
  committee system, 203
  election of deputies to, 42
  elections (1937), 30-1
  legislative acts, 45
Ustinov, Viktor, 276
Uzbekistan, 50, 207

Vasil'ev, V. (All-Union Scientific Research Centre of Soviet State Construction and Legislation, 51
Vasil'ev, V. (St Petersburg psychologist), 111
Vedernikov, Nikolai, 251
Velikii Novgorod, 266
Verba, Sidney, 125
vice-president, position abolished, 218
Vil'chek, Vsevolod, 106
village assembly, 16
Vishnyakov, Viktor, 262
Vitruk, Nikolai, 251
Vladimir region, 120
Vladislavlev, Aleksandr, 272
Vlast' sovetam, 77
Volgograd, 81-2
volost' (village election), 18
Vol'sky, Arkadii, 70, 72, 100, 110, 179, 271, 272
Voronezh *oblast'*, 254
voters
  1993 election, 124-42
  weariness and election overload, 157-8
votes, multiple, 18, 19
voting
  one person - one vote principle, 47, 48
  pre-1989, 37-8

procedures (1993), 80
rights (1989), 44
voting patterns, and social stratification, 151-4
VR *see* Russia's Choice
VTsIOM (All-Russian Centre for the Study of Public Opinion), 98, 108
Vybory: pryamoi efir, 74, 78
War Industries Committees, 22
Welch, Stephen, 185
Western political models, 229-30
White, Stephen, i, 8, 9, 41, 49-50, 66, 75, 240
Whitefield, Stephen, 86
Wishnevsky, Julia, 158, 251
Women of Russia (ZhR), 70, 110, 160
  programme, 269-70
Workers' Opposition, 29
World War I (1914-18), 22
Writers' Union, 43
Wyman, Matthew, 8, 66, 75, 240

Yabloko (Yavlinsky-Boldyrev-Lukin bloc), 69, 73, 130-1, 134, 136, 139, 179, 256
  media coverage, 99, 102, 110, 114, 120
  programme, 265-6
  proposed ban on, 80
Yakutsk *oblast'*, 20
Yanaev, Gennadii, 206
Yanitsky, O.N., 182
Yaroshinskaya, Alla, 45
Yaroslavl', 27
Yaroslavtsev, Vladimir, 251
Yarov, Yurii, 76, 253
Yasmann, Victor, 252
Yavlinsky, Grigorii, 69, 99, 113, 114, 116, 120, 179, 181, 213, 256, 266
Yavlinsky-Boldyrev-Lukin Bloc *see* Yabloko
Yebzheev, Boris, 251
Yeltsin, Boris, 75, 76, 174, 250
  candidacy in Moscow, 45
  Charter for Civic Accord (1994), 181, 187
  on constructive criticism, 80-1
  criticism of actions, 64-5
  degree of government, 1, 6
  disbanded soviets (1993), 25
  dissolution of Russian parliament (1993), 6, 124, 175, 211, 214, 238
  economic reform programme (1991), 209
  election as Russia's first president (1991), 202, 207-9
  on Gorbachev's presidency, 206-7
  on himself, 218-19
  image, 83
  and the KPRF, 274, 275
  leaves CPSU, 219
  on the media, 101, 104
  media exposure, 113, 114

on nomination meetings, 50
popularity 212-13, 215, 216-17 Table, 9.2
potential candidacy in 1996, 256-7
Presidential Decree No. 1400 (1993), 63, 66
as prime minister, 237
relations with parliament, 249-53
rule by decree, 185, 230-1, 234-8
on Russia's Choice, 178-9
strength in new political order, 71, 85, 87
supporters and opponents, 251
Yermakov, S.N., 147, 150, 159
Youth Movement in Support of the People's Party of Free Russia, 270
Yugoslavia (former), 125
Yurasova, Tat'yana, 53-4
Yurgens, I., 116
Yushenkov, Sergei, 264

Zadornov, Mikhail, 266
Zatulin, Konstantin, 267
Zaveryukha, Aleksandr, 76, 273
Zavtra, 117
zemstvo elections, 16-17
Zemstvo Statutes (1864), 16
Zhadanova, L.A., 147, 152
Zhenshchiny Rossii see Women of Russia
Zhirinovsky, Vladimir, 102-3, 116, 121, 129, 160, 180, 181, 195, 213, 249, 276
leadership images, 114, 143, 236, 240
television exposure, 102, 107-13, 116, 120
ultra-nationalism, 32, 70, 98, 124, 131, 136-9
Zhitomir, 45
ZhR *see* Women of Russia, 127, 130, 136
Zhuravlev, Vitalii, 262
Zhurnalist, 73
Zorkal'tsev, Viktor, 275
Zor'kin, Valerii, 78, 81, 181, 251
Zyuganov, Gennadii, 70, 120, 188, 240, 274